Reagan's War on Terrorism
in Nicaragua

Reagan's War on Terrorism in Nicaragua

The Outlaw State

Philip W. Travis

LEXINGTON BOOKS
Lanham • Boulder • New York • London

Published by Lexington Books
An imprint of The Rowman & Littlefield Publishing Group, Inc.
4501 Forbes Boulevard, Suite 200, Lanham, Maryland 20706
www.rowman.com

Unit A, Whitacre Mews, 26-34 Stannary Street, London SE11 4AB

British Library Cataloguing in Publication Information Available

Library of Congress Cataloging-in-Publication Data

Names: Travis, Philip W., author.
Title: Reagan's war on terrorism in Nicaragua : the outlaw state / Philip W. Travis.
Description: Lanham, MD : Lexington Books, [2016] | Includes bibliographical references and index.
Identifiers: LCCN 2016041488 (print) | LCCN 2016057718 (ebook) | ISBN 9781498537179 (cloth : alk. paper) | ISBN 9781498537186 (Electronic)
Subjects: LCSH: Nicaragua--History--1979-1990. | United States--Foreign relations--Nicaragua. | Nicaragua--Foreign relations--United States. | Terrorism--Prevention--Government policy--United States--History. | International law--United States--History--20th century. | Counterrevolutions--Nicaragua--History. | United States--Military policy--History--20th century.
Classification: LCC F1528 .T75 2016 (print) | LCC F1528 (ebook) | DDC 327.7307285--dc23
LC record available at https://lccn.loc.gov/2016041488

Printed in the United States of America

Contents

Acknowledgments

There are a number of individuals that contributed fundamentally to my own development and to which I owe a debt of gratitude. Foremost among these are my mother, Elizabeth Anne Travis, and my late father, Charles Gary Travis. Many things in life arrive at us upon chance and circumstance, and I have the great fortune of being blessed with the best parents any person could want. Even though my father suffered a massive heart attack while I was only in the ninth grade his contribution to my life and development remains profound. Gary Travis taught me work ethic, compassion, and respect. He was a serviceman of twenty-eight years with the United States Coast Guard, and he introduced me to history at a young age. Our family toured museums, shipyards, submarines, and many other sites integral to the historical development of the United States. It was through my early development living near US Coast Guard facilities that exposed me to things that ultimately steered my interest toward US international relations history. Despite the short period of time that I was blessed to have a father on this earth Gary Travis was of profound influence, and I am forever grateful for the fortune to have had such a special father figure. This book is dedicated to his memory. I only wish Gary Travis were here to read this book.

I also dedicate this book to my mother, Elizabeth Travis. Without the support and encouragement of Elizabeth Travis nothing that I have ever achieved could have been possible. My mother sacrificed everything she could for her children. When I questioned whether I should pursue a career as a historian my mother encouraged me. When I needed assistance of any kind my mother helped me. I cannot quantify the extent of her contribution to my life and my career. I am indebted to her and am grateful for her making achievements such as this possible.

In addition to my parents, I have also been fortunate to have received exceptional guidance from inspiring mentors. Noriko Kawamura, Matthew Avery Sutton, and Thomas Preston provided invaluable guidance as I developed the basis of this project, first, as a doctoral dissertation at Washington State University. George C. Herring, too, provided invaluable feedback and guidance as I developed this project. In addition, my colleagues Ryan Dearinger and Nicole Howard provided important support as not only friends but mentors while I matured as a scholar. In addition, undergraduate professors Matthew Oyos, Glen Martin, Kim Kipling, John Davis, and Mike Montgomery provided fundamental inspiration that helped shape my thoughts in my early development as an academic. These teachers and mentors provided critical insight in the development of this project as well as in my development as a professional.

I also want to thank my siblings James and Laurie Travis as well as my closest friends John Wurtz, James Scanlon, Nathan Brown, Jody Waddell, Mike Burroughs, Jeff Fisher, Alex Marris, Ginger Travis, Shawna Herzog, Jason Erdey, Beth Erdey, Lydia Borowicz, Johnny Waddell, Rodney Alwang, Ryan Weyers, Zach McCoy, Manan Desai, and Darcy Crisp. These individuals are not only friends, but over the years engaged me with in-depth discussions on topics of politics and international relations that helped further shape and inspire my thinking and encouraged me to delve into primary source research out of a desire to search for answers to many of the big questions that our numerous conversations left us asking.

Finally, I must thank President Oscar Arias Sanchez and Keith Graham, MD. Both President Arias and Dr. Graham were gracious enough to allow me to conduct firsthand interviews that provided invaluable and unique insight in the development of this project. Likewise, I thank the Ronald Reagan and George Bush Presidential Libraries, the National Security Archive at George Washington University, and the Costa Rican National Archives. Lastly, I thank Alex Marris, and James Scanlon for providing the maps and artwork for the book. All of these individuals and archives were invaluable in the development of this project and I am grateful for such positive assistance.

Map

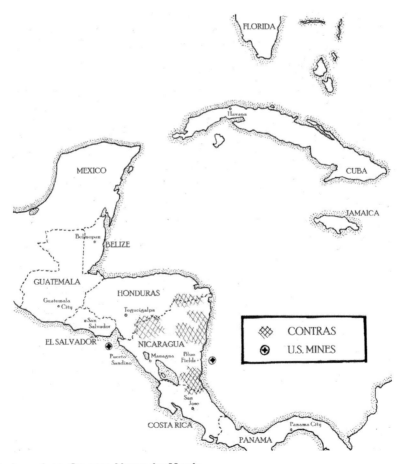

Harbor mines. *Source*: Alexander Marris.

Introduction

It was a warm, partly cloudy June afternoon in Maryland. President Ronald Reagan and his wife Nancy took the thirty-minute helicopter ride in "Marine One" from Camp David to Andrews Air Force base located just outside of the nation's capital. Reagan carried four Purple Heart medals with him. It was Saturday, June 22, and the medals were posthumous decorations for the families of four Marines that died in San Salvador, El Salvador, a few days earlier. The assailants used disguises and automatic weapons. They sprayed bullets throughout an outdoor café, killing nine. The gunmen escaped in a vehicle that retreated to the heart of El Salvador's capital city. As Reagan spoke amid four coffins draped in American flags, two things were apparent: the nation's grief was acute, and the president intended to act with resolve to combat a new and troubling national security threat, terrorism.[1] With his characteristic passion Reagan exclaimed, "They say the men who murdered these sons of America escaped, disappeared into the city streets. But I pledge to you today they will not evade the justice of the United States any more than they can escape the judgment of God. We will move any mountain, ford any river to find the jackals and to bring them, and their colleagues in terror, to justice."[2] The Reagan administration's war on terrorism began in the aftermath of these remarks.

The event in El Salvador was a capstone to an escalation of terrorist incidents throughout the world. In particular, the ten days prior to President Reagan's speech was a time of hardship for the nation. On June 14, hijackers seized TWA flight 847 shortly after it departed from Athens, Greece. The hijackers took the plane to Beirut, Lebanon. Americans were horrified to learn of the murder of a US navy service member during the ordeal. The terrorists demanded that the United States force Israel to release up to 700 Palestinian Liberation Organization (PLO) fighters from its prisons, and a

1

Figure I.1.   President Reagan with his wife Nancy attaches a Purple Heart on the coffin of one of the marines slain in the El Salvador killing. *Source*: **National Archives and Records Administration.**

standoff ensued.[3] When those four Marines died in San Salvador, this crisis was nearly a week old. The front page of the *New York Times* on June 21 covered three different terrorist incidents, the El Salvador killings, the TWA hijacking, and a deadly bombing at the airport in Frankfurt, Germany.[4] These events caused the then Deputy Director for the Office of Counterterrorism Parker Borg to recall, "There seemed to be hijackings or terrorist incidents almost continuously." The ubiquity of terrorist acts in the 1980s provided a catalyst for the development of a US counterterrorism offensive against Nicaragua and other alleged state sponsors of terrorism.[5]

This is a story about international terrorism and how this threat emerged in the late Cold War and influenced the development of US international relations. When the United States first began to recognize terrorism as a unique security threat it was a relatively minor aspect of world affairs that only periodically garnered some public attention. In the 1970s there were some high profile hijackings and kidnappings, but terrorists rarely targeted US citizens and casualties for such attacks were relatively low. In some cases, terrorists even went to significant lengths to avoid the killing of hostages. In the 1970s, terrorism was often used by militants but typically for compromises, prisoner swaps, and other crude forms of negotiation rather than the shock killings that were associated with this in the post–September 11th world.

By the early 1980s, terrorist violence was a commonplace characteristic of regional conflicts throughout the developing world, and particularly in Latin America and the Middle East. As global revolutions and international terrorism appeared to escalate, the United States took an increasingly firm stand against those that it identified as complicit in terrorism. The United States labeled the perpetrators of terrorism uncivilized and pledged to never negotiate with the villains. By the middle of the 1980s, the United States defined terrorism broadly and made no meaningful distinction between a leftist revolutionary guerrilla army and international terrorists. The Reagan administration used the rhetoric of terrorism as a propaganda device and as a way of characterizing international relations policy against revolutionary groups and nations. Terrorism was made a tool for describing the actions of enemies and by contrast defending the actions of allies within the broader context of the Cold War. This study is about how the Reagan administration used terrorism to characterize its conflict with Sandinista-led Nicaragua in order to facilitate an aggressive policy of regime change that represented an alteration of the norms of international law and national sovereignty.

Following the attack in El Salvador, Ronald Reagan declared Nicaragua, which the administration held responsible for the conflict that raged in El Salvador, an "outlaw state." While Reagan's accusation was part of a long running campaign to slander the Nicaraguan government and gain authorization from Congress for the use of military force against it, the choice of terminology in 1985 signified an important shift in US international relations. Reagan's use of the term "outlaw state" reflected a culmination of the United States' efforts at addressing the threat from state sponsors of terrorism. It suggested that the government violated international law for an alleged complicity in sponsoring terrorism. This allegation justified a new course for the use of force and other hardline measures. The administration relied on the selected use of preemptive war, largely through proxy armies, as a tool of forcible regime change. The approach challenged the norms of international law precisely because the administration suggested that a government affiliation with international terrorism amounted to a surrender of rights as a sovereign nation, and authorized the United States, under the guise of preemptive self-defense, to violate those rights and forcibly remove the government.

Regan's use of the term "outlaw state" was not the same as classifying a country as a failed state. Identifying a state as failed suggests that the government has ceased to function and is incapable of governing. In this case, the charge of "outlaw state" referred to governments that were either undertaking or collaborating with those that carryout acts that violate international law, particularly terrorism. "Outlaw state" implied that a country was a national security threat, and was so primarily because of an intent to challenge US hegemony and influence through the use of international terrorism. This term suggested the criminal intent of a government, and therefore its illegitimacy.

The international rights of a nation centers on the concept of sovereignty. National sovereignty is a relatively straightforward idea. At its most basic level, it prohibits one country from violating the territory of another country unless in a case of clear self-defense. All nations possess certain rights within the international system. The concept of national sovereignty goes back to the seventeenth century and the conclusion of the Thirty Years War. Virtually every European nation participated in that war, and used it as a vehicle for the expansion of self-interest. The Peace of Westphalia ended the conflict and is credited with creating the foundation for the modern nation-state system and the concept of sovereignty. European nations agreed to basic premises about national rights, and established the framework for the modern nation-state system. According to this agreement all sovereign nations possessed a right to freedom from violations of territorial borders.[6] The most fundamental characteristic of the nation-state system is sovereignty, which refers to the right of a nation to be free from foreign designs on its government and is further meant to deter aggressive actions by a more powerful nation seeking to maximize its self-interest at the expense of a weaker country.[7]

When the George W. Bush administration preemptively invaded Iraq and Afghanistan, two governments that it implicated as security threats and potential sponsors of terrorism, national security specialists acknowledged that the use of a preemptive policy of regime change challenged the traditional nation-state system. This, some feared, was a possible precedent to the less restrained use of military power on the part of not just the United States but, potentially, other governments as well. However, despite the tendency to assert the Bush doctrine as the beginning of this challenge to the old nation-state system, the history is rooted in the late Cold War and, particularly, with the Reagan administration's own war on terrorism. The term "outlaw state" referenced a move by the United States to alter the old ordering principle of the modern world. In its place, and in the name of counterterrorism and self-defense, the Reagan administration sought to promote a policy in which the United States possessed the power and freedom to preemptively alter the leadership of a sovereign nation in the pursuit of its own interests. In the 1980s, Nicaragua was a primary target of this policy.[8]

In the confusing and tumultuous twenty-first century the terms terrorism and war on terrorism are often tossed around by the media and the political leadership in the United States, but few Americans really understand that these commonplace terms signify a landmark transformation in how the United States uses and justifies its use of power in the world. The basic definition of terrorism involves a range of violent actions perpetrated on non-combatants with the goal of achieving some kind of political objective. Acts of terrorism are carried out by non-state agents, terrorist organizations, and are often facilitated directly by state sponsors of terrorism. Likewise, a war on terror occurs anytime a government, in this case the United States, uses counterterrorism as a primary justification for taking hardline actions to combat a terrorism threat from or within another nation. These seem like fairly simple concepts, however, let us look a little deeper.

The standard definition of terrorism is primarily concerned with only the act of targeting innocents. From this standpoint, any side in a conflict regardless of affiliation or ideology might be guilty of conducting acts of terrorism. In the 1970s and the 1980s, many Americans understood this and accurately highlighted both rightist and leftist forms of terrorism in the bloody Central American wars that raged during this period. However, as the problem of international terrorism evolved alongside the emergence of revolution in the developing world, the United States came to increasingly define the threat of terrorism within the parameters of the Cold War. The United States tended to identify international terrorism as a uniquely leftist problem, and upon this it based a global counter-offensive against its Cold War enemies.

By the mid-1980s, the Reagan administration defined terrorism in such a way that it applied to a broad array of enemies and justified an aggressive foreign policy. In terms of acts, the Reagan administration defined terrorism loosely and included drug trafficking and insurgency, but it centered the definition specifically around the anti-US motive for the action. According to the Reagan administration, terrorism was fundamentally a product of a global war carried out by radical leftists, and particularly a group of "outlaw states" that represented an alliance of its Cold War enemies and radical Middle Eastern agents like Libya and Palestine. Such a broad and one-sided characterization the Reagan administration promoted with a thorough propaganda and public diplomacy campaign that painted its enemies with the broadest brush while simultaneously denying its own complicity in the terrorism issue.[9]

While the attacks of September 11, 2001, represent an important moment of change this project scales the perspective of analysis back and demonstrates a continuity between the Cold War and the war on terror.[10] For years scholars argued that around 1985 the Reagan administration adopted an offensive policy against hostile governments in the developing world. The United States pursued a two pronged approach referred to as the Reagan doctrine and the Reagan offensive. The former referred to the Reagan administration's insistence on its right to pursue the democratization of governments in the developing world. The Reagan offensive referred to the administration's assertion that it reserved the right to use hardline measures of regime change, particularly through the use of proxy guerrilla armies, in the pursuit of its goal of democratization. Both of these concepts were most relevant to the situation in Nicaragua. The Reagan doctrine amounted to a demand for the democratization of Nicaragua on the terms of the United States, and a justification of its use of proxy armies dedicated to ending the rule of the Sandinistas. This move represented a step away from a containment-oriented policy with Nicaragua to an offensive policy of regime change.[11]

Numerous and acclaimed scholars acknowledge the transformation from containment to offensive during the 1980s, but due to the classification of important materials earlier narratives left out a significant component. Scholars of this conflict argue that the primary thrust of the Reagan administration's policy was exclusively connected to the Cold War. That is, the Reagan offensive represented a casting off of the containment policy in favor of a more aggressive rollback policy that involved the Reagan administration's goal of pushing back the gains of communism in the developing world by overthrowing revolutionary leftist regimes like the one in Nicaragua. This interpretation is accurate, but because of the classification of important documents older interpretations miss a significant component of this offensive.

The Reagan offensive was not exclusively about communism. The Reagan offensive was also a war on terrorism. It was an offensive directed at developing world nations like Nicaragua that was significantly constructed around the notion that these governments were "outlaw states" and sponsors of international terrorism. When the Reagan offensive began in 1985 counterterrorism was in the forefront of its justification for a policy of preemptive regime change. During the Reagan offensive, terrorism was a ubiquitous justification for the policy against Nicaragua. The Reagan offensive was an anti-communist Cold War phenomenon, but it was also a war on terrorism and introduced new foreign policy principles that factored centrally into the post–2001 war on terror. With respect to the later, the Reagan offensive established a precedent for a policy future. The Reagan offensive against Nicaragua was an early example of the use of preemptive regime change designed to thwart an alleged threat from a state sponsor of terrorism, and provided a lesson for the danger of a hardline and military oriented counterterrorism policy, which I suggest rarely creates peaceful solutions and often radicalizes the opposition, exacerbates war, and reduces the chance for peace.

In addition to contributing to existing scholarship on US-Nicaraguan relations this book engages with an ongoing debate over the historical position of the George W. Bush administration's preemptive attack on Saddam Hussein's Iraq, and more broadly the role of terrorism in the making of US foreign and domestic policy. Following the attacks on September 11, 2001, the United States targeted Iraq, and launched an aggressive and large-scale military assault on that nation. Since the outset of this conflict historians and political scientists debated whether this development represented a new precedent in

US international relations or a variation of older practices. Was the Bush doctrine, the use of preemptive military force on an alleged state sponsor of terrorism, an unprecedented development or a variation of long established patterns in US international relations? In 2006, historian Lloyd Ambrosius provided an answer to this question in a compelling article for *Diplomatic History*.

Ambrosius addressed the arguments of several significant scholars like Melvin Leffler and John Lewis Gaddis, who insisted that President Bush's invasion of Iraq was not new, and that his preemptive operation was a variation of an older principle used in other ways by prior administrations. Ambrosius, however, claimed that these scholars discounted the nature of the means that the United States applied against Iraq. He insisted that the Iraq War represented an unprecedented development because the United States utilized a full-scale conventional force against a sovereign nation that posed an alleged, but still dubious, security threat. [12]

I accept Ambrosius' position that the central thrust of the Bush doctrine, an overt and large-scale conventional offensive, represented an unprecedented form of preemption taken in a time of great national urgency. However, the invasion of Iraq was not the first time that the United States used the allegation of state sponsorship of terrorism to pursue a policy of regime change. I demonstrate that the Reagan administration also used the allegation of state sponsorship of terrorism to target Nicaragua with an aggressive policy of preemptive regime change during the late Cold War.

From the United States' standpoint international terrorism often developed far less as a legitimate foreign policy concept and far more as a political tool developed for the purpose of alienating enemies and justifying hardline measures. Scholars such as Paul Chamberlin, Robert Fisk, and John Collins demonstrate that the allegation of terrorism has, at times, developed as a political tool and a way of justifying war rather than an evenly applied analytic concept. [13] This book engages the works of these scholars and others by providing another example in which the United States used terrorism as a propaganda device to unwarrantedly justify hardline measures as in the interest of counterterrorism.

The terms terrorism and counterterrorism refer to a new kind of global war fought across the developing world that emerged in earnest during the late Cold War. The United States engaged in a global irregular war with leftist revolutionary groups and states. It was an irregular war because the battlefield was unconventional and global. No longer were revolutions limited geographically to a particular location. Instead, the new war blurred the distinction between political boundaries and of combatant and non-combatant. While the United States understood international terrorism as a distinct development and national security problem it often addressed it by itself adapting to this new reality of warfare and using terrorism to combat terrorism.

Over the course of the Cold War, the United States sponsored, or carried out itself, hostile international acts of sabotage, provocation, assassination, threat, and preemptive regime change. Its policies often ran counter to traditional norms of international law. In the 1980s, the Reagan administration believed it witnessed a global leftist offensive that utilized irregular war against the United States and its allies. The Reagan offensive, as a response, was an adaptation of the tactics of this global irregular war. It relied on a myriad of unconventional an unsavory tactics and some of which were rightly identified as acts of terrorism. In Central America its primary ally against Nicaragua, the transnational guerrilla army known as the Contras, were a product of a policy of state sponsored war against leftism and engaged in acts that many rightly criticized as terrorism. Over the course of Ronald Reagan's Presidency, the administration went to extensive lengths to deny the narrative that it, too, was a complicit sponsor of terrorism across the Americas. In this, terrorism emerged as a powerful political term. Terrorist, effectively, was another word for the enemies of the United States in a new global irregular war. Counterterrorist forces, a more positive connotation, referenced its allies. A war on terrorism was a new way of justifying the application of the power of the United States abroad in offensive conflicts against and within other sovereign nations.

NOTES

1. Itinerary, "Schedule of the President for Saturday, June 22 1985," Folder "Ceremony for Marines Killed in El Salvador," Box OA 16003, Office of Presidential Records: Series II, Domestic Events, Ronald Reagan Library.

2. Speech, "Presidential Remarks: Ceremony for Marines Killed in El Salvador, Andrews Air Force Base, June 22, 1985," Folder "Ceremony for Marines Killed in El Salvador," Box OA 16003, Office of Presidential Records: Series II, Domestic Events, Ronald Reagan Library.

3. Dena Kleiman, "Those Still Captive: 40 Remaining Hostages: A Diverse Group United by the Random Nature of Their Plight Hostages in Lebanon: Who the Captives Are," *New York Times*, June 21, 1985, http://search.proquest.com/docview/111148555?accountid=14902.

4. Shirley Christian, "Four Marines Slain in Rebel Raid in El Salvador," *New York Times*, June 21, 1985, http://search.proquest.com/docview/111140226?accountid=14902.

5. Parker Borg, interview by Charles Stuart Kennedy, *Foreign Affairs Oral History Project*, Association for Diplomatic Studies and Training, August 12, 2002.

6. Clifford Bachman, *Cultures of the West: A History, Volume 2, Since 1350, 2nd ed.* (New York: Oxford University Press, 2016), 529–530.

7. "Reagan Doctrine: Assisting Anti-Marxist Guerrillas," Folder 5, Box 11, David S. Addington, Series II: Chron File, 1987–1988, Ronald Reagan Presidential Library.

8. D. E. Sanger, "Bush to Outline Doctrine of Striking Foes First," *New York Times*, September 20, 2002, http://search.proquest.com/docview/92235253?accountid=45760. This is but one of many articles during the early twenty-first century that deals with the topic of the Bush doctrine and preventative war.

9. Propaganda, generally, refers to the work of a particular agency or group to use written, visual, and spoken communication to promote its own biased perception of events. Public

diplomacy refers to a more broad going campaign that includes propaganda, but also extends to building relationships with lawmakers, media outlets, and so forth, in pursuit of one promoting a group's goals and interpretation of events in the world.

10. By war on terror, I am referring to post–September 11, 2001, period in which US foreign policy turned to global offensive and preemptive counterterror operations against states and groups.

11. "Reagan Doctrine: Assisting Anti-Marxist Guerrillas," 1987–1988, Ronald Reagan Presidential Library.

12. Lloyd E. Ambrosius, "Woodrow Wilson and George W. Bush: Historical Comparisons of Ends and Means in their Foreign Policies," *Diplomatic History* 30, no. 3 (June 2006): 509–543.

13. Paul Chamberlin, *The Global Offensive: The United States, The Palestinian Liberation Organization and the Making of the Post-Cold War Order* (New York: Oxford, 2012); Robert Fisk, *Pity the Nation: Lebanon at War* (New York: Oxford, 2001); and John Collins and Ross Glover, *Collateral Language: A User's Guide to America's New War* (New York: New York University Press, 2002).

Chapter One

Imperialism, the Cold War, and the Roots of Revolution

On November 17, 1909, early on in William Howard Taft's presidency, two American warships, the Cruiser USS Des Moines and the slightly smaller gunboat the USS Vicksburg, steamed for Nicaragua. Both ships symbolized the transformations of the industrial and pre-industrial age, and the technological power that made the most accelerated period of imperialism possible. The vessels were steam powered, but were also outfitted with schooner sail configurations. Nicaragua faced deep rooted and intense political rivalries between conservatives and liberals, and the Vicksburg and Des Moines responded in support of a conservative uprising against the government of Jose Santos Zelaya. At the outset of the revolt, government forces captured two Americans, Leroy Cannon and Leonard Grace. Grace and Cannon were summarily executed by firing squad. Apparently, the two US citizens were involved in a plan to sabotage government vessels with dynamite. The executions, which some in the Zelaya leadership opposed, caused outrage from the United States. Following a strong statement from Secretary of State Philander Knox the United States sent the Vicksburg and Des Moines to protect citizens and interests.[1]

The United States did more than simply protect the interests and lives of American citizens in Nicaragua. The Zelaya government had made overtures that challenged the hegemonic influence of the United States in the region, and this caused the Taft administration to question the efficacy of its remaining in power. Preceding the uprising, the Zelaya government approached two of the United States' most significant imperial rivals, Great Britain and Japan, asking for loans and offering the right to a canal zone. The United Kingdom made a substantial loan to the Zelaya government, and Nicaragua contemplated offering Japan, like the United States, a newer upstart empire

11

and destined to rival the United States in the Pacific, exclusive rights to build a canal across the country.[2] These steps irritated the Taft administration as it feared a weakening of US interests and profits in a critical part of its empire. Preventing foreign investment and involvement was a hallmark of this era of informal empire in the Americas; in places like Cuba and Nicaragua this was a primary way that the United States prevented foreign powers from undermining its influence.

As the conflict deteriorated the United States landed marines at the port of Bluefields on the east coast and helped facilitate the overthrow of the Zelaya regime. Ultimately, the United States supported his replacement, the conservative Adolfo Diaz, and over the course of the next two decades a small contingent of US Marines remained stationed in the country. Following this, the first Nicaraguan Civil War, the United States compelled the Diaz government to turn over control of many commerce and banking institutions to the United States, which it did after signing the Bryan-Chamorro Treaty.[3]

The roots of the Nicaraguan Revolution of 1979, like so many of the independence struggles of the twentieth century, were linked to a violent legacy of imperialism. Nicaragua was a hub of the United States' informal empire that stretched across the Americas. Our historical understanding of this empire is owed most to scholars like Walter Lafeber and William Appleman Williams. Lafeber defined the United States as an informal empire and published several highly influential works demonstrating its development.[4] The term informal empire refers to an empire that is held together more through coercion than direct colonization. The United States created an empire that was tied together by business interests, military power, and cooperative political associations, i.e., dictatorships that owed a sort of fealty to the United States and likewise profited handsomely from the relationship. The United States, like European and Asian empires of the time, fought numerous conflicts in an effort to secure a hegemonic influence over smaller regional powers.

Typically, when one hears the word decolonization they think about the end of colonialism in Africa and Asia. However, this term refers more broadly to an end of empire and the emergence of independent nations primarily during the twentieth century. The Americas also experienced the effect of decolonization during the Cold War period. Many countries in the Caribbean as well as Central and South America went through a long two phased process of decolonization: phase one occurred with the revolutions that brought independence from Spain during the nineteenth century, and phase two occurred when revolutionaries began to struggle against the United States empire that took the place of the Spanish empire in the nineteenth and twentieth centuries.

Shortly after the countries of Central and South America obtained independence from Spain in the nineteenth century, the United States issued its most significant policy principle for Latin American relations, the Monroe Doctrine. Composed by John Quincy Adams and declared by President James Monroe in 1823, the Monroe Doctrine was a declaration that acknowledged a unique relationship between the United States and Latin America. In 1823, the policy was a largely symbolic gesture meant as a statement of support for anti-monarchial revolutions. It was meant as a declaration that the United States would not tolerate a return of monarchial rule to the Americas. This statement, however, marked the symbolic starting point for an informal American empire across much of Latin America, and focused on Central America and the Caribbean. It was against this empire that figures like Fidel Castro, Che Guevara, and Carlos Fonseca led their revolutions in the twentieth century.

The United States took its strongest step toward building an empire at the turn of the twentieth century. It annexed Hawaii, made Puerto Rico a territory, the Philippines a colony, and asserted a right to shape and direct the governments of many Latin American states through economic, political, and military force. Of the countries effected by the United States' empire building Nicaragua was toward the top of the list. US involvement in Nicaragua went back to the middle of the nineteenth century, and included the involvement of numerous private and non-government agents. In many respects, private imperialism in Nicaragua preceded the government directed program. In one curious case in the 1850s a Tennessean named William Walker, took over the country, made himself president, and legalized slavery. Walker's triumph, though, was short-lived as not long after his foray he was captured and executed by firing squad. During this period US railroad magnates and canal builders, too, invested in the country, as did the United Fruit Corporation. By the time of the inauguration of President William Howard Taft in 1909 United States businesses dominated the banana, lumber, gold, and coffee industries across the country. Effectively, the United States private sector had monopolized Nicaragua's most significant export products. [5]

Historian and author of the monograph *The Business of Empire*, Jason Colby, demonstrated that private businesses were the original architects of the United States empire in the Americas. [6] The dawn of the twentieth century, however, brought a new involvement by the United States government in the Americas. This was the age of the Roosevelt Corollary to the Monroe Doctrine and President William Howard Taft's Dollar Diplomacy. Teddy Roosevelt's corollary effectively granted the United States the right to use military force in the region in pursuit of stability and national interest while his successor William Howard Taft further pressed the idea that United States investment and economic influence in the region might extend the global power and influence of the country as well as enhance the economy of the industrialized United States. Both of these Progressive Era Presidents accelerated a government-led imperialism in Nicaragua and across the Americas.

During the first half of the twentieth century Nicaragua experienced two civil wars, which were effectively conflicts fought in the backdrop of the imperial influence of the United States. This period produced, perhaps, Nicaragua's greatest revolutionary figure, Augusto César Sandino. The icon of the future Sandinista movement Sandino was a liberal leader that resisted the United States' influence, which forced itself on Nicaragua following the civil war of 1909–1912. Sandino led armies made up significantly of peasants and workers. He was an anti-imperialist and nationalist whose message focused on the importance of true national sovereignty for Nicaragua. Among his foremost concerns were for complete and permanent withdrawal of the United States' Marines. Sandino was well-spoken, and wrote about his experiences in the struggle with the United States and its political allies in Nicaragua.

The war that Sandino described in his letters shared similarities with other US interventions in the developing world during the twentieth century. The United States entered with greater organization and technological power. It sought more conventional engagements and relied on heavy fire power and aerial bombardment from its planes. The Marines relied largely on conventional tactics, what Sandino called "school tactics," while Sandino's army used guerrilla tactics. The Marines sought pitched battles and defended garrisons with trenches and barbed wire. Sandino described the United States defensive posture at Telpaneca in 1927 as "imitating the system of entrenchment used in the European War." Sandino's forces possessed submachine guns, but lacked formal training and sought instead to fight a guerrilla war that frustrated the more powerful US Marines. As the United States sought to maintain and/or extend its hegemony in the developing world it fought several such guerrilla wars against nationalist and anti-imperialist indigenous armies: first, the Philippines, then Nicaragua, then Vietnam. [7]

Most in the United States know of the Vietnam War, and possess a basic understanding of the nature and controversy of this conflict. Generally, far fewer understand that the Vietnam War was only the more recent of a long line of guerrilla wars in which the United States fought on the side of imperialism and against the forces of self-determination. Scholars like Michael Hunt, Steven Levine, and Stuart Creighton Miller identified the Philippine-American War as the beginning of a string of Pacific wars brought on, in part, by the expanded global power and influence of the United States. [8] Even more forgotten than the war in the Philippines are the two Nicaraguan civil wars that the United States intervened in out of a desire to shape the government and maximize its national security interests.

From 1926 to 1933, the United States struggled against the guerrilla army lead by Sandino who continued to fight long after the Nicaraguan government had begun normalization with the United States. The United States struggled to fully pacify the people of Nicaragua. It bombed the mountainous jungle headquarters of Sandino's guerrillas, and eventually forced him into Mexico. By the time of Herbert Hoover's administration the United States grew tired of fighting the conflict directly and instead decided to turn the fighting over to the Nicaraguan government. The United States sought to shape the policy of the Nicaraguan government. Such control enabled it to protect US economic interests as well as prevent the Mexican government, which tended to support the liberal anti-US opposition, from expanding its influence and creating a pro-Mexican Central America. By contrast, Sandino insisted that he fought for national sovereignty, and fashioned himself as a peoples leader.[9]

Even after the government normalized relations with the United States Sandino pledged to continue to fight until the Marines left. In 1933, the United States decided to remove the Marines, and Sandino appeared to make peace with the leadership in Nicaragua, including soon to be dictator Anastasio Somoza Garcia. The removal of the Marines, however, resulted in the consolidation of a powerful dictatorship led by Garcia rather than the beginning of true independence for the people of Nicaragua, for which Sandino hoped.

The United States facilitated the emergence of the infamous Somoza family dictatorship. To keep the new government stable, thereby sustaining US interests, it helped organize the Nicaraguan National Guard to provide a military police force to prevent the overthrow of the regime and stabilize the United States-Nicaraguan relationship. The National Guard acted, effectively, as a military police force above the law, and it often acted in complete disregard for the Nicaraguan Constitution or for individual human rights. On February 21, 1934, following a cordial and diplomatic meeting of the Nicaraguan leadership, the National Guard stopped Sandino's car. Sandino was arrested, and summarily executed in a move that proved critical to the emergence of an over four decades long Somoza family dictatorship. However, while Sandino's death and the rise of the Somoza dictatorship appeared like the end of the independence struggle it actually marked a phase in a long revolutionary process that emerged again during the Cold War.[10]

The Cold War profoundly altered the behavior of the United States in the world. No longer a regional power, the United States emerged from World War II a superpower prepared to compete with the Soviet Union and its leftist affiliates across the developing world. Increasingly, the United States defined friend and foe on the basis of ideological affiliation. The emergence of the Cold War transformed how the United States viewed revolution and stability in the developing world and this carried potentially devastating ramifications.[11]

Not only did the end of World War II bring on the Cold War, it also accelerated the collapse of the nineteenth and twentieth century empires. The roughly forty years following the end of the Second World War embodied the intersection of two powerful global processes: the Cold War and decolonization. The destruction wrought by the Second World War on the great nineteenth century empires accelerated revolutionary movements for independence across the developing world. As empires crumbled the United States and the Soviet Union struggled to maintain influence over these regions with aid, advisors, armies, and ideology. The Cold War helped turn the process of decolonization into a traumatic and bloody affair. Numerous assassinations, unprecedented global arms dealing, and brutal wars resulted, indirectly, and sometimes directly, from the struggle of both the United States and the Soviet Union to maintain or expand its hegemony within the chaos of a rapid, and often violent, decolonization process.

The Second World War and the emergence of the Cold War transformed anti-imperial struggles across the developing world. The Soviet Union was a global superpower and it offered an anti-imperial ideology that appealed to many revolutionaries. It also came with material aid and assistance, and the hope of international recognition. Leninism and Marxism influenced many guerrilla movements across the developing world, and in each region revolutionaries adapted these ideas to their own experiences. The Cold War, too, changed how the United States approached the world. Instead of democracy being understood as the true recipe for peace and stability the administration of Harry Truman, which witnessed the emergence of the Cold War, began an approach that involved positioning anti-leftist stability as the most critical component to maintaining its hegemony against the overtures of movements sympathetic to communism. Whether in Southeast Asia or in Latin America the United States justified support for sometimes repressive governments and waged conventional and unconventional war in the name of anti-communism. As a result, during the Cold War the United States often accepted dictatorship in exchange for stability and advantage in a world struggle against the forces of leftism.

Fidel Castro, Che Guevara, and the Nicaraguan revolutionary Carlos Fonseca represented the core of leftist revolution in Latin America and the Caribbean during the Cold War. Castro and Guevara's shocking success in the Cuban Revolution of 1959 had a lasting effect on the Nicaraguan Revolution two decades later. These revolutionary figures successfully carried through a people's rebellion against a US-friendly government, and gained recognition from the international community. As Matilde Zimmerman demonstrated in her book *Sandinista*, Nicaraguan Carlos Fonseca was among those influenced and encouraged by Cuba's success. Fonseca was integral to the formative years of the Sandinistas. According to Zimmerman, Carlos Fonseca molded the FSLN around two themes, "the fight for national liberation and against U.S. imperialism and . . . the struggle for socialist revolution."[12] Fonseca charted the ideological objectives of the movement, and shaped the revolution around the ideal of a Cuban-style Marxism. Eventually Fonseca and the Sandinistas grew from a small student based body in the 1960s to a legitimate guerrilla army during the 1970s.

The late Cold War witnessed a transformation in how revolutionary struggles were waged. The revolutions of the late Cold War were global events and developments in Central America and the Caribbean intersected with the consolidation of leftist leaderships in places like China, Cuba, Vietnam, and with movements in the Middle East. In the late 1960s, the Palestinian Liberation Organization (PLO) led by Yasser Arafat began to emerge as a central group in a more consolidated Palestinian resistance (at the time there were several different groups). The movement consolidated out of general opposition to the United States' ally Israel. The PLO represented a primary example of global revolutionary struggle, and what the United States called international terrorism, in the late Cold War.[13]

Technological change is fundamental to how people live, think, and also how they resist. During the late Cold War, technology accelerated globalization and the speed of communication and movement was unprecedented in human history. Just as technology like the steamboat facilitated imperialism, revolutionary groups used technological advancements to resist imperialism and dictatorship. Revolutionary groups moved, fought, and communicated on an international level. In the populated and globalizing world, terrorism was a new tactic designed to force opposing governments into negotiation or to acceptance of demands. The revolutions of the late Cold War were also facilitated by a global arms trade never before as robust, and this provided ample small arms. Fighting was unconventional and it bled across borders and extended even to the sky on the new jet airliners that speedily transported people throughout the world. During the late Cold War, terrorism emerged as a tactic carried out by insurgencies and state sponsors (governments supporting irregular fighters) alike. In the fall of 1972, one event, perhaps more than any other, signified the new reality of irregular war in the late Cold War.

On September 5, 1972, a horror unfolded at the Olympics in Munich, Germany. While sleeping in the Olympic village, Israeli athletes were awakened in a panic. They were under attack by members of a Palestinian militant group known as the Black September Organization. The masked terrorists carried assault weapons, and intended to take hostages. The innocent Olympians, the assailants hoped, could act as a negotiating chip to force the Israeli government to release Palestinian fighters held in its prisons. That night, the militants forced their way into the athletes' sleeping quarters. Heroic individuals attempted to bar the door as the young Olympians ran for their lives. In the melee, two were killed and the terrorists took nine hostages. The Black September militants used the hostages to acquire helicopters that flew to the airport. There they prepared to board a Boeing 707 operated by Lufthansa. On the tar mac a gunfight ensued and the helicopter carrying the hostages was exploded by a grenade. In the end, eleven Israeli Olympians were dead. The world was shocked.[14]

The Black September attack on the Munich Olympics was the most publicized of a series of terrorist attacks in the early 1970s. In addition to this attack, however, there were numerous cases of hijackings as well as kidnappings, bombings, and shootings. Palestinian groups reacted to its involvement in a gritty war with Israel and frequently carried out terrorist actions that involved hijackings, kidnapping, and even letter bombings. Groups like the PLO conducted a new kind of global irregular war. The most significant such event prior to Munich occurred on September 6, 1970, and is sometimes referred to as "skyjack Sunday." On that day Palestinian terrorists simultaneously took over four hundred hostages when they carried out a massive and coordinated hijacking of multiple passenger airlines. Not all of the hijacking attempts succeeded, but the militants did gain the release of prisoners from the British, German, and Swiss governments, which cooperated out of the hope of avoiding a massive catastrophe.[15]

In the United States, two of the terrorists involved caught the attention of the media. Leila Khaled and Patrick Argüello were revolutionaries of unique backgrounds, and on that September in 1970 the two participated in the attempted hijack of a Boeing 707 flying out of Amsterdam. Prior to the operation Patrick Joseph Argüello, an American of Nicaraguan heritage, was living in Nicaragua and working as a leftist political activist with the Sandinistas, the small revolutionary organization struggling to oust Nicaragua's dictator Anastasio Somoza Debayle.[16] The hijack operation was botched. Argüello and Khaled, however, attempted to take the plane alone. The couple's efforts failed and Argüello was killed. The unusual male-female hijacking combination and the presence of an FSLN operative and US citizen captured the minds of many in the media.

Argüello and Khaled symbolized the global and transnational nature of revolutions in the developing world during the late-Cold War. As Paul Chamberlin demonstrated in his 2012 work, *The Global Offensive*, the PLO represented a revolution that fought in multiple countries and locations, even airplanes, and built connections with revolutionaries across the developing world.[17] The Argüello and Khaled connection demonstrated the broad transnational nature and global interconnectedness of the revolutions of the late Cold War. In Latin America and, as evidenced by Argüello, the FSLN, too, built these connections and conducted an irregular war against the United States' ally in Nicaragua. These types of conflicts bled over into the civilian sector and blurred national boundaries. Many revolutions of the late Cold War made hijacking, kidnapping, and other forms of civilian targets across national boundaries an integral tactic and overall strategy for obtaining its goals. The PLO was a primary example of a revolutionary organization that made the use of terrorism for the pursuit of political objectives an integral tool for achieving its goals.

The problem of terrorism was not unique to the Palestinian and Israeli conflict. Latin America, with revolutions simmering, was also an increasingly common location for terrorism. In his 2015 article, "Take Me to Havana," Teishan A. Latner demonstrates that hijacking in the Americas was an increasingly common theme in the late 1960s and early 1970s. Hijacking, he argues, was representative of the political culture of the time. It was a way in which individuals both expressed a resistance to the revolutionary Castro regime, the heart of leftism in the hemisphere, or uplifted it as a symbol of leftism in the world. The hijackers in the 1970s, he insists, should not be treated as villains or heroes, but rather as "transnational historical actors who belong within conversations about social change and U.S.-Cuba relations."[18]

The revolutionary nation of Cuba was the most common terminus for planes hijacked from the United States or other Latin American countries. Cuba was a revolutionary leftist regime, and it built connections with the FSLN and with groups throughout the Americas and across the Atlantic to Africa. Cuba was the original country deemed a state sponsor of international terrorism by the United States. Cuba supported revolutionaries that sought to undermine the interests of the United States. It was also a sort of bastion of leftism in the Americas and the central point for hijacking and haven, which the Cuban government was not always keen on. In one such case, in 1971, a group of Nicaraguans hijacked a flight from Managua, Nicaragua, to Miami, Florida. The hijackers sought passage to Cuba; however, when the plane was forced to land in Costa Rica for refueling, Costa Rican President Jose Figueres led police forces in fighting the Nicaraguan hijackers. The battle left two hijackers dead and Figueres claimed the Nicaraguans were FSLN agents of "communist subversion."[19] There were also a number of successful and unsuccessful events involving planes hijacked within the United States.[20]

On September 14 and 15, 1972, shortly following the Munich attacks, there were several bombings on United States businesses in Mexico. Small bomb blasts shook office buildings for IBM, Coca Cola, and Pepsi Cola. The bombs did minimal damage though IBM lost some costly and expensive equipment. There was also a blast at a Mexican government building. Following the string of attacks the Central Intelligence Agency (CIA) was asked to provide an assessment for the Nixon administration that determined the degree to which global coordination, i.e. international terrorism, was a serious problem in Latin America and elsewhere. On September 29, Henry Kissinger summarized to President Richard Nixon that the CIA believed that the attacks in Mexico were of little concern and were not coordinated events by legitimate groups or states. In the 1970s, the United States grew increasingly concerned over the emergence of international terrorism as an extension of revolutionary and guerrilla war. Further, following the Munich attacks the administration became increasingly aware of the possibility that guerrilla conflicts could internationalize in a more dangerous and coordinated way and leave difficult to defend areas as potential targets for war.[21]

In 1972 the only group that concerned the CIA with respect to international terrorism was the PLO, which seemed encouraged by the Black September attack, and which actively established international connections.[22] In contrast to the Middle East, Latin America seemed relatively stable. There existed problems, but most of the violence the CIA chalked up to uncoordinated attacks by small groups that reacted out of a sense anti-imperialism. The perception of stability, however, was short lived. Below the surface there were numerous problems. Countries like Nicaragua faced poverty, anger, and a reactionary dictatorship. In many countries nationalist groups motivated by a desire to overthrow the government remained active, but relatively quiet. In Nicaragua, the FSLN remained a relatively small group that few in the United States gave much consideration. While the PLO dominated headlines in the United States, revolutions were poised to escalate in Latin America.

Following the Munich attack Richard Nixon decided that his administration needed to respond and address the terrorism issue. The Nixon administration's response was most significant for what it symbolized for the future of US counterterrorism policy. The administration, for the first time, created a cabinet-wide group to combat terrorism. The body was chaired by Secretary of State William Rogers and was designed to provide an arena through which the United States could consider issues of diplomacy, intelligence, and responses to terrorist incidents. The move marked an important turning point for the United States. The statements and actions taken by the Nixon administration in the early 1970s demonstrated that it began taking terrorism seriously as a unique security threat. Eventually, leaders in the United States realized that by addressing terrorism as a unique threat, rather than evaluating insurgencies/revolutions individually, it could challenge the legitimacy of leftist revolutions more broadly and enhance its Cold War struggle.[23]

Whether or not terrorism was considered a form of unconventional warfare linked to bloody irregular conflicts or whether it was defined as an exclusively criminal act was a significant matter. Was terrorism understood, first, as an offshoot of revolutionary conflict and of long-term regional problems or as a form of criminal behavior? The answer to this question factored centrally into the decisions made by the United States throughout the 1970s and 1980s. The answer was significant because it determined the course of action. If terrorism was understood as symptom of imperialism, inequality, and regional conflict then diplomacy, intelligence, and law might prove the best response to keep civilians safe. However, if defined as a barbaric and criminal behavior than the United States was more likely to establish a hardline position that wholly disregarded the causes of conflict and involved a refusal of negotiation and a repudiation of the legitimacy of leftist revolutionary movements.

For the Nixon administration, how to react to the Munich attacks and to terrorism was not a straightforward matter. The leadership understood that such incidents outcropped from revolutionary conflicts across the developing world. Nixon and his closest advisor Henry Kissinger played a delicate balancing act with respect to Israel and Palestine, by far the most pressing such conflict of the time. On the one hand, the United States could not simply ignore the events, but on the other hand if it demonstrated an obvious favoritism toward Israel or a broad repudiation of terrorism it could alienate potential allies across the Arab and African world. Because of the sensitivity of this issue both Nixon and Kissinger agreed that the United States would not fly flags at half-mast or have the President appear at the United Nations (UN) following the Munich terrorist attack. The United States did support a UN convention that sought the punishment and/or extradition of those individuals that were involved in "the export of politically motivated terrorism but not domestic terrorist acts committed where, for example, wars of liberation are [were] taking place."[24] This measure on terrorism was rather moderate in nature. It was not designed to deal with acts of domestic terrorism, but only with acts of international terrorism that involved violence beyond the territorial boundaries of the conflict with which the acts were associated. The resolution, however, remained controversial among a number of developing world nations, which remained resistant to a measure that seemed a potential strike at legitimate insurgencies in the region. The measure was, as a result, challenged by Arab states that supported the PLO and African states that backed liberation conflicts in Africa. Both perceived this as a strike against legitimate insurgencies that waged anti-imperial conflicts that often extended across boundaries.

Despite a lukewarm response at the UN for the convention on terrorism the Nixon administration joined members of Congress and called for global cooperation and the severing of ties with any state deemed to sponsor terrorists. The leadership in the United States adopted the language that the enemy, the terrorist, represented "outlaws" and were "uncivilized" international criminals.[25] Nixon had, in 1970, insisted that terrorism was an "International disease [and that] the cause [bringing an end to terrorism] justified the means."[26] The United States joined the Nicaraguan dictatorship and other Latin American states in denouncing acts of international terrorism as crimes rather than political actions and/or part of ongoing revolutionary conflicts.[27]

In November 1972, with the strong passage of the UN anti-terrorism convention unlikely the United States representative W. Tapley Bennett spoke before the New York based organization. Bennett voiced the views of President Nixon and Secretary of State Rogers and insisted that the world should join together and create a directive that condemned terrorist acts and allowed for the aggressive targeting of states that support terrorism and the groups that carried the acts out. Nations like Egypt, Lebanon and other Middle Eastern states resisted the call for an ultimatum on terrorism. These governments understood that the causes of terrorism that occurred on "sky-jack Sunday" or during the Munich attacks were unconventional components of gritty wars. Many Middle Eastern states wanted greater awareness of the problems that brought about instances of terrorism with the hope that international awareness of the conflict with Israel might secure peace. The United States, however, was not interested in such investigations, which Bennett claimed were only delaying decisive action.[28]

According to Bennett and the United States representatives at the UN, terrorism was a crime, and was never a permissible form of warfare, regardless of the nature of the conflicts that brought it about. There should be no negotiation with terrorists and only the most decisive and crushing action would supplant such a criminal evil. According to Bennett, terrorism was a "cancer" that had to be immediately expunged. He insisted that the Middle Eastern governments that suggested greater understanding of the conflicts that brought such a threat about "is to say that no treatment can be given the cancer patient until we know all the causes of cancer." For the United States terrorism was a criminal and barbaric evil that targeted innocent civilians, and from this standpoint it should target it decisively regardless of the causes that brought it about.[29]

The Nixon administration's position on the issue of terrorism that the perpetrators were uncivilized, criminal, and that there should be no negotiating or diplomatic involvement with states or groups associated with the terrorism problem was an important symbolic development. Over time the position taken by the Nixon administration on terrorism encouraged the United States to blur the distinction between terrorist groups and legitimate insurgencies. Insurgencies that fought revolutionary wars in which terrorism occurred were eventually characterized as identical to groups that used terrorism as a primary tactical tool. The United States determined that terrorism was a criminal behavior and established a tradition of non-negotiation in US counterterrorism strategy. Despite moments in which the non-negotiation strategy was contradicted by action, like during the Iran-Contra affair a decade later, the United States has since consistently adhered to an ideal of non-negotiation with those deemed by the administration as affiliated with terrorism. Over the long term this principle is the underlining hallmark of the war on terrorism. Simply stated, the United States does not negotiate with those associated with terrorism. Of course, the catch to this decisive assertion is that those which were or were not associated with terrorism was a determination made by the United States. Nonetheless, the small steps taken by the Nixon administration established a precedent that later allowed the Reagan administration to use counterterrorism as a tool for waging a more aggressive Cold War in the following decade.

The perpetrators of terrorism were often guerrilla fighters and were connected to war and revolutionary activity. Often terrorist hijackers and kidnappers during the 1970s almost always sought an exchange and in many cases the exchanges were made without serious harm. Common demands were the release of political prisoners or military fighters or transport to a friendly nation, like Cuba. Hijacking as an aspect of revolution and civil struggle was surprisingly sane when compared to suicide events like September 11, 2001, or the frequent bombings of the more recent past. In one case, Palestinian terrorists in Egypt actually exploded a hijacked airline to send a message only after having evacuated all the passengers to safety. International terrorism was often a form of unconventional warfare connected to conflicts and revolutions, and in many cases terrorist acts were used as leverage for negotiation. Non-negotiation as a firm United States policy, over time, made the deterioration of conflicts that had legitimate diplomatic solutions more likely and tended to radicalize the opposition, but it was also a way for the United States to address the revolutions of the late Cold War in the decade to come.[30]

While Nixon never used counterterrorism exclusively to justify an invasion of another country, he did, in the aftermath of the Black September attacks, create a basic groundwork for the future. Political scientist Joseph H. Campos demonstrated in his book, *The State and Terrorism*, that the rhetoric of the United States following the terrorist events of the early 1970s established a basis for characterizing terrorism not in terms of local and regional problems that brought such action about, but rather as associated with the uncivilized, the irrational, and with which negotiation was impossible.[31] The Nixon administration identified terrorism as a security threat that was unique in its criminal and barbaric nature. It was from this standpoint that a policy of non-negotiation with those alleged of terrorism was created and has remained the most consistent component of US counterterrorism strategy ever since.

Throughout the 1970s and 1980s the United States grew increasingly concerned over terrorism primarily as a problem related to leftism. In the 1970s, the PLO was recognized as the primary international terrorist group while Cuba was perceived as the primary global state sponsor of terrorism, and the United States was already considering the use of hardline measures to remove the leadership. In a meeting between President Gerald Ford and Secretary of State Henry Kissinger in February 1976, the Secretary, agitated over Cuban interventions in Angola and the Americas suggested to President Ford that, "I think we are going to have to smash Castro." The Secretary proposed a preemptive attack on Cuba. Kissinger believed that the controversial action needed to wait until after the election that November, 1976. To this President Ford only gave a two word response, "I agree."[32]

Kissinger was, at the time, a highly respected diplomat. Despite controversy and protest toward of some of his decisions, his sharing of the Nobel Peace Prize with Le Duc Tho to end the United States involvement in the Vietnam War was a tremendous success in the eyes of many. In the twenty-first century, Kissinger, while still beloved by many conservatives and the political establishment, has grown increasingly controversial over his handlings of the Vietnam peace and his involvement with the hard rightist regimes of South America: particularly, Chile and Argentina. Kissinger was a realist, he believed that decisions should be in the best interests of the United States, and from his view it often seemed that economic and political alliances mattered more than human rights. Of course, 1976 was an election year, and Ford's loss to Jimmy Carter meant the world would not see how the Ford and Kissinger policy on Cuba and the Cold War might have developed.

State sponsored terrorism was hardly a problem limited to forces on the left. Indeed, in the Americas in the late 1970s the most vigilante and aggressive state sponsors of terrorism were hardline rightist governments that sought a no limits war on leftists and potential subversives. However, because of global Cold War competition and Henry Kissinger's strict realism with respect to friend and foe in the developing world, the United States during the Nixon and Ford administrations felt compelled to overlook, and even act in complicity with the problem of rightist state sponsored terrorism. Allies like Garcia's son and successor, Anstasio Somoza Debayle, in Nicaragua were among the hardline dictatorships in the 1970s supported by the Nixon and Ford administrations. However, following a military coup in 1976 Argentina's new military rightist government proved, along with Chile, a most efficient, ruthless, and aggressive state sponsor on the right.

On September 1, 1976, Director of Policy Planning Winston Lord sent a lengthy brief to Secretary of State Henry Kissinger. The brief was titled "Latin America: A Deceptive Calm?" and it conveyed a cautious optimism with respect to the Americas. Overall, Latin America appeared relatively stable and moving toward the orbit of the United States. Lord affirmed that the region witnessed a resurgence of conservative governments that were interested in closer economic ties with the United States while the leftism driven by Cuba, the Soviet Union, and others had fallen in popularity. However, the stability and apparent pro-US shift in the leadership of many Latin American governments came alongside a deep seated concern. Lord expressed concern with a particular problem in the region, terrorism from the right.[33]

Several South American governments, including Argentina, Chile, Paraguay, Uruguay, and Brazil, participated in sweeping counterterrorism operations against leftists in the region. The program was designed to arrest, assassinate, and destroy those elements in the region affiliated with leftism. The governments were militaristic and supported "indiscriminate counterterrorist operations, some of which [were] carried out with anti-Semitic fury by defiant local Nazis, apparently with police connections and even some official tolerance." Lord feared that such a militant rightist crackdown would victimize the innocent, and make a negative blowback a possibility. [34]

Following a successful military coup in Argentina a new hard right government seized power in 1976. During a meeting with the new leadership that June, Henry Kissinger opened with a casual conversation about soccer. The world cup, he acknowledged, was in Argentina in 1978 and Kissinger said he would be there and, further, he enthusiastically expected Argentina to take the cup. Despite the fact that his prediction was actually correct, Argentina did win the cup two years later, the purpose of the meeting was to confirm the support of the United States and the process of consolidating and stabilizing the new government. The new military regime needed to consolidate its control, and it sought to target what it defined as leftist terrorism that threatened the country. In meetings with Kissinger, individuals like Foreign Minister César Augusto Guzzetti lamented with paranoid fear the presence of leftists, many of whom had allegedly been forced to Argentina by the hardline leaderships in Chile and Uruguay. In somewhat veiled language the Argentinians spoke to Kissinger of the need to purge the country of leftist terrorism. The conversations with the Secretary of State acknowledged the beginning of what historians call the Dirty War: a period of several years in which the government of Argentina conducted a brutal terror war against its people that resulted in thousands kidnapped, tortured, and murdered indiscriminately. State Department officials of both the Ford and Carter administration's acknowledged that a significant number of the victims of this purge were innocent civilians or immigrants. [35]

In April 1977, President Jimmy Carter's Human Rights Coordinator Patricia Derian described the treatment of political prisoners in Argentina. She explained that those picked up, often at random, were

> tortured with water, electricity and psychological disintegration methods. Those thought to be salvageable [were] sent to regular jails and prisons where the psychological process [was] continued on a more subtle level. Those found to be incorrigible [were] murdered and dumped on garbage heaps or street corners, but more often [were] given arms with live ammunition, grenades, bombs and put into automobiles and sent out of the compound to be killed on the road in what [was] then reported publicly to be a shootout or response to an attack on some military installation. [36]

From Derian's perspective her primary question was, why, why had such violence occurred? The answer was complex and multifaceted, but part of the reason for its escalation related to the failure of Henry Kissinger's State Department to make a coordinated and clear effort to stop the slaughter in Argentina. A year prior to Derian's report, Kissinger responded to Argentina's intended use of domestic terrorism against leftists with a short and concise statement: "If there are things that have to be done, do them quickly."[37]

Henry Kissinger's stance with the government of Argentina at the outset of the Dirty War revealed a dangerous double standard in the United States' handling of the terrorism problem that continued in the coming decade. Kissinger was a consummate realist. The Secretary seemed to have believed that the United States needed to support its allies, and as long as that relationship facilitated the interests of the United States then the means thru which stability was achieved were less relevant. Judging from his policy, human rights really only mattered to Kissinger if it undermined the United States' interests and those of its allies. His was a cold realism and a grand vision. The global fight against leftism was far more important than human rights and the use of terrorism. For this reason, Kissinger kept himself at an arms distance from openly discussing the tactics that the Argentine leadership implemented, but made it known that as long as it did not last long the State Department's policy was to support Argentina virtually with no regard at all for the kinds of actions the government undertook. On several occasions Kissinger went out of his way to convey support for the Argentine government even as it carried out widespread acts of domestic and international terrorism.[38]

Kissinger's policy of ignoring Argentina's human rights abuses caused a division with the then-Ambassador to Nicaragua, Robert Hill. Hill seemed to take it as a commonsense decision to issue a démarche to the Argentine government over human rights. The abuses were obvious and widespread. Hill strongly felt that the United States needed to make it known to the leadership of Argentina that such abuses were unacceptable. Kissinger, however, fearing damage to the diplomatic relationship with the United States, refused to support issuing such a firm statement to the government. This policy shocked Ambassador Hill, who regarded Kissinger's treatment of the Argentine leadership as basically providing a "green light" to begin a domestic terror war of massive proportions.[39]

As terrible as Patricia Derian's assessment of the domestic terrorism issue in Argentina was, it was only part of the story. Argentina and Chile were also the leading architects in an international terror operation against leftism across the region, but also extending to the United States and Europe. Argentina, ally of the United States, was a state sponsor of international terrorism. As a leading agent of extreme rightist governments that dominated the Southern Cone states of South America, Argentina prepared and conducted a state sponsored international terror campaign. During 1976, the extreme right states comprised of Argentina, Chile, Uruguay, Paraguay, and, to a lesser extent, Brazil hatched a plan known as Operation Condor. The purpose of Condor was to conduct an international irregular war against leftism. The plan involved acts of international assassination, sabotage, and support for rightist governments and militants. Assistant Secretary of State Harry W. Schlaudemen described the governments as "paranoid" and expressed concern that these states together began privately referring to the campaign as a global and Christian "third world war." The parties intended to use the same kind of irregular war used by Cuba and the PLO in fostering a global irregular war against the left. [40]

Even on the issue of international assassination, which involved coordination of multiple Southern Cone countries and the organization of irregular units designed to operate globally in pursuit of leftist targets, the State Department under Kissinger responded in a questionable fashion. Initially, Operation Condor and the discussion of a coordinated third world irregular war appeared to create a consensus of disapproval in the State Department. The Assistant Secretary of State Harry W. Schlaudemen, Ambassador Robert Hill, and Secretary of State Henry Kissinger agreed that an internationally coordinated irregular counterterror war might escalate the terrorism problem, and suggested US involvement in illegal violations of sovereign territory by aligned states that was morally indefensible. The Assistant Secretary of State provided a long brief that explained how diplomats could help dismantle the southern cone states attempt at a coordinated international terror program. Kissinger prepared a formal message on the issue for the United States' ambassadors to deliver to their respective governments. [41] However, before the message was delivered to Argentina and Chile (the two foremost states involved) Kissinger, apparently feeling that the southern cone governments were not going to act on the plan after all, repealed the messages and directed the ambassadors to "take no further action." [42]

The refusal to send the message of opposition on Operation Condor was a mistake. On September 21, 1976, former Chilean Ambassador Orlando Letelier was traveling with Ronni and Michael Moffitt thru the busy embassy row area of Washington, DC. The three were heading to *The Institute for Policy Studies*. Shortly after entering Sheridan Circle an explosive device affixed to bottom of the car detonated and killed Letelier and Ronni Moffitt. [43] The car bombing, which coincidentally occurred shortly after Kissinger called off the cease and desist message on Condor, was the first major international assassination for the operation. Later, the southern cone alliance botched an attack on a leftist headquarters in Paris, France. The states, also, apparently used an American communication site in the Panama Canal Zone as the base to coordinate with states and groups throughout the region. [44] From Kissinger's vantage the United States would and should stand by its allies regardless of human rights issues. It seems that a fear of harassing or upsetting US allies led Kissinger to not issue the démarche on human rights or on matters of international assassination. On October 7, Kissinger, along with Schauldemen and Undersecretary of State Philip Habib, testified to Foreign Minister Guzzetti that, "we want you to succeed. . . . I have an old fashioned view that friends should be supported . . . the quicker you succeed the better."[45] The controversial position taken by the Secretary of State implicated the United States in a program of both domestic and international terrorism.

By 1979, Argentina turned its state sponsorship toward Central America, which was gripped by revolutionary violence. It influenced El Salvador and Guatemala, which incorporated the use of death squads to purge leftists. It also began the assistance and training of rightist militants in the region, eventually referred to as the Contras, whose purpose involved attacking the new leftist Sandinista government of Nicaragua.[46] The United States, through the CIA, were complicit in the activity of the Argentines in the region and when the Reagan administration took over in 1981 and 1982 it assumed full responsibility for what was, in truth, a state sponsored terror war against Nicaragua, and a militant global irregular war against leftism.

The problem of terrorism developed alongside regional conflicts across the developing world. In the period following September 11, 2001, Americans were trained to consider terrorism as an act conducted by irrational fanatics with no reasonable motivation other than an extreme and barbaric perspective on the world. The historical development of the modern terrorism problem, however, accompanied regional conflicts that related, often, to the long historical roots of imperialism and inequality. Historically, terrorism was not limited to Islamic radicalism or to the Middle East. Instead, this form of unconventional warfare was an outcropping of conflicts throughout the world, and significantly in the Americas.

By the end of Gerald Ford's presidency an important segment of the leadership in the United States increasingly evaluated international terrorism most on the basis of ideological affiliation within the Cold War rather than by the specific action (violence against non-combatants). The actions of individuals like Henry Kissinger pushed the United States toward defining terrorism as a political term meant to justify its posture in the world. Across the Americas the Nixon and the Ford administrations supported countries like Chile and Argentina that used domestic terrorism and hatched plans for international sponsored acts of terrorism while simultaneously identifying Cuba and the PLO as barbarous criminals. A trend was being set in US foreign relations that supported using unconventional irregular war, which included acts of terrorism, in pursuit of the national security interests and hegemony of the United States.

The course on foreign policy for the 1980s, however, was not yet charted. When Jimmy Carter was elected president in November 1976 he pledged a foreign policy doctrine built on the idea that the United States needed to depart from the morally and legally questionable Cold War realism that embodied the period. Carter insisted that the United States supported far too many human rights abusers that terrorized populations. For Jimmy Carter, the policy outlook of the United States was so obsessed by the left-right struggle of the Cold War that it was morally indefensible. Following the beginning of the Nicaraguan Revolution the President made the small Central American state and its despised dictator a testing ground for a departure from the Cold War realism of a Henry Kissinger driven State Department. The administration hoped to chart a course in which the United States treated human rights and terrorism equally regardless of political or ideological affiliation.

NOTES

1. "Zelaya Insisted on Death of Americans: Overruled Advisors, Vice Consul," *New York Times*, November 21, 1909, http://db15.linccweb.org/login?url=http://search.proquest.com. db15.linccweb.org/docview/96937486?accountid=45760; "Two Americans Shot for Aiding Revolt," *New York Times*, November 19, 1909, http://db15.linccweb.org/login?url=http:// search.proquest.com.db15.linccweb.org/docview/96908373?accountid=45760.

2. Neill Macaulley, *The Sandino Affair* (Micanopy, Fl.: Wacahoota Press, 1998), 20–23.

3. Matilde Zimmerman, *Sandinista: Carlos Fonseca and the Nicaraguan Revolution* (London: Duke University Press, 2000), 1–11; Macaulay, *The Sandino Affair*, 1–30.

4. Walter Lafeber, *Inevitable Revolutions: The United States in Central America* (New York: W. W. Norton, 1993); Walter Lafeber, *The New Empire: An Interpretation of American Expansion, 1860–1898* (London: Cornell University Press, 1963).

5. Macaulay, *The Sandino Affair*, 22–23.

6. Jason Colby, *The Business of Empire: United Fruit, Race and U.S. Expansion in Central America* (Cornell: Cornell University Press, 2011).

7. Sandino accounts of battles of Telpaneca, San Fernando, and Las Flores, as compiled in Sergio Ramirez and Robert Edgar Conrad, *Sandino: The Testimony of a Nicaraguan Patriot, 1921–1934* (Princeton: Princeton University Press, 1990), 101–104.

8. Michael Hunt and Steven Levine, *Arc of Empire: Americas Wars in Asia from the Philippines to Vietnam* (Chapel Hill: University of North Carolina Press, 2012); Stuart Creighton Miller, *Benevolent Assimilation: The American Conquest of the Philippines, 1899–1903* (London: Yale University Press, 1982).

9. Macaulay, *The Sandino Affair*, 1–30.

10. Ramirez and Conrad, *Sandino*, 492–497.

11. Paul Coe Clark, Jr., *The United States and Somoza, 1933–1956: A Revisionist Look* (London: Praeger, 1992).

12. Zimmerman, *Sandinista*, 6–7.

13. Paul Thomas Chamberlin, *The Global Offensive: The United States, the Palestinian Liberation Organization, and the Making of Post-Cold War Order* (New York: Oxford, 2012).

14. David Binder, "9 Israelis on Olympic Team Killed with 4 Arab Captors as Police Fight Band that Disrupted Munich Games," *New York Times*, September 6, 1972.

15. Joseph H. Campos II, *The State and Terrorism: National Security and the Mobilization of Power* (London: Ashgate, 2013), 34.

16. "Slain Airline Hijacker a U.S. Citizen," *New York Times*, September 15, 1970.

17. Chamberlin, *The Global Offensive.*

18. Teishan A. Latner, "Take Me to Havana: Airline Hijacking, U.S.–Cuba Relations, and Political Protest in Late Sixties' America" *Diplomatic History* 39, no. 1 (January 2015): 16–44.

19. "President Says No," *New York Times*, December 19, 1971.

20. "Two are Wounded in New Hijacking: Stewardess and Passenger Shot in Flight to Cuba," *New York Times*, June 25, 1971.

21. "Terrorist Attacks on US Companies," Memorandum From the President's Assistant for National Security Affairs (Kissinger) to President Nixon, Washington, September 29, 1972, National Archives, Nixon Presidential Materials, NSC Files, Subject Files, Box 310, Cabinet Committee on Terrorism.

22. "Terrorist Attacks on US Companies," September 29, 1972, Nixon Presidential Materials.

23. NSDD 207-NSC Staff, "Trends in Terrorism," Folder "NSDD 207-NSC Staff: Craig Coy, Robert Earl," Box 1-91956, Counterterrorism and Narcotics Directorate NSC Records, NSC Office of: Records, Ronald Reagan Library.

24. National Archives, Nixon Presidential Materials, NSC Files, Subject Files, Box 310, Cabinet Committee on Terrorism.

25. Tad Szulc, "U.S. Moves for World Campaign to Counter Political Terrorists" *New York Times*, September 7, 1972.

26. Warren Weaver Jr., "President Scores Tide of Terrorism: Campaigning in the Midwest, He Asserts Violence is an International Disease," *New York Times*, October 20, 1970.

27. "11 Nation Unit Sets Pact on Terrorism," *New York Times*, September 28, 1970.

28. Robert Alden, "U.S. Challenges UN on Terror: Legal Committee Told It Can No Longer Afford Rhetoric," *New York Times*, November 14, 1972.

29. Alden, "U.S. Challenges UN on Terror: Legal Committee Told It Can No Longer Afford Rhetoric."

30. "4 Jets Hijacked; One, a 747, is Blown Up: Arab Group Says it Took Planes, El Al Foils Move," *New York Times*, September 7, 1970.

31. Campos, *The State and Terrorism: National Security and the Mobilization of Power*, 34–40.

32. Kissinger to Ford, Memorandum of Conversation, February 25, 1976, *The Digital National Security Archive*, "Argentina, 1975–1980: The Making of U.S. Human Rights" (Ann Arbor: Proquest, 2012).

33. Briefing Memorandum From the Director of the Policy Planning Staff (Lord) to Secretary of State Kissinger, National Archives, RG 59, Policy Planning Council (S/PC), Policy Planning Staff (S/P), Director's Files 1969–77, Lot 77D112, Box 361, September 1976.

34. Briefing Memorandum From the Director of the Policy Planning Staff (Lord) to Secretary of State Kissinger, National Archives, September 1976.

35. Kissinger and Guzzetti, "Memorandum of Conversation, June 10, 1976," *The Digital National Security Archive*, "Argentina, 1975–1980: The Making of U.S. Human Rights" (Ann Arbor: Proquest, 2012).

36. Notes from US State Department Human Rights Coordinator Patricia Derian, April 1, 1977, *The Digital National Security Archive*, "Argentina, 1975–1980: The Making of U.S. Human Rights" (Ann Arbor: Proquest, 2012).

37. Kissinger and Guzzetti, "Memorandum of Conversation, June 10, 1976," *The Digital National Security Archive*.

38. "Patricia Derian's conversations with Ambassadors Hill and Siracusa, April 1, 1977," *The Digital National Security Archive*, "Argentina, 1975–1980: The Making of U.S. Human Rights" (Ann Arbor: Proquest, 2012).

39. "Patricia Derian's conversations with Ambassadors Hill and Siracusa, April 1, 1977," *The Digital National Security Archive*.

40. "Department of State, Cable, 'Operation Condor,' drafted August 18, 1976, and sent August 23, 1976," *The Digital National Security Archive*, "Argentina, 1975–1980: The Making of U.S. Human Rights" (Ann Arbor: Proquest, 2012).

41. "Department of State, Cable, 'Operation Condor,' drafted August 18, 1976, and sent August 23, 1976," *The Digital National Security Archive*.

42. "Department of State, Cable, 'Operation Condor,' September 20, 1976," *The Digital National Security Archive*, "Argentina, 1975–1980: The Making of U.S. Human Rights" (Ann Arbor: Proquest, 2012).

43. David Binder, "FBI Gets Tip in the Letelier Bombing Case That High Chilean Secret Policeman Flew to U.S. Last Month," *New York* Times, September 23, 1976.

44. State Department Cable, US Ambassador Robert White (Paraguay) to Secretary of State Cyrus Vance, October 13, 1978, *The Digital National Security Archive*, "Argentina, 1975–1980: The Making of U.S. Human Rights" (Ann Arbor: Proquest, 2012).

45. Secretary's Meeting with Argentine Foreign Minister Guzzetti, October 10, 1976, *The Digital National Security Archive*, "Argentina, 1975–1980: The Making of U.S. Human Rights" (Ann Arbor: Proquest, 2012).

46. Noam Chomsky, *What Uncle Sam Really Wants* (Berkeley: Odonian, 1992).

Chapter Two

Revolution in Nicaragua

On the night of December 27, 1974, in a quiet area of Managua, Nicaragua, the United States Ambassador Turner B. Shelton attended a dinner party for the Nicaraguan Minister of Agriculture. Shortly after the ambassador left, over a dozen armed men from the Sandinista Liberation Front (FSLN) approached the location unseen. Then, after entering the grounds, the militants raided the party and caught the occupants by surprise. The targets were high profile figures that the guerrillas intended to use as leverage for the release of captured fighters held by Nicaragua's authoritarian leader Anastasio Somoza Debayle. The militants succeeded and took several hostages including corporate executives from both *Exxon* and *Bank of America*.[1] Somoza was infuriated at the successful operation, and was further embarrassed for ultimately having no choice but to capitulate to the guerrillas demands. In exchange for the release of the hostages Somoza released several FSLN fighters and arranged for them a flight to Cuba.[2] The dictator declared that the act was carried out by Sandinista and Cuban terrorists. He promised a response to the terrorist act. This rather obscure event marked an early catalyst in the development of the Nicaraguan Revolution.

In the 1970s, Nicaragua was a nation of many problems. A devastating earthquake in 1972 destroyed much of the capital city, Managua, and left some 10,000 people dead. After the tragedy Somoza assumed complete power over the foreign aid and reconstruction of the country. However, he did little to help the people and instead took personal business opportunities and profited from the crisis.[3] The Somoza family was long supported by the United States in the rule of the country. The United States facilitated the rise of the Somoza family to power during the 1930s. Over the course of the following decades many Nicaraguans suffered. Trade agreements with the United States reduced the population of Nicaragua to the status of servitude.

The Somoza's, meanwhile, controlled much of the business in the country and profited handsomely despite the suffering of the people.

Hardship in the small Central American country expanded nationalist resistance and helped bolster the ranks of the FSLN. Tomas Borge, Carlos Fonseca, Silvio Mayorga, and Daniel Ortega made up the leadership of this revolutionary movement. For over a decade this group agitated for reform. The FSLN formed in the early 1960s. The group portrayed itself as Marxist and drew influence from Fidel Castro's success in Cuba. The Sandinistas oriented itself in firm opposition to the pro-United States and staunch anti-communist Somoza.[4] In fact, the wanton aggression of Somoza was the key ingredient to the development of the FSLN as a legitimate and consolidated group. Prior to the late 1970s the group was actually a collection of different entities with different leaders that competed against one another and lacked continuity or even a remotely popular national backing. What, in fact, created the popular backing of the FSLN was an aggressive war on terror conduct by President Anastasio Somoza Debayle.[5]

Terrorism is not only a type of action, something one does, it also can provide a framework for power and control by justifying repressive measures at home and in some cases offensive measures abroad. It is not uncommon for national leaders to use the threat of terrorism to characterize and ground its own aggressive domestic and military policies. Terrorism is often mobilized as propaganda against a state's citizens. This form of domestic coercion is powerful because it implies that the enemies are criminal, immoral, and will attack citizens and the government with suddenness and without cause. The propaganda surrounding terrorism draws on the instinctive emotions of fear and self-preservation held by citizens. If the situation is urgent enough citizens will accept significant limitations on personal liberty out of feelings of revenge and prevention of sudden and impending death. Because it implies the criminal and immoral targeting of a civilian population the rhetoric of terrorism is sometimes used by governments as a tactic of defending a policy that is aggressive internationally and domestically. In the aftermath of the FSLN attack that December, Anastasio Somoza Debayle, not unlike other rightist regimes across the Americas, began his own anti-leftist terror war.

The December attack embarrassed Somoza. Following the event the dictator began a concerted effort against the FSLN in his country. He insisted that the Sandinistas were complicit in Cuban backed terrorism. The CIA could not confirm that this was a reality, but Somoza was convinced and used the situation to justify a state of martial law in the Nicaragua. Somoza redoubled the training of the National Guard in unconventional warfare and counterterrorism, he censored the media, and began sweeping arrests of potential FSLN operatives. The suspects were swiftly prosecuted in military courts or simply murdered in cold blood. Somoza claimed that the purpose of these measures was to address a coordinated terrorist enemy, and he used this to attack the FSLN and other critics like Pedro Joaquin Chamorro and his critical newspaper *La Prensa*.[6]

As part of Somoza' domestic war on terror pro-government groups harassed the population. The groups made threatening phone calls, kidnapped, tortured, and murdered those considered either complicit in FSLN activity or for openly criticizing the Somoza regime.[7] On multiple occasions Somoza ordered the National Guard to attack towns, which it did so aggressively and at times with indiscriminate fire bombings.[8] On Sunday, November 7, 1976, government forces ambushed and killed Carlos Fonseca, the ideological leader of the FSLN. Somoza reportedly received the news of Fonseca's death with jubilation. The National Guard had killed the most significant leader of the FSLN. 1976 was a difficult year for the FSLN as the group suffered not only the death of Fonseca, but also of a number of leaders including the organizer of the December 1974 raid.[9] However, any feelings of success that Somoza may have possessed were soon washed away as his regimes brutality increasingly fueled the growth of a popular uprising.

On January 10, 1978, four assassins allegedly linked to the Somoza family shot and killed Pedro Joaquin Chamorro in an event that was a culmination of a violent domestic war on terror unleashed by Somoza following the attack of December 1974.[10] In a country increasingly angry with Somoza's corrupt leadership Chamorro, not a member of the FSLN, was the leading voice for democratic change. The silencing of Chamorro unleashed the final momentum needed for the FSLN to bring Somoza down. Following the killing the FSLN grew in strength and widespread opposition to Somoza swelled to an unprecedented level. *La Prensa* was a leading source of criticism to the actions of what it called a pro-government "White Hand" group that terrorized the society. According to the United States embassy in Nicaragua such a group did exist, but it also emphasized that the amount of terrorism from the left, most likely, eclipsed pro-government terrorism. Regardless, the populace moved against Somoza, and by 1978 the dictator was locked in a civil struggle for his government and his life.[11] What happened next likely gave Somoza the greatest surprise of his life.

While Somoza clinched Nicaragua in a violent terror war the United States President, Jimmy Carter, inaugurated in 1977, attempted to chart a bold new course in US foreign policy. The election of Carter was a bad sign for Somoza. Jimmy Carter, elected specifically because he was not a Washington insider, began his presidency with the hope that his election ushered in a new age in US foreign relations. At a speech at Notre Dame University on May 22, 1977, President Carter called for a correcting of the flaws of the Cold War foreign policy of his predecessors. He claimed, "We are now free of that inordinate fear of communism which once led us to embrace any dictator who joined us in that fear . . . this approach failed, with Vietnam the best example of its intellectual and moral poverty."[12] Carter believed that the

Cold War policy of the Vietnam era was inherently flawed. He insisted that, "Our policy during this period was guided by two principles: a belief that Soviet expansion was almost inevitable but must be contained, and the corresponding belief in the importance of an almost exclusive alliance among non-communist nations on both sides of the Atlantic . . . we can no longer separate the traditional issues of war and peace from the new global questions of justice, equity and human rights."[13] Carter wanted human rights and democracy as the hallmarks of his policy.

Carter's approach hinged on the idea that the United States needed to set a moral standard in the world, and that the United States had, in Vietnam, lost much of the country's moral credibility. The basis of Carter's human rights initiative was that the country would not align itself with dictatorial human rights violators for the sake of Cold War competition. Latin America was one of the first regions where Carter pursued this new policy agenda. Under Carter the United States, for the first time, signed on to the Inter-American Convention on Human Rights, and began selectively refusing aid to human rights violators.[14] For liberal critics, the Vietnam War called into question the American utilization of non-democratic regimes in the pursuit of containment and the consolidation of the United States' sphere of influence. In sharing this view, Carter "did not regard communism as the chief enemy" in the world.[15] As President he felt that the United States should act "as a protector of democracies", and should define policy through human rights, not communism.[16] His policy was a break from that of his predecessors, which had often placed human rights as secondary to anti-communism.

As a result of Somoza's tyrannical war on terror the dictatorship was an ideal candidate for Jimmy Carter's new human rights centered foreign policy. The Somoza's were educated in the United States. Anastasio Debayle attended West Point, spoke perfect English, and had friends in the Defense Department and in the United States Congress.[17] Under his leadership Nicaragua acted as a virulently anti-communist servant to the United States. Nicaragua was also an authoritarian state and Anastasio Somoza Debayle was a repressive leader and consistent human rights violator. Somoza's exceptionally bad record on human rights following the December attack made the leadership a primary target for the Carter administration's new policy approach. In an attempt to force democratization and improve the condition of human rights the administration eliminated virtually all military aid to the Somoza regime.[18]

The Carter administration underestimated the potential strength that the removal of support might give to Somoza's revolutionary opponents. It did not support the FSLN, which it perceived as a radical and a potentially dangerous Marxist organization. Carter also was concerned with Cuban and Soviet influence. The Carter administration hoped to use the economic and military pressure on Somoza to encourage a democratization of Nicaragua.

However, the democratization that the administration envisioned was moderate and centered around the existing governmental structure and included the National Guard and the state legislature. The administration hoped it could remove the leadership, but yet maintain the governing structure for elections in 1980 that would end Somoza's control, but also disenfranchise any ability of the FSLN to seize control of the new government. It was a risky policy and one that the administration was unable to control once the revolution, led by the FSLN but carried through by the people, gained momentum.[19]

Since the 1950s, decolonization swept through the developing world and it was often fueled ideologically by leftist visions of Leninism and Marxism. Revolutionary writers like Frantz Fannon and Le Duan made the call for the people to rise up against imperialism. The FSLN in Nicaragua and the Farabundo Marti National Liberation Front (FMLN) in El Salvador both represented examples of revolutionary movements that heeded the call for revolution throughout the developing world. While these two groups developed in the 1960s and 1970s both fashioned its organizations as leftist nationalist movements symbolized by fallen leaders, Augusto César Sandino in Nicaragua and Agustín Farabundo Martí Rodríguez in El Salvador. During the 1930s, both had sought to evict brutal military dictators. Neocolonialism forced a desperate poverty on the people in Central America and this led to unrest and eventually revolution in both Nicaragua and El Salvador. These revolutions were part of a series of events that challenged the Carter administration's approach with Nicaragua.

Following Chamorro's death the revolution in Nicaragua gained momentum as a true popular uprising.[20] There were countrywide marches, and work strikes from wide sectors of the populace. Somoza and his National Guard repressed dissent and killed thousands. Among the dead included ABC news correspondent Bill Stewart.[21] Somoza's resistance to democratic change and his increased use of force played into the hands of the dictators' foremost opposition, the FSLN. The Sandinista Liberation Front's ranks swelled as the political movement against Somoza, known as the Broad Opposition Front, began to work directly with the FSLN. Many Nicaraguans were increasingly disgruntled with the regime, and looked for a movement that could bring effective change.

By 1978, the Somoza regime received virtually no military support from its former ally the United States. The leadership relied on whatever small military shipments it could receive from Honduras and Guatemala. However, Somoza remained defiant. By September the National Guard had temporarily stopped an FSLN offensive that escalated following the Chamorro killing, the cost was around 10,000 dead, a figure that included substantial numbers from the civilian population.[22] Throughout the twentieth century the United States openly reserved the right to intervene in the affairs of Nicaragua and to support military strongmen like Somoza. The rise of Somoza's father Anastasio Somoza Garcia came amid the influence of the United States. Anastasio Somoza Debayle was a product of a long running history of intervention. In July of 1978, understanding the historical connection of the United States, the embattled dictator told reporters that, "I don't think that the United States would have the nerve to ask me to resign . . . if they ask me to resign the implications would be tremendous."[23] Somoza confidently insisted that, "The United States has not lost interest in its ultimate geopolitical mission."[24] For the dictator, a leader whose family had consciously served the geopolitical interests of the United States for so long, it was incomprehensible that the United States might facilitate its collapse. Somoza's confidence, however, proved poorly placed. By July 1979, Somoza's end was imminent, and the Carter administration secretly demanded his resignation.[25]

Fearful of the radicalism of the FSLN and equally insistent on separating itself from Somoza the Carter administration tried to control the endgame in Nicaragua and played an increasingly delicate balancing act. Its goal was a moderate democratization that would alienate the FSLN and oust Somoza while introducing a democratic transition that maintained the legislature and the National Guard as central structures in the country. To achieve this the administration arranged a series of meetings between the new Ambassador Lawrence Pezzullo and Somoza. Pezzullo had just come to Nicaragua from Uruguay after the serving Ambassador simply packed up and left amid an increasingly dangerous and violent situation.[26] The purpose of the meetings were to communicate the United States' objectives to Somoza and convince the embattled dictator to behave in a manner consistent with the Carter administration's goals. By 1979, the most important objective was to convince Somoza to resign, but only at the moment of the United States' choosing.[27] The Carter administration attempted to sever its ties with the United States' long time imperial client, but it still secretly worked to control the governing structure of the country.

The Pezzullo-Somoza meetings were icy and full of resentment. By July, Somoza feared for his life and was eager to flee the country. The United States, however, urged him to stay on until the time was right so as not to allow a poorly timed resignation to facilitate a Sandinista take over, which the administration viewed as a potential disaster. Somoza, visibly exhibiting the anger of betrayal, only cooperated because it appeared that the United States was likely the only player capable of protecting him after the resignation. In the fourth meeting with Pezzullo, he lamented that, "I realize that I am a captive and am willing to go along with your plans."[28] Somoza viewed the deterioration of the situation as linked primarily to the lack of military support from the United States and the abundant support of nations like Cuba to the FSLN. The Carter administration resented Somoza and the FSLN on almost equal grounds. Somoza was intransigent and continually refused to recognize human rights and to democratize his country. In the meetings with

Pezzullo, Somoza was most concerned about his life, his financial assets, and the lives of the members of his high command, but the ambassador gave the embattled dictator few assurances. When Somoza asked the ambassador about the fate of his assets in Nicaragua, Pezzullo responded that his wealth would be "nationalized." The ambassador remarked that when he was told this Somoza "did not blink an eye."[29] Pezzullo told Somoza that the administration made no guarantee that he might receive asylum in the United States or that the Carter administration would do anything to assure his safety.[30]

Undoubtedly during those final meetings with Pezzullo, Somoza, who had originally expressed certainty of the United States' support, surely felt shock as the imperial neighbor to the north dictated his dismissal. As perhaps a final gesture of anger toward the United States' leadership, which Somoza felt had betrayed him, the dictator released details from these meetings to journalists. The information revealed the administration's attempt to leave Somoza in power until a time right for the United States. Somoza revealed that the United States attempted to manipulate the future leadership of the country. In a different situation, perhaps, such information posed potential problems, but the actual plan that the Carter administration hoped to hatch was unlikely to work anyway.[31]

For the Carter administration Somoza had to go, but it did not want the FSLN to replace the dictator. Instead, it wanted the National Guard in place and as the backbone for a new moderate democratic leadership. The United States hoped to orchestrate a change of government by directing Somoza to appoint a temporary replacement that would oversee a democratic transition after he fled the country.[32] At least a few in the State Department perceived this tightrope policy as folly. Mark L. Schneider, Senior Deputy Assistant to Human Rights in the State Department and Ambassador William Bowdler criticized the approach. According to Schneider the administration needed to ensure protection for Somoza after resignation and needed to consider a truly democratic approach that included the FSLN. Both Bowdler and Schneider rightly understood that the administration's goal of a democratic transition built around Somoza's National Guard and upon the ideal of alienating the Sandinistas promised increased revolutionary violence and was unlikely to work.[33]

Somoza resigned his position on July 17, 1979. He fled the country in the early morning. The dictator was frightened for his life. However, perhaps unsurprisingly, Somoza double crossed the United States. His replacement met with Ambassador Pezzullo, but rather than turn over power to a transitional junta as was agreed to he planned to stay in power and acted as though he possessed no knowledge of the scheduled transition on which he was briefed. The popular uprising at this time, however, was truly victorious, and Somoza's secret plan of maintaining a hard anti-leftist friend in power lasted almost no time at all. The next day the dictator's duplicitous appointee fled the country. Likewise, the National Guard was largely hemmed into its barracks and people of all ages attacked the group with whatever implements that might be found. It was a genuine popular uprising, the people ousted the government. Before the end of August the FSLN paraded uncontested into the capital Managua and took control of the country. Many of the surviving elements of the National Guard fled to remote border sanctuaries.[34] Somoza initially went to Miami, but after the United States learned of his betrayal the deposed dictator organized two huge yachts and left the South Florida coast.[35] He ultimately was given refuge by the President of Paraguay, Alfredo Stroessner. It was perhaps fitting that Stroessner was the one to give Somoza asylum. The two rulers were cut from the same cloth. Paraguay under Stroessner's long rule was a corrupt dictatorship that often declared martial law to persecute potential political opponents with kidnapping, torture, and death. He had already granted asylum to controversial figures that included the infamous Nazi doctor Mengele.[36]

The Sandinistas rise to power in Nicaragua brought immediate concern from the State Department. Shortly following the successful Sandinista revolution the government of the tiny island nation Grenada also fell to leftist revolutionaries, and the government of El Salvador found itself threatened by the FMLN, a guerrilla army supported closely by the Sandinistas. Unlike Reagan, the Carter administration did not consider the use of a military option against Nicaragua, but instead hoped that the Sandinistas were a leadership with which it could work. Carter's State Department increasingly feared the expansion of Soviet-Cuban influence throughout the region, but preferred to rely first on a sound diplomacy.

National Security Adviser Zbigniew Brzezinski led Carter's foreign policy in the final two years. The administration perceived a global move for power by the Soviet Union and Cuba in areas of critical importance, the Persian Gulf and Latin America.[37] In both regions the Carter administration pledged to support allies militarily and economically in order to prevent an expansion of Soviet influence. In Central America, Brzezinski and the NSC focused its concern at Cuba, which was increasingly involved in support for insurgency in Central America. Presidential Directive 52, signed by Carter on October 4, 1979, pledged "to undercut Cuba's drive for third world leadership."[38] According to the administration, Cuba was closely connected to the Sandinistas and the FMLN.

According to members of the State Department there was significant reason to believe that the Sandinistas were a threat to regional stability, and the primary way that the Carter administration understood this was through the growing issue of terrorism in Central America. The conflict in El Salvador increasingly deteriorated and was exacerbated by brutal violence. The Carter administration believed that the FMLN's guerrilla fighters were supported by the Sandinistas and from this ground insisted that the Sandinistas were directly engaged in terrorist activity from Nicaragua. The brutality of the conflict in El Salvador led the Carter administration to consider evoking powers granted by the Export Administration Act of 1979. This act empowered the executive to use its resources to withhold deliverable aid to countries engaged in the sponsorship of terrorism.[39] In Nicaragua, the Carter administration recognized and acted upon terrorism conducted from both the right and the left.

The Export Administration Act gave the executive branch the power to control exports for reasons of National Security. The United States faced a significant national security crisis, and the action allowed the president to use economic and trade sanctions as a policy tool. One of the key components of the legislation gave the president the specific right to use complicity in acts of terrorism as a reason for a cut off of US aid to regimes deemed involved in acts of international terrorism. The Carter administration was the first to pursue these powers. The administration began the process of creating a list of potential state sponsors of terrorism. It used this to consider the application of economic sanctions as way of punishing states involved in acts of terrorism. Just as the removal of aid for states violating human rights placed Nicaragua as a central focus so too did the new policy of using allegations of terrorism as a standard for withholding economic support.[40]

Though not intent on using the allegation of state sponsorship of terrorism as a justification to make war on Nicaragua, as the Reagan administration did, the Carter administration did seriously consider identifying Nicaragua as a state sponsor of terrorism and to place economic restrictions on the country for this reason. The apparent internationalization of weapons trafficking by the Sandinista government was a primary cause for concern. Many in the Carter administration believed that Cuba and Nicaragua directly supported the FMLN in El Salvador. This action, if verified, the administration insisted represented an act of international terrorism and justified the refusal of economic aid that was promised to the new Nicaraguan leadership.[41]

After the success of the Sandinistas, which capitalized on a massive popular uprising, the Carter administration struggled over the issue of whether or not to classify Nicaragua as a state sponsor of terrorism. Leading officials agreed that Nicaragua supported the FMLN in El Salvador, and that such activity amounted to involvement with international terrorism. However, the administration also feared that denying the aid to the Sandinistas could cause the Central American situation to deteriorate, and might even lead to retaliatory attacks on Americans throughout the region. The Carter administration felt it was at an important moment in US–Central American relations, and the embassy in Managua reported that the Sandinista government was weak and unstable and that it might bargain. The White House did not want to accuse Nicaragua of support for international terrorism unless the evidence was conclusive. On September 12, 1979, President Carter approved the scheduled humanitarian and economic assistance.[42]

While in Paraguay, Somoza lived in a large walled compound. Armed guards were with him at all times, and he was increasingly paranoid about assassination. However, Somoza did not keep a low profile. Prior to his flight from power the former dictator had, allegedly, moved some $100 million out of Nicaragua, and this formed the basis for the playboy lifestyle he so infamously flaunted in the area around the capital of Paraguay. Somoza bought land outside of the Paraguayan capital and took a young and extravagant girlfriend.[43] However, despite all of his military protection Somoza's refuge was short lived. The deposed leader was hunted down by Sandinista militants who sought revenge on the leader. On September 17, 1980, while traveling in his yellow Mercedes sedan, Anastasio Somoza Debayle was brutally assassinated in Asunción, Paraguay, by a group of militants that wielded automatic weapons and rocket propelled grenades. Somoza's car was lined with bullet holes and the blast from a rocket propelled grenade ripped the roof off of the car and threw the former dictator several feet away. Somoza's body was barely identifiable.[44]

The September 17 killing of Somoza caused the Carter administration to revisit the issue of Sandinista complicity in acts of international terrorism. The administration found the entire situation disheartening. The Carter administration clearly believed that the Sandinistas were involved in both supporting the FMLN in El Salvador and the killing of Somoza, and it regarded the actions as the export of terrorist violence. However, whether or not to use this to cut off humanitarian and economic support to the Sandinistas was a decision that the Carter administration preferred not to make. If the Carter administration found that the Sandinistas were involved in either supporting the FMLN or in the assassination of Somoza it could enact executive powers that would halt any further support and demand immediate repayment of money already delivered. Both the Department of State and the United States embassy again suggested that only the most conclusive evidence should lead to such a determination.[45]

The decision over whether or not to cut-off the new Nicaraguan government was not an easy one. By early January 1981 it appeared that United States supported government of El Salvador faced collapse amid pressure from the FMLN. The Carter administration was concerned over the security threat that Nicaragua and Cuba posed to the region. In the wake of the Sandinista victory, National Security Advisor Zbigniew Brzezinski and the Special Coordination Committee (SCC), tasked with addressing key policy matters, outlined the Carter administration's objectives in the region. The SCC insisted that, "We are at a watershed in our relations with Central America and possibly the hemisphere as a whole." In stark contrast to the administration's policy several years earlier the group insisted that the principle objective was the "containment of Cuba: to prevent the consolidation of extreme left regimes in Nicaragua, or in other Central American countries."[46] The Carter administration failed to maintain a moderate government in Nicaragua and then it faced the issue of addressing the emergence of a potentially radical leftist regime to replace the rightist dictatorship of Somoza.

On January 2, 1981, the Carter administration gave the newly elected president, Ronald Reagan, a final brief on the situation in Central America. The picture was not pretty, and the Carter administration confirmed fears of Nicaragua's export of terrorism and subversion. The brief addressed the imminent concern in the Americas at this time: the escalating revolution in El Salvador and the role of Nicaragua and Cuba in facilitating the overthrow of the United States supported government. According to the document, "An imminent leftist offensive supported by . . . large numbers of international volunteers from Cuba, Nicaragua, and Panama will participate in a major offensive this month."[47] The document remarked that Nicaragua had escalated its military activity, and the goal of the international insurgents that Nicaragua harbored was "to sustain a high level of assassinations and other spectacular terrorist attacks."[48] The Carter administration set the stage for Ronald Reagan.

Despite the dire warnings and serious concerns, on January 12, 1981, President Carter signed off on continued delivery of humanitarian and economic support to the Sandinista government. Both the Embassy and the State Department concerned that if the United States cut-off Nicaragua that the action threatened to exacerbate the crisis. Ambassador to Nicaragua Lawrence A. Pezzullo feared the development of "another Tehran" hostage crisis and planned to remove the United States mission in Nicaragua if the administration cut-off support.[49] The SCC likewise insisted that to cut-off Nicaragua "would dangerously undercut the position of those Nicaraguans that are willing to work with us, and the demand for repayment could unleash a violent anti-U.S. reaction."[50] Following these suggestions, the Carter administration again decided not to cut-off the Sandinistas, but instead continued the aid deliveries and suggested that if Nicaragua participated conclusively in the export of terrorism and violence in the future that withholding support remained a potential option for the Reagan administration.

This decision identified a key difference between the Carter White House and the Reagan administration. Carter wished to prevent a further deterioration of the Central American situation, the administration wanted to find a way to work with the Sandinistas by using diplomacy to prevent a continued escalation of war in the region. The Reagan administration, on the other hand, had far less patience and, instead, pursued a policy of military pressure as a method of forcing Sandinista complicity. This difference, undoubtedly, worsened the situation and prolonged and expanded the crises in Central America.

Terrorism factored fundamentally into the Central American crisis during the 1970s. Whether it was Somoza's use of terrorism as a tool for a further militarization of his leadership or the FSLN's increasing complicity in support for guerrillas in neighboring countries like El Salvador or in the assassination of Somoza, terrorism was at the heart of the conflict and the United States' future policy would have to tackle this issue. How it would do so was of critical importance.

The 1970s witnessed an escalation of terrorism coupled with revolutionary violence and rightist repression. The end of Carter's presidency was riddled with bloody controversies. In Central America, revolutions raged. On the other side of the world the Soviet Union invaded Afghanistan, and in the most troubling incident, the Iranian revolution and the controversy over the Shah led to a hostage crisis. In response to these situations, the Carter administration entered a phase that demanded greater direct activity in the world. Infamously, the administration ordered special forces into Iran in a failed attempt to free the hostages held in Tehran. However, often overlooked by scholars were the critical problems in Central America. Following the Sandinista take over and the assassination of Somoza the Carter administration increasingly defined the Nicaraguan government as potentially complicit in state terrorism.

A central component in the development of US counterterrorism strategy centered on what terrorism was: was it exclusively a criminal behavior or was it also linked to revolutions and regional conflict and a component of war? Was terrorism, the act of targeting civilians for political objectives within larger conflicts, a motive for an offensive policy against revolutionary movements and governments and if so should the United States define the problem in such a way as to include guerrilla and paramilitary movements and governments? These questions rested at the core of US counterterrorism policy in the 1970s. By the end of Jimmy Carter's term in office the United States appeared to increasingly define guerrilla and revolutionary movements in Central America as complicit in the global threat of international terrorism and as criminal actors rather than political fighters within complex conflicts. In the years ahead, the Reagan administration built its own aggressive policy of preemption and regime change on this precedent.

NOTES

1. Defense Intelligence Notice, "Nicaragua: Government Declares Martial Law as Terrorists Hold Prominent Figures Hostage," December 1974, *Digital National Security Archive* (Ann Arbor: Proquest 2012), NI00004, http://gateway.proquest.com/openurl?url_ver=Z39.88-2004&res_dat=xri:dnsa&rft_dat=xri:dnsa:article:CNI00004.

2. Alan Riding, "Nicaragua will Free 26 to Win Hostage's Release, Special to the New York Times: Nicaragua Agrees to Free 26 to Win Release of Hostages," *New York Times,*

December 30, 1974, http://ntserver1.wsulibs.wsu.edu:2184/docview/120132453?accountid= 14902.

3. Alan Riding, "Somoza, Long U.S. Ally was Bitter Over Betrayal," *New York Times*, September 18, 1980.

4. Riding, "Somoza, Long U.S. Ally was Bitter Over Betrayal."

5. Lawrence Pezzullo, interview by Arthur Day, *Foreign Affairs Oral History Project*, Association for Diplomatic Studies and Training, February 24, 1989.

6. Staff Notes, "Latin American Trends," Central Intelligence Agency, February 12, 1975, *Digital National Security Archive* (Ann Arbor: Proquest, 2012), NI00007, http://gateway. proquest.com/openurl?url_ver=Z39.88-2004&res_dat=xri:dnsa&rft_dat=xri:dnsa:article: CNI00007.

7. Memorandum from US Embassy to Secretary of State, "Analysis of White Hand Existence," February 1979, NI00650, http://gateway.proquest.com/openurl?url_ver=Z39.882004& res_dat=xri:dnsa&rft_dat=xri:dnsa:article:CNI00650.

8. Lawrence Pezzullo, interview by Arthur Day.

9. Matilde Zimmerman, *Sandinista: Carlos Fonseca and the Nicaraguan Revolution* (London: Duke University Press, 2000), 201–204.

10. Memorandum from US Embassy to Secretary of State, "Chamorro Assassination: Assassins Confess, but Opposition Denounces Cover-up," January 18, 1978, *Digital National Security Archive* (Ann Arbor: Proquest, 2012), NI00032, http://gateway.proquest.com/openurl? url_ver=Z39.88-2004&res_dat=xri:dnsa&rft_dat=xri:dnsa:article:CNI00032.

11. Memorandum from US Embassy to Secretary of State, "Analysis of White Hand Existence," February 1979.

12. Jimmy Carter, "Power for Humane Purposes," speech given at Notre Dame University, May 22, 1977. As seen in Ernest W. Lefever, *Morality and Foreign Policy: A Symposium on President Carter's Stance* (Washington, DC: Ethics and Public Policy Center, 1977), 4–5.

13. Carter, "Power for Humane Purposes," 4–5.

14. Kenneth A. Oye, Donald Rothchild, and Robert J. Lieber, *Eagle Entangled: U.S. Foreign Policy in a Complex World* (Longman: New York, 1979), 293.

15. Herbert D. Rosenbaum and Alexej Ugrinsky, *Jimmy Carter: Foreign Policy and Post Presidential Years* (Westport, Conn.: Greenwood Press, 1994), 245.

16. Rosenbaum and Ugrinsky, *Jimmy Carter*, 245.

17. Riding, "Somoza, Long U.S. Ally was Bitter Over Betrayal."

18. "U.S. To Give Nicaragua Some Humanitarian Aid," *New York Times*, March 16, 1978.

19. Memorandum from Schneider to Secretary of State, "Nicaragua," July, 3, 1979, *Digital National Security Archive* (Ann Arbor: Proquest, 2012), NI00864, http://gateway.proquest. com/openurl?url_ver=Z39.88-2004&res_dat=xri:dnsa&rft_dat=xri:dnsa:article:CNI00864.

20. Lawrence Pezzullo, interview by Arthur Day.

21. Department of State Telegram, July, 3, 1979, *Digital National Security Archive* (Ann Arbor: Proquest, 2012), NI00863.http://gateway.proquest.com/openurl?url_ver=Z39.88-2004& res_dat=xri:dnsa&rft_dat=xri:dnsa:article:CNI00863.

22. Riding, "Somoza, Long U.S. Ally was Bitter Over Betrayal."

23. Alan Riding, "Somoza and His Foes Both Looking for U.S. Aid," *New York Times*, July 26, 1978.

24. Riding, "Somoza and His Foes Both Looking for U.S. Aid."

25. State Department Memorandum from Lawrence Pezzullo, "Somoza: Fourth Meeting," *Digital National Security Archive* (Ann Arbor: Proquest, 2012), NI00866, http://gateway. proquest.com/openurl?url_ver=Z39.88-2004&res_dat=xri:dnsa&rft_dat=xri:dnsa:article: CNI00866.

26. Lawrence Pezzullo, interview by Arthur Day.

27. State Department Memorandum from Lawrence Pezzullo, "Somoza: Fourth Meeting," *Digital National Security Archive*.

28. State Department Memorandum from Lawrence Pezzullo, "Somoza: Fourth Meeting," *Digital National Security Archive*.

29. State Department Memorandum from Lawrence Pezzullo, "Somoza: Fifth Meeting," *Digital National Security Archive* (Ann Arbor: Proquest, 2012), NI00868, http://gateway.

proquest.com/openurl?url_ver=Z39.88-2004&res_dat=xri:dnsa&rft_dat=xri:dnsa:article: CNI00868.

30. State Department Memorandum from Lawrence Pezzullo, "Somoza: Fifth Meeting," *Digital National Security Archive.*

31. State Department Memorandum from Lawrence Pezzullo, "Somoza Tell Post Reporter He Made Commitment to USG to Resign," *Digital National Security Archive* (Ann Arbor: Proquest, 2012), NI00873, http://gateway.proquest.com/openurl?url_ver=Z39.88-2004&res_dat=xri:dnsa&rft_dat=xri:dnsa:article:CNI00873.

32. Lawrence Pezzullo, interview by Arthur Day.

33. Memorandum from Schneider to Secretary of State, "Nicaragua," July, 3, 1979, *Digital National Security Archive.*

34. Lawrence Pezzullo, interview by Arthur Day.

35. Lawrence Pezzullo, interview by Arthur Day.

36. Riding, "Somoza, Long U.S. Ally was Bitter Over Betrayal."

37. Presidential Directive PD/NSC-62, "Modifications in U.S. National Strategy," January 15, 1980, Jimmy Carter Presidential Library and Museum.

38. Presidential Directive PD/NSC-52, "U.S. Policy to Cuba," October 4, 1979, Jimmy Carter Presidential Library and Museum.

39. Memo from McFarlane to Meese, "Background Material on Terrorism," August 15, 1984, *The Digital National Security Archive* (Ann Arbor: Proquest, 2012), TE00715, http://gateway.proquest.com/openurl?url_ver=Z39.88-2004&res_dat=xri:dnsa&rft_dat=xri:dnsa:article:CTE00715.

40. Memo from McFarlane to Meese, "Background Material on Terrorism," August 15, 1984, *The Digital National Security Archive.*

41. "El Salvador: Military Prospects," January 2, 1981, *Digital National Security Archive* (Ann Arbor: Proquest, 2012), EL00050, http://gateway.proquest.com/openurl?url_ver=Z39.88-2004&res_dat=xri:dnsa&rft_dat=xri:dnsa:article:CEL00050.

42. Telegram from Ambassador William Bowdler to the State Department, "Nicaraguan Certification on Terrorism: The Somoza Assassination," *The Digital National Security Archive* (Ann Arbor: Proquest, 2012), NI01202, http://gateway.proquest.com/openurl?url_ver=Z39.88-2004&res_dat=xri:dnsa&rft_dat=xri:dnsa:article:CNI01202.

43. Riding, "Somoza, Long U.S. Ally was Bitter Over Betrayal."

44. Edward Schumacher, "Somoza, Ousted Nicaraguan Leader, is Ambushed and Slain in Paraguay," *New York Times*, September, 18, 1980.

45. Telegram from Ambassador William Bowdler to the State Department, "Nicaraguan Certification on Terrorism: The Somoza Assassination," *The Digital National Security Archive.*

46. Memorandum for Dr. Zbigniew Brzezinski, "PRC Meeting on Central America," August 1, 1979, *Digital National Security Archive* (Ann Arbor: Proquest, 2012), EL01327, http://gateway.proquest.com/openurl?url_ver=Z39.88-2004&res_dat=xri:dnsa&rft_dat=xri:dnsa:article:CEL01327.

47. "El Salvador: Military Prospects," January 2, 1981, *Digital National Security Archive.*

48. "El Salvador: Military Prospects," January 2, 1981, *Digital National Security Archive.*

49. Special Coordinating Committee Meeting, January 12, 1981, *Digital National Security Archive* (Ann Arbor: Proquest, 2012), EL01364, http://gateway.proquest.com/openurl?url_ver=Z39.88-2004&res_dat=xri:dnsa&rft_dat=xri:dnsa:article:CEL01364.

50. Special Coordinating Committee Meeting, January 12, 1981, *Digital National Security Archive.*

Chapter Three

Counterinsurgency-Counterterrorism

After Somoza's defeat loyalist elements, ultimately referred to as the Contras, established operations in border regions of Honduras and Costa Rica. By 1980 these guerrillas conducted hit and run attacks as well as acts of sabotage within Nicaragua.[1] The militants were, initially, a product, in part, of the rightist Argentine government's attempt to sponsor the group as a transnational guerrilla army capable of overthrowing the new leftist government. The program was markedly similar to actions by the leftist government of Cuba, which the United States held as the epitome of a state sponsor of terrorism. Argentina was a rightist state sponsor of terrorism and the militants that made up the Contras were, in part, the product of its attempt to support unconventional irregular war against leftists groups. Simultaneous to this development the government of El Salvador, Nicaragua's bantam sized Pacific coast neighbor, descended into a conflict that carried the same hallmarks as the revolutions in Nicaragua and the tiny island nation of Grenada, which had fallen to leftist revolutionaries in the same year as Nicaragua. On the eve of Ronald Reagan's inauguration as President of the United States, Central America, so long considered a haven of US imperial control seemed a chaotic morass of anti-Americanism. To those close to Reagan, the situation represented a dangerous trend and sign that leftism was undermining areas of traditional US strength.

The Nicaraguan revolution was one of a series of revolutions and conflicts throughout the developing world between 1978 and 1980. In Central America and the Caribbean there were leftist rebels in multiple countries. Both the Carter and the Reagan administration defined the new Nicaragua as a danger to the region and part of a revolutionary campaign driven mostly by Cuba. The Reagan administration, though, was different because it believed that the best way to address this problem was through force. Over subsequent years, the administration placed military measures with the CIA and the Contras as the primary instrument of a policy to contain and ultimately overthrow the sovereign government of Nicaragua. The United States under Reagan applied a policy that involved the application of military pressure as the primary method of achieving a solution dictated by the United States.[2] The primary objective was similar to that of the Carter administration just prior to the overthrow of Somoza: a moderate democracy that was within the orbit of the United States and that marginalized the influence of the Sandinistas. However, whereas the Carter administration sought to rely on diplomacy, the Reagan administration treated it with disdain, never at any point using a fair and respectful diplomacy with Nicaragua. Over the course of Reagan's time as president the administration applied economic and diplomatic measures, but these were consistently secondary to the use of military pressure exerted through proxy guerrilla armies.

In the 1980 Presidential election Ronald Reagan swept into office in the United States on his charisma and nostalgia. Economic and foreign policy controversies that hurt the Carter campaign also enhanced his candidacy. As a candidate, Reagan struck a nostalgic chord among the American people. He campaigned largely on the principle that the invasiveness and power of the federal government weakened the country and resulted in a loss of vigor for the Cold War. Reagan's ideas did not always make a lot of sense. His future Vice President George H. W. Bush campaigned against him in 1980 and perplexed at some of Reagan's economic ideas. Reaganomics, the trickle down economic perspective that rested on the federal government cutting taxes while simultaneously increasing military spending Bush criticized as "fuzzy math." For Bush, the numbers simply did not line up. Bush's criticism was well placed and, certainly, Reagan was no policy wonk. His skill was, instead, in his ability as an orator. Reagan spoke of better times and suggested that the United States' best days were still to come. His speaking style appealed most to the emotion of the voting populace rather than its ability to understand major issues. This was Reagan's decisive talent. The overwhelming feeling that America could return to a bygone era conveyed by a passionate but calm elder canceled out claims of "fuzzy math" for many in the United States.

Reagan's nostalgia over the Vietnam War resonated with many Americans. During the Vietnam War the United States tore itself apart. The conflict acted as an umbrella for culture wars, political corruption, and civil disobedience that shook the country to its core. By the election of 1980 Americans remained in a state of shock as the people tried to understand the meaning of that sorry foray in US foreign policy. For many, and most scholars, Vietnam was a mistake. The United States, and most significantly the people of Vietnam, Laos, and Cambodia, paid a terrible price for an unnecessary conflict caused by a misguided global containment policy.[3] While many sectors of the population understood Vietnam as a testament to an aggressive and overstretched foreign policy that needlessly drew the country into a civil war, a large section of the populace struggled more with the cause of veterans. Was it all just a waste? Why had the United States failed? A large element of the American public was far less concerned with whether the policy was wrong or right from the standpoint of international law and sovereignty and far more with why the United States lost and seemed to leave veterans disgraced. Numerous pop-culture songs and films struggled with the toll of a lost cause and of a generation of soldiers seemingly forgotten and lost in the shadows.

Ronald Reagan famously, or infamously depending on one's perspective, led a revision of the history of the Vietnam War that remains strong with many Americans. According to Reagan, the United States had won every battle, the soldiers were heroes, and any failure in overall objectives was simply due to the meddling of a government that forced American patriots to fight "with one arm tied behind their backs." While giving a speech in 1980 to the Veterans of Foreign Wars in Chicago, Reagan insisted with convincing sincerity that, "It is time we realize that ours was, in truth, a noble cause . . . we dishonored the memory of fifty thousand young Americans who fought and died for that cause when we give way to feelings of guilt as if we did something shameful."[4] This revision of the Vietnam War, that it was just and right and that the Cold War and feared domino theory were real, was the backbone of the debate over Central America during Reagan's first term. The administration sought to convince Americans and Congress that Nicaragua was a Cold War conflict worth fighting.

Military support for the United States' allies in Central America was established by the Carter administration as it sought to minimize the spread of the Nicaraguan Revolution. In January 1980, President Jimmy Carter established military aid and sent nineteen advisors to El Salvador to prevent the collapse of the government. When Reagan took command in 1981 the United States had these same nineteen advisors in El Salvador and had loaned the struggling regime half a dozen Huey UH-1H helicopters.[5] In January 1981, the situation in El Salvador worsened considerably. On January 3, rebels killed two US workers involved in farm assistance. One week later the revolutionaries went on the offensive and seized parts of the capital city, San Salvador. The conflict was brutal and much of it occurred within population areas. Rightists terror squads appeared responsible for the kidnapping and murder of many people including priests. In October 1980 when the body of Rev. Manuel Antonio Reyes Monico was found filled with bullet holes it brought the tally of priests killed in the war to seven. Leftist guerrillas, too, made public places a battleground. The insurgents blasted into the Organization of American States (OAS) building and held hostages there for nearly three weeks. Kidnapping and murder, terrorism of the right and the left, dominated the conflict.[6] Some 9,000 people died in El Salvador in 1980, and at the outset of 1981, the situation deteriorated.[7]

Unlike the Carter administration, Ronald Reagan's team of advisors possessed a vigor for the Cold War and the fight against leftism that drew the United States into the conflicts in Central America. Two publications at this time most embodied the Reagan administration's doctrine on the Cold War and terrorism. Jeane Kirkpatrick, Reagan's Ambassador to the UN, and journalist Claire Sterling together captured the administration's outlook on the Cold War. Kirkpatrick, a political scientist at Georgetown, wrote *Dictatorships and Double Standards* while Sterling penned her influential and controversial book *The Terror Network*. Together the two publications, which came out in 1979 and 1981, asserted that there was a global leftist terror network. Accordingly, the terrorist problem was, uniquely, leftist and a product of communist totalitarian influence. The United States, it was implied, needed to shirk off the containment policy or the guilt of collaborating with rightist dictatorships and take the fight to the leftists that embodied the new global terror threat. These works symbolized the Reagan administration's outlook on Nicaragua, terrorism, and the Cold War. The idea that the problems of terrorism and revolution were reducible to a global left-right struggle encouraged aggressive hardline measures that ensured the escalation of hostilities in Central America. Alongside such escalation the administration pursued a propaganda operation hinged, in part, on the implementation of terrorism as a political term designed only to characterize enemies and justify aggressive actions that violated norms of international law.[8]

On January 18, 1981, the State Department sent a telegram to all regional diplomatic posts emphasizing the role of the Soviet-Cuban-Nicaraguan states in the El Salvadoran Civil War. According to this secret message, "The guerrilla offensive launched on January 10 with major Cuban and other foreign military support and participation has changed the character of the conflict to a military struggle between the legitimate government of El Salvador and Marxists-Leninist guerrillas backed by Cuban, Nicaraguan and Soviet bloc supplies."[9] On Capitol Hill the Reagan administration responded by requesting that the House of Representatives approve an additional $25 million in aid for El Salvador. The White House also expanded the number of advisors from nineteen to fifty-four.[10] Over the next four years, aid requests and CIA/advisor activity expanded continually. By 1983, the administration asked Congress for $110 million for military aid to El Salvador, and journalists and politicians rumored about the possibility of direct military intervention in the region.[11] The yearly need for funding and the lack of any formal resolution or war declaration gave Congress the ability to play a central role in evaluating policy with Central America. Over the course of Reagan's presidency debates in the House and Senate provided a critical platform for the shape of the United States' Central American policy. Many in Congress, now fully recognizing the potential damage of the Vietnam conflict to congressional war powers, engaged in annual debate and analysis of the conflicts in Central America and the role of the United States.

At the beginning of 1981, kicking off a period of intense debate over the United States commitment to El Salvador, PBS aired a documentary film, titled, "El Salvador: Another Vietnam." This represented one of the earliest critical comparisons of Central America to Vietnam. Directed by Glenn Silber and Tete Vasconcellos, the fifty-three-minute film examined the recent history of El Salvador in the twentieth century and the role that the United States played in this period and, particularly, following the growth of the El Salvadoran Civil War. The film revealed the brutality of the United States-supported dictatorship as well as the presence of American advisors or 'so-called' "technicians." Silder and Vasconcellos made it clear: they understood the role of the United States as "analogous to the circumstances under which the United States was drawn into Vietnam." From the outset of the conflict with El Salvador and Nicaragua, Americans questioned policy in terms of Vietnam.[12]

During Reagan's first term there were no less than seventy newspaper articles in prominent publications like the *New York Times*, the *Boston Globe*, and the *Washington Post* that discussed policy in Central America in terms of the Vietnam War. For low-level conflicts, ones that did not command the front page very often, this represented an impressive statistic. Congress also repeatedly engaged in drawn out battles over the administration's policy that involved questioning the meaning of America's earlier conflict in Southeast Asia. Americans fought over what Vietnam meant and how its legacy should or should not apply to Central America. Increasingly, high-level figures like Reagan, Jeane Kirkpatrick, Secretary of State Alexander Haig and his successor George Shultz tried to influence Congress, the public and the media with a revised understanding of the Vietnam analogy in Central America. The legacy of the Vietnam War channeled the debate on policy. Virtually every critical statement one way or the other formed around the Vietnam comparison.

Initially, Secretary of State Alexander Haig led the Reagan administration in articulating the details of the new Cold War conflict taking shape in Central America while tip-toeing around the popular imaginings of Vietnam, the memory of which was a lasting impediment to the pursuit of Cold War interventions in the developing world. Haig served during the Vietnam War and as, first, a national security adviser and then White House Chief of Staff for the Nixon and Gerald Ford administration. Haig spent his years prior to his appointment as Reagan's Secretary of State as the seventh Supreme Allied Commander in Europe. He earned a reputation as a Hawk, and in the Reagan cabinet a person that was rather difficult to get along with. In one case in 1981, while others like Defense Secretary Caspar Weinberger pushed for moderation, Haig announced, to the shock of individuals present, "Just give me the word, and I'll make that fucking island [Cuba] a parking lot." He was a hardliner and at times a loose cannon in the administration. [13]

Ambassador Lawrence Pezzullo, the one man most in tune with what happened in Nicaragua and who the Sandinistas were, sensed that the Reagan administration was beginning to chart a dangerous military course with Nicaragua, and it troubled him deeply. The people that came down to Nicaragua to the embassy seemed rather unsavory, and the administration was increasingly defining the small country as a leftist nation that acted as frontline of a global communist offensive. Pezzullo was concerned and, frankly, wanted out as he feared that his job as a diplomat in Nicaragua was about to end amid a policy of military force that might negate his effectiveness. Because of this concern he went to see Secretary of State Haig. [14]

When Pezzullo met Haig the administration had already cut off assistance to the new government. Pezzullo was shocked, and calmly expressed his feelings to the Secretary of State. The Ambassador remembered exclaiming to Haig,

> Look, what the heck are we doing? You know, if we want to sanction this bunch, then you don't need me. I mean, I think we can still work with these guys. . . . I'm not saying they're going to turn Nicaragua into Connecticut, but I think we can deal these fellows. And I think we can prevent them from doing stupid things, and causing problems in the hemisphere. I think that is a cheaper way to go about it, than to get into some sort of John Wayne approach. You're going to lose going down that track.

Haig responded simply, "I buy that." Unknown to Pezzullo at the time, however, was that Haig was already overseeing the United States use of the covert Contra military operations. Not knowing this, Pezzullo left the meeting feeling at least somewhat reassured. [15]

One week after his meeting with Haig, Pezzullo experienced something that truly demonstrated that the Reagan administration had barely given a thought to diplomacy, and were instead going to pursue an aggressive militaristic approach with little respect or regard for the new government of Nicaragua. Pezzullo went to a meeting with a member of the new ruling government who exclaimed to him, "Why do we have to get insulted by you people!?" Pezzullo, was taken aback, what was he talking about? After all, he was the Ambassador and should have a knowledge of the happenings and dealings between the United States and Nicaragua. In a public "diplomatic reception" in the United States, Haig, in front of other diplomats, went up to the Nicaraguan Ambassador, Sergio Ramirez, and gruffly confronted her with a finger in the face. Haig said to her that, "You better tell the boys down south, you know, your government, that they better behave themselves, otherwise they're really going to be in for it." Pezzullo was shocked to hear this and after making calls back to the states determined that the testimony was accurate. At this point he pressed to get out of the position, which he did later that year. The exchange was a first demonstration that the Reagan administration never intended a fair diplomacy with Nicaragua, but rather sought a policy based on threat, intimidation, and use of military force. For Pezzullo it was a terrible sign, and left him only able to exclaim to himself, "What the hell?"[16]

In March 1981, Haig went before the Senate Foreign Relations Committee and the House Foreign Affairs Committee to answer questions about the administration's aid requests for Central America. Haig expressed concern with Cuba. He argued that Fidel Castro's communist regime represented the primary facilitator of revolution and weapons trafficking in Central America. Furthering fears, he did not mention any details other than the fact that the President did "not exclude anything" when it came to options for dealing with the Castro regime. This caused concern for many in Congress that the Reagan administration sought an expanded conflict.[17]

In these meetings, Undersecretary of State Walter J. Stoessel supported Haig and acknowledged that the United States did not exclude the military option when it came to addressing the situation in Central America. Instead, all possibilities remained on the table. His testimony resulted in widespread concern on Capitol Hill. Republican Senator Charles Percy of Illinois asked the undersecretary, "If Central America could turn into another 'quagmire' like Vietnam?" To this, Stoessel replied that the administration stood "determined that this situation will not develop into another Vietnam . . . the situation is containable." Shortly after, Haig explained his version of a "four phased" communist plan to take over Central America, Representative Robert (Bob) Dornan, Republican from California, clumsily questioned Haig as to whether this represented a "Caribbean domino theory," to which Haig, obviously aware that accepting this analogy directly might cause political backlash, responded that he felt the communist plan looked more like a "hit-list." Haig used the phrase to distance the administration from directly citing the Vietnam War. Nonetheless, the Reagan administration defined the crisis in Central America in a logic embedded in and drawn from the Vietnam War and the Cold War, a global struggle against leftism. A Central American domino theory was the way in which the White House defended policy, and US politicians and journalists made the comparison to Vietnam from the outset. Central America, for the Reagan administration, was about Cold War grand strategy and the prevention of world communism undermining the United States in an area of long-time US influence.[18]

Concerned politicians feared a repeat of Vietnam in which the government escalated a war without public support and with an authoritarian ally that violated human rights and could not win its people over. A 1981 *Gallup Poll* confirmed such fears: the survey posed the question, "How likely do you think it is that the US involvement in El Salvador could turn into a situation like Vietnam?"[19] Of those polled, 38 percent felt it "fairly likely" that US involvement in El Salvador might deteriorate into a Vietnam like conflict.[20] This number represented an American public concerned and aware of Reagan's policy. Many Americans feared that the Cold War might cause policy makers to overlook warning signs and embark on another fool's errand.

In general, Democrats criticized the administration's actions most widely, but that March on Capitol Hill Republicans voiced disagreement with Reagan's Central American policy as well. Senator Claiborne Pell (R) from Rhode Island expressed that, "Every time that government forces are involved in acts of violence against Salvadoran civilians. It is the communists who benefit. As we learned too painfully in Vietnam, no amount of American arms or military advisers will have any lasting effect if the government we are supporting is losing the battle for the hearts and minds of its own people."[21] Senator Mark Hatfield (R) followed Pell, he claimed, "I do not think that strong public support will ever be forthcoming because the nation's heart is not in this war."[22] These statements came in the shadow of continuing reports from El Salvador that the United States supported-regime involved itself in civilian killings and widespread human rights abuses. The Reagan administration denied the claims.[23]

1982 began in a similar fashion to 1981, with a significant offensive in El Salvador by insurgents fighting to overthrow the United States supported government. However, during 1982 the focus of concern in the United States shifted away from El Salvador to Nicaragua. While the fighting was in El Salvador, the White House implicated Nicaragua in the conflict. National Security Decision Directive number 17 (NSDD-17), signed by Reagan in early 1982, represented an escalation of intervention by the United States. Implicating Nicaragua and Cuba in the conflict in El Salvador, the National Security Council (NSC) proposed a variety of operations including expanded assistance to El Salvador.[24] Significantly, this document authorized the support for a legally dubious proxy war against Nicaragua. The NSC allocated "secret funds" through the CIA of $19.5 million for the development, equipping, and training of Nicaraguan rebel "commandos," known as the Contras or counterrevolutionaries, to interdict weapons trafficking to El Salvador.[25]

There were several different groups and several different leaders, but the administration used the singular term Contras for simplicity. In the south, on the border of Costa Rica, the Revolutionary Democratic Alliance (ARDE) operated along with the Nicaraguan Revolutionary Armed Forces (FARN). These two groups conjoined in May of 1986. The Costa Rican front was organized by two former FSLN members, Eden Pastora and Alfonso Robelo, and represented the smaller front in terms of numbers. The largest proxy group was the Nicaraguan Democratic Force (FDN) led by Adolfo Calero. The FDN numbered roughly 20,000 soldiers by 1986, and operated on the

Nicaraguan-Honduran border. There were also rebel bands of Miskito Indians operating on the Atlantic side of Nicaragua. The FDN, over time, developed as the most significant unit in the United States proxy war on Sandinista-led Nicaragua.[26] These rebels, some of whom were former members of Somoza's National Guard and others defectors from the FSLN, harassed the Nicaraguan government with sabotage attacks against bridges, harbors, oil storage, communication, and power plant facilities.[27]

The Reagan administration's first major public action against Nicaragua was the suspension of aid to the Sandinista government and the affirmation of its view of Nicaragua's terrorist activity. Its alleged role in assisting the FMLN in El Salvador was the reason for the executive action.[28] Only a few months earlier the Carter administration refused to take this step primarily out of a concern that such restrictions threatened to exacerbate the crisis and limited the chances of a diplomatic solution and productive relationship between the two governments in the future. The Reagan administration's decision was a first step in a proxy war against the government of Nicaragua and toward establishing terrorism as a broader justification for the use of pre-emptive and overt force against another sovereign nation. This represented the beginning of a process by which communist inspired insurgencies and revolutionary movements were characterized as illegitimate for an alleged association with international terrorism. Journalists acknowledged the Reagan administration's policy with Nicaragua as, "The first testing ground of its campaign against Soviet-inspired-international terrorism."[29] When it really took hold in 1984–1985 international terrorism as a concept rested at the core of the Reagan offensive. This new way of defining foreign policy lumped leftist revolutionary governments and groups with those non-communist Middle Eastern elements like the PLO, Libya, and Iran in a diabolical global alliance dedicated to the destruction of the United States. Over time this outlook justified a more aggressive and hardline United States.

The Reagan administration's concern with the role of Middle Eastern terrorist states and organizations acting in Nicaragua was apparent from the outset. In a special report prepared by the administration in October of 1981, the new leadership remarked with concern that while, "Arms and other supplies are said to arrive by air and sea from Nicaragua. . . . Libya is apparently taking a larger role."[30] In November 1981, an issue brief produced by the Congressional Research Service confirmed the administration's concerns. According to this brief, the PLO, Libya, and Algeria were expanding activity in Nicaragua. The report stated that, "The PLO may have training camps in Nicaragua and has trained Salvadoran guerrillas there . . . [and] took an important role in introducing Nicaragua to Arab states."[31] It insisted that Soviet-communist designs and non-communist politically motivated groups like the PLO and Libya fueled international terrorism.

Nicaragua was a central point of intersection for a US policy past and future. During Reagan's first term, the administration defended its war in Nicaragua most as a Cold War conflict. However, a shifting international environment and escalation of war in Central America began to factor more and more in the administration's perspective on the conflict. Early in the spring of 1982, CIA intelligence noted a significant growth in the role of "Palestinian terrorist groups" as well as Libyans in Nicaragua. According to this information, the Palestinians were training guerrillas and pilots, and Libya was committing money and advisors to Nicaragua.[32] The administration noted a significant increase in PLO activity in Nicaragua, and in El Salvador, and connected this directly to the alleged Sandinistas export of arms and terrorist violence throughout the region. The administration started to frame Nicaragua as not just a member of the communist bloc, but also as a terrorist state.[33]

In 1981 and 1982, the United States sent military personnel and CIA operatives to Honduras to train, equip, and organize the Contras. Reports in July described the Honduran border with Nicaragua as an "armed camp waiting for a war."[34] Through the CIA, the United States organized a transnational paramilitary force that launched military incursions into Nicaragua.[35] Honduras acted as an important staging area. More advisers went there than to El Salvador, which seized the concern in Congress over the possibility of an expansion of the Salvadoran Civil War.[36] In order to stabilize the government in El Salvador the administration applied a two pronged strategy that sought to bolster the government's struggle against the FMLN while simultaneously denying the Nicaraguan government the ability to support the Marxist guerrillas. NSDD-17 authorized a policy designed to contain Nicaragua, but to do this meant violating the sovereignty of Nicaragua, Honduras, and Costa Rica as well as arming a group of guerrillas that sought to overthrow the Sandinista government.

In early March 1982, only a few months after the president signed NSDD-17, the *Washington Post* revealed the United States' covert proxy operation against the Nicaraguan government.[37] The *New York Times* reported incursions into Nicaragua and the shocking revelation that the CIA trained Contra troops in South Florida.[38] Throughout the year, the media exposed the United States-backed war against Nicaragua. Dozens of articles in the *New York Times,* the *Washington Post,* and the *Boston Globe* covered the crisis. Many, including members of Congress, accused the administration of conducting a policy that violated international law and represented an attempt to overthrow the Nicaraguan government. These accusations resulted in a congressional measure to prohibit the use of aid "for the purpose of overthrowing the government of Nicaragua."[39] With the revelations of a US-led military escalation directed against Nicaragua in 1982, Congress acted to restrict funding to US-supported covert paramilitary operations against Nicaragua. Marking the beginning of a battle on Capitol Hill for Reagan's policy Congressman Edward Boland from Massachusetts championed the Boland Amendment. The measure, which began a process of limiting funds to the guerrillas, was first approved in the House of Representatives in December 1982. The Reagan administration's attempt to direct a war against the Sandinistas moved the Salvadoran conflict to the side and seized the spotlight on Capitol Hill.

The Reagan administration insisted that the goal of its policy was to use the Contras to harass the Nicaraguan government in such a way as to eliminate its effectiveness in funneling arms to El Salvador. According to the Reagan administration, the policy was containment carried through by surrogate guerrillas. Opponents of the administration, however, insisted that the Reagan administration sought the overthrow of the Nicaraguan government. The Boland amendment originally passed as a rider in an allocation for defense expenditures for 1983. The budget, signed by Reagan in January 1983, allowed limited funds to the Contras in order to minimize arms smuggling to El Salvador, but denied the Reagan administration the right to use the aid to overthrow the government of Nicaragua. Formally classified policy documents and statements asserted a policy of containment and weapons interdiction but Democrats at the time were, nonetheless, suspicious that the overthrow of the government of a sovereign nation was the central motivation.

In his massive metanarrative, *A Twilight Struggle,* Robert Kagan, former Reagan insider and scholar, noted the apparent contradiction in the United States-Nicaragua policy debate at this time. The Reagan administration was emphatic that it did not seek the overthrow of the Nicaraguan government, and that the United States merely sought to use the Contras to stop Sandinista weapons shipments to El Salvador through harassing border assaults and weapons interdiction. In 1983, Congress recognized this goal as acceptable, in principle. However, the contradiction involved the motivations of the Contra guerrillas themselves. Could the Contras actually be fighting and putting themselves on the line to contain the Sandinistas? The answer was, of course, no. The Contras were soldiers without a homeland that operated illegally and across several international sovereign boundaries. Many of these proxies had belonged to the National Guard of Somoza and prior to the success of the Sandinistas were intended by the Carter administration to remain the backbone of a new democratic government. The goal of these guerrillas was not simply to help the United States prevent the collapse of El Salvador. The Contras wanted to reassert a place in Nicaragua.[40]

In contending with accusations of regime change and most importantly the actions of Congress, the administration accepted responsibility for the covert operations. However, officials denied that the Reagan administration sought to overthrow the Nicaraguan government. The administration justified the action as defensive and aimed at preventing the "Marxist-Leninist"

leadership in Managua, Nicaragua, from undermining the United States supported regime in El Salvador.[41] Reagan asked for support not only to stop
communism and to interdict weapons, but also to back the proxies that waged
war on the government of Nicaragua, and harassed the Sandinistas making it
incapable of expanding the revolution.[42] Administration documents, like
NSDD-17, confirm that the administration's stated objective at this time was
a defensive policy of containment. If the Contras did bring about the collapse
of the Sandinista government the administration, undoubtedly, would have
celebrated the occasion, but during the first several years of Reagan's presidency the stated objective from Washington remained centered on the primary aim of containing Nicaragua, and preventing a Vietnam-like domino
theory.

To complicate matters, the situation in El Salvador continued to deteriorate adding fuel to a debate already inflamed by the Nicaraguan revelations.
In early 1983, five hundred Salvadoran rebels seized Berlin, El Salvador. In
the fight to extradite the guerrillas from the city journalists confirmed the
first US advisor wounded in action. Sargent J. Thomas Stanley received a
bullet wound to the leg.[43] Widespread media reports, from notable personalities like Mike Wallace, further complicated the Reagan administration's
aims by exposing human rights abuses carried out by the Salvadoran government.[44]

In response to the changing situation in El Salvador, the Reagan administration proposed an increase in the number of advisors in country beyond the
limit of fifty-five.[45] In appealing for support, Reagan insisted, "If El Salvador
fell to the rebels, other countries in Central America would fall too."[46] Many
in the media identified a similarity with the rhetoric of Vietnam. Major
television news personalities like Dan Rather and Lesley Stahl understood
the language in these terms. On the CBS evening news, Rather remarked,
"The President's language recalled Southeast Asia." Likewise, Stahl acknowledged that Reagan "echoed . . . Vietnam era rhetoric."[47] Vietnam
continued to swirl around the debate over the United States' efforts in Central America.

In 1983, Congress and the administration continued to argue over policy,
and the success of its Central American initiatives hinged on shaping the
public narrative. In 1983, the Reagan administration was losing in this important area. Americans continued to draw a negative association with the
United States' activities in Central America and the tragic memory of the
Vietnam War. In 1983, media coverage drew widely on the Vietnam analogy. In an April op-ed piece for the *New York Times* Lewis Flora claimed, "It
is accurate to compare El Salvador to Vietnam, Central America to Indochi-
na, in the sense that Washington's policy has no positive goal."[48] Flora
repeated the fears of many that an inability to form a clear objective would
lead the United States wandering into another Vietnam War.

In the spring of 1983, the administration faced further resistance from Congress. The House Intelligence Committee, headed by Boland, took the first step to eliminate any kind of assistance to the Contras for the next fiscal year, 1984. The committee decided, in a partisan vote, to support an amendment that rejected all appeals by the Department of State and the CIA to fund the Contras in any capacity in the coming fiscal year.[49] This decision created a tense environment in the House of Representatives and the summer months ahead promised a fight over policy. Of the opponents of Boland's measure Minority leader Robert Michel (R) and Senator Strom Thurmond (R) provided thought provoking comments. Michel lamented the decision recalling the injustice of Vietnam. He drew a connection with the crisis in Cambodia and Vietnam, and claimed that this, "Would leave Nicaragua as a sanctuary for guerrillas in El Salvador and a festering sore for American interests in the region."[50] Strom Thurmond, a supporter of Reagan's policy, proclaimed a position that conjured up the familiarity of rhetoric from the Vietnam era. He insisted that if "we turn our backs on the people of El Salvador and other Central American countries, we do great harm to the future of democracy itself, and we send a dangerous message to friends and foes alike."[51] Michel and Thurmond espoused a position taken by many proponents, a position that did not refute the connection to Vietnam, but rather appealed to a different interpretation of that past.[52] However, as politicians on Capitol Hill argued about Central America and the lessons of Vietnam, something happened that represented the beginning of a change that over the next several years significantly altered the course of the debate and of policy regarding Nicaragua.

On May 25, 1983, Lt Commander Albert Schaufelberger sat in his green Chevy Malibu, from which he had removed the bullet resistant glass that all such vehicles were outfitted. The sealed bulletproof windows made the sweltering heat of San Salvador unbearable. As he waited, a vehicle pulled in from behind, gunmen jumped from the small van and gunned down the deputy commander of the United States Military Advisory Group while he sat in his car.[53] Schaufelberger was shot while he waited for a friend in a parking lot outside of Central American University in San Salvador. A resident of San Diego, California, he was a member of the small contingent of American advisors helping the government of El Salvador fight the Nicaraguan backed insurgency in the country.

Alongside the escalation of violence in Central America during 1983 two massive attacks on American foreign service and military personnel in Beirut, Lebanon, seized the country's attention. Earlier that spring a suicide bomber attacked the United States embassy in Beirut, Lebanon. Dozens lay dead and wounded.[54] Later on October 23, a Mercedes Benz truck carrying six tons of dynamite rammed into a barracks for United States marines in Beirut. The explosives detonated and the death and destruction that resulted was unprecedented. Two hundred and forty US servicemen lay dead in the

rubble.[55] While civil wars raged in regions of US interest and military involvement meant that servicemen were increasingly targeted by militants
aligned against the United States and its allies.

During 1983 administration officials observed an escalation of terrorist
violence in Latin America and throughout the world. Of the 170 attacks
against US citizens and property that year, Latin America led all regions with
nearly eighty incidents. Likewise, by 1985 Latin America made up 15.2
percent of international terrorism in the globe, this was the third highest
percentage following the Middle East and Western Europe. More importantly, just short of 50 percent of all international terrorist attacks on US citizens
and property occurred in Latin America. That year marked the emergence of
a terrorism crisis.[56]

While Americans struggled over the legacy of Vietnam, conflict was
escalating in the Americas and the Middle East. As the Schaufelberger killing in San Salvador earlier that May showed, urban terrorism had increased
alongside the escalation of the conflict in El Salvador. Likewise, the Beirut
attack, a symptom of the increasingly violent Lebanese Civil War, also demonstrated that the United States faced a profoundly more deadly and aggressive security threat than in the 1970s. The issue of international terrorism was
not a mere anomaly. Instead, what was once a somewhat overlooked problem
was, in the 1980s, far more deadly as it expanded alongside the escalation of
regional conflicts. The terrorism problem in Central America was not limited
to leftist terrorism. It also involved rightist "death squads" that hunted down
anti-government affiliates in El Salvador as well as violent Contra attacks on
civilian communities in Nicaragua.

The escalation of terrorism in Central America, from both the right and
the left, forced the White House to consider the emergent danger more closely. In November 1983, Ambassador to El Salvador Thomas Pickering spoke
for the administration and denounced terror from the right. Pickering said
that the leadership in Washington believed that "extremist terror [was] another case of fascists serving the communist cause."[57] In December 1983, the
activity of rightist death squads in El Salvador also led Vice President
George H. W. Bush to speak for the administration. On December 11, 1983,
Bush visited El Salvador and at a dinner with President Alvaro Magana
proposed a toast in which he insisted, "These cowardly death squad terrorists
are just as repugnant to me, to President Reagan, to the United States Congress, and to the American people as the terrorist on the left."[58] An escalation
of terrorism in Central America and in other parts of the world led the
Reagan administration to recognize this threat in a more serious manner.
This, however, was the last time that a lead spokesman for the administration
publically acknowledged the problem of rightist terrorism. In the coming
years the administration increasingly constructed terrorism as a problem that
emanated from leftism. It increasingly ignored rightist terrorism and used

propaganda to reconstruct this threat from the basis of the administration's political interests.

In 1983 a shifting international environment and escalation of war in Central America drove a change. CIA intelligence noted a significant growth in the role of Palestinian groups and Libyans in Nicaragua. According to this information, the Palestinians were training guerrillas and pilots, and Libya was committing money and advisors to Nicaragua. The CIA noted a significant increase in PLO activity in Nicaragua, and in El Salvador, and connected this directly to the allegation that the Sandinistas exported arms and terrorist violence throughout the region. In 1984, George Shultz, who replaced Alexander Haig as Secretary of State, led the administration in defining the new concept of international terrorism. Despite terrorism from the right or the left in Central America, the administration used international terrorism over subsequent years to develop a propaganda angle that defined the problem as associated with an expanded leftist threat. In the coming years, the terrorism problem redefined the narrative and the policy with Nicaragua. This development encouraged a departure from containment and the adoption of offensive measures that further challenged the norms of international behavior.[59]

NOTES

1. "Around the World: Honduras Reports Raids by Nicaraguan Aircraft," *New York Times*, November 12, 1980, http://ntserver1.wsulibs.wsu.edu:2184/docview/121227731?accountid= 14902.

2. In this case, military force refers to any policy that places military pressure as a means to an end. Proxies, governments supported by the United States, the United States' armed forces or covert operations are all aspects of a military oriented policy in which the use of such force is integral to the achievement of policy goals. Military force, though carried out by proxies, foreign governments and covert operations, was integral to the Reagan administration's policy against Nicaragua and in El Salvador. I am careful to avoid a narrow definition of war as only when US armed forces are directly involved. A narrow definition absolves the role of the United States in conflict abroad. In the case of Nicaragua and Central America, the Reagan administration actively waged war, the actions should be considered as a war, as the use of military force as the primary route to achieving the interests of the United States.

3. The publication of *America's Longest War* by George C. Herring in 1979 embodied the scholarly understanding of the Vietnam War at this time. Herring argued that the containment policy was based on a flawed global national security model. Herring insisted that the United States containment policy mislead leaders and led to the travesty of Vietnam.

4. Howell Raines, "Reagan Calls Arms Race Essential to Avoid and Surrender or a Defeat," *New York Times*, August 10, 1980.

5. "US: More Arms Head For Rebels in El Salvador," *Boston Globe*, February 28, 1981, http://ntserver1.wsulibs.wsu.edu:2184/docview/294026790?accountid=14902.

6. "Leftists Free Ten Held in El Salvador: They Evacuate Offices of O.A.S. in Capital and Release Hostages After Three-Week Siege Government Rejected Concessions Kidnapped While Shopping Rights Violations Denounced," *New York Times*, October 8, 1980, http://db15. linccweb.org/login?url=http://search.proquest.com.db15.linccweb.org/docview/121027818? accountid=45760.

7. *Foreign Affairs Chronology 1978–1989* (New York: Free Press, 1990), 121.

8. Claire Sterling, *The Terror Network: The Secret War of International Terrorism* (New York: Readers Digest, 1981); Jeane Kirkpatrick, *Dictatorships and Double Standards: Rationalism and Reason in Politics* (New York: Simon and Schuster, 1982).

9. "US policy in El Salvador in Response to Guerrilla Offensive," January 18, 1981, *The Digital National Security Archive* (Ann Arbor: Proquest, 2012), ES01228, http://gateway. proquest.com/openurl?url_ver=Z39.88-2004&res_dat=xri:dnsa&rft_dat=xri:dnsa:article: CES01228.

10. Judith Miller, "15 U.S. Green Berets to Aid Salvadorans," *New York Times*, March 14, 1981, http://ntserver1.wsulibs.wsu.edu:2184/docview/424070851?accountid=14902.

11. "The Coming Showdown in Central America," *New York Times*, April 10, 1983, http:// ntserver1.wsulibs.wsu.edu:2184/docview/424620344?accountid=14902.

12. Glenn Silber, Tete Vasconcellos, *El Salvador: Another Vietnam*, 16mm, 1981: Icarus Films.

13. Elliot Brownlee and Hugh Davis Graham, *The Reagan Presidency: Pragmatic Conservatism and Its Legacies* (Lawrence, Ka.: University Press of Kansas, 2003), 97.

14. Lawrence Pezzullo, interview by Arthur Day, *Foreign Affairs Oral History Project*, Association for Diplomatic Studies and Training, February 24, 1989.

15. Lawrence Pezzullo, interview by Arthur Day.

16. Lawrence Pezzullo, interview by Arthur Day.

17. "Panel Wants Haig to Tell All on Cuba," *Boston Globe*, March 19, 1981, http:// ntserver1.wsulibs.wsu.edu:2184/docview/294049563?accountid=14902.

18. "Panel Wants Haig to Tell All on Cuba," *Boston Globe*.

19. *The Gallup Poll* (Wilmington, Delaware: Scholarly Resources Inc., 1982), 63.

20. *The Gallup Poll*, 63.

21. 97 Cong. Rec. S16549 (March 1981) (Statement of Senator Pell).

22. 97 Cong. Rec. S16549 (March 1981) (Statement of Senator Hatfield).

23. Alma Guillermoprieto, "Salvador Raids into Honduras, Refugees Charge," *The Washington Post*, January 7, 1981.

24. National Security Council, "National Security Security Decision Directive on Cuba and Central America," in Simpson, *National Security Decision Directives of the Reagan and Bush Administrations*, 53–54.

25. Simpson, *National Security Directives of the Reagan and Bush Administrations*, 18.

26. "Reagan Doctrine: Assisting Anti-Marxist Guerrillas," Folder 5, Box 11, David S. Addington, Series II: Chron File, 1987–1988, Ronald Reagan Presidential Library.

27. Simpson, *National Security Directives of the Reagan and Bush Administrations*, 18.

28. Nina Serafino, "Nicaragua: Conditions and US Interests," November 19, 1981, *The Digital National Security Archive* (Ann Arbor: Proquest, 2012), 15–17, NI01409, http:// gateway.proquest.com/openurl?url_ver=Z39.88-2004&res_dat=xri:dnsa&rft_dat= xri:dnsa:article: CNI01409.

29. "US: Nicaragua Backs Marxists in Salvador," *Boston Globe*, February 21, 1981.

30. "Exporting the Revolution," October 1981, *The Digital National Security Archive*, EL00066, http://gateway.proquest.com/openurl?url_ver=Z39.88-2004&res_dat=xri:dnsa&rft_ dat=xri:dnsa:article:CEL00066.

31. Serafino, "Nicaragua: Conditions and US Interests," November 19, 1981, *The Digital National Security Archive*.

32. "Background Information for Your Briefings on Central America," March 9, 1982, *The National Digital Security Archive* (Ann Arbor: Proquest, 2012), HN02040, http://gateway. proquest.com/openurl?url_ver=Z39.88-2004&res_dat=xri:dnsa&rft_dat=xri:dnsa:article: CHN02040.

33. "Nicaraguan Military Build-Up," March 22, 1982, *The Digital National Security Archive* (Ann Arbor: Proquest, 2012), 12–14, NI01474, http://gateway.proquest.com/openurl? url_ver=Z39.88-2004&res_dat=xri:dnsa&rft_dat=xri:dnsa:article:CNI01474.

34. Raymond Bonner, "War in El Salvador Threatens to Spread," *New York Times*, July 7, 1982, http://ntserver1.wsulibs.wsu.edu:2184/docview/424384316?accountid=14902.

35. Philip Taubman, "U.S. Backing Raids Against Nicaragua," *New York Times*, November 2, 1982, http://ntserver1.wsulibs.wsu.edu:2184/docview/424491778?accountid=14902.

36. Alan Riding, "Nicaragua Rebels Build up Strength," *New York Times*, November 7, 1982, http://ntserver1.wsulibs.wsu.edu:2184/docview/424491257?accountid=14902.

37. "U.S. Said to Authorize Anti-Nicaraguan Force," *New York Times*, March 10, 1982, http://ntserver1.wsulibs.wsu.edu:2184/docview/424320378?accountid=14902.

38. "The Worst-kept Secret War," *New York Times*, December 8, 1982, http://ntserver1.wsulibs.wsu.edu:2184/docview/424508081?accountid=14902.

39. Anthony Lewis, "Road to Disaster," *New York Times*, April 10, 1983, http://ntserver1.wsulibs.wsu.edu:2184/docview/424620468?accountid=14902.

40. Robert Kagan, *A Twilight Struggle: American Power and Nicaragua, 1977–1990* (New York: Free Press, 1996), 218–220.

41. Francis X. Clines, "U.S. Acting Legally About Nicaragua, President Asserts," *New York Times*, April 15, 1983, http://ntserver1.wsulibs.wsu.edu:2184/docview/424602196?accountid=14902.

42. Steven R. Weisman, "President Calls Nicaragua Rebels Freedom Fighters," *New York Times*, May 5, 1983, http://ntserver1.wsulibs.wsu.edu:2184/docview/424641490?accountid=14902.

43. Lydia Chavez, "Salvadoran Troops Reoccupy City after Withdrawal of 500 Rebels," *New York Times*, February 4, 1983, http://ntserver1.wsulibs.wsu.edu:2184/docview/424560027?accountid=14902.

44. John Corry, "TV: El Salvador Coverage on the Evening News," *New York Times*, March 22, 1983, http://ntserver1.wsulibs.wsu.edu:2184/docview/424574395?accountid=14902.

45. Bernard Weinraub, "Reagan Weighing More U.S. Advisers for El Salvador," *New York Times*, March 1, 1983, http://ntserver1.wsulibs.wsu.edu:2184/docview/424567940?accountid=14902.

46. Corry, "TV: El Salvador Coverage on the Evening News."

47. Corry, "TV: El Salvador Coverage on the Evening News."

48. Lewis Flora, "Oil On The Fire," *New York Times*, April 29, 1983, http://ntserver1.wsulibs.wsu.edu:2184/docview/424592896?accountid=14902.

49. David Rogers, "House Panel Approves Bar on Covert Aid to Nicaragua," *Boston Globe*, May 4, 1983, http://ntserver1.wsulibs.wsu.edu:2184/docview/294129902?accountid=14902.

50. Rogers, "House Panel Approves Bar on Covert Aid to Nicaragua."

51. 98 Cong. Rec. S10157 (1983) (statement by Senator Thurmond).

52. 98 Cong. Rec. S10157–10158 (1983).

53. Bureau of Diplomatic Security, US Department of State, "Lethal Terrorist Actions Against Americans 1973–1986," in Robert A. Friedlander, *Terrorism: Documents of International and Local Control* (New York: Oceania, 1990), 220.

54. "News Summary," *New York Times*, April 19, 1983, http://search.proquest.com/docview/122151717?accountid=45760.

55. "The U.S. Marine Tragedy: Causes and Responsibility, an Inquiry," *New York Times*, December 11, 1983, http://search.proquest.com/docview/122212027?accountid=45760.

56. US Department of State, "Patterns of Global Terrorism: 1985," in Friedlander, *Terrorism*, 80–81.

57. Lydia Chavez, "U.S. Envoy Castigates Salvadorans on Terrorism," *New York Times*, November 26, 1983, http://search.proquest.com/docview/122157525?accountid=14902.

58. Lydia Chavez, "In Salvador, Bush Assails Death Squads," *New York Times*, December 12, 1984, http://ntserver1.wsulibs.wsu.edu:2184/docview/122220867?accountid=14902.

59. Defense Department Background Paper, Nicaragua's Military Build-up and Support for Central American Subversion, Folder "The Sandinistas and Middle Eastern Radicals," Box 16, David S. Addington Files, Ronald Reagan Presidential Library.

Chapter Four

Harbor Mines

Shortly after lunchtime on March 20, 1984, the Soviet tanker, Lugansk, cruised into the waters near Puerto Sandino on Nicaragua's Pacific coast. The vessel carried petroleum supplies destined for delivery to the Sandinista government. Then, suddenly, at 1:40 pm an explosion rocked the ship. When the smoke lifted, five Soviet seamen were injured. The cause of the explosion was immediately apparent. The *Lugansk* had hit a mine. It was a small mine not capable of sinking the vessel, but a mine nonetheless. Shortly after the incident, the Nicaraguan Ministry of the Interior released a statement. The ministry insisted that the explosive device was planted by the United States and its paramilitary ally, the Contras. The Nicaraguan government argued that this was part of a criminal US-led terror war, and undeclared blockade against Nicaragua. Other vessels received damage in Nicaragua's two other major ports of Bluefields on the Gulf of Mexico and Corinto on the Pacific coast.[1]

The US mining of Nicaragua's ports catapulted the Reagan administration's war against the Sandinistas to a new level of controversy. CIA personnel directed the construction and placement of the weapons. Together with the Contras the operatives placed the explosives using small boats that moved as close as twelve miles from Nicaragua's coast. As from 1981 to 1982, when the Reagan administration began covert assistance to the Contras, it again did not inform Congress of the activities.[2] From January to March 1984 US-Contra mines damaged six ships and wounded at least ten non-combatant sailors. Nicaragua and the Soviet Union condemned the action. Nicaragua went before the United Nations and the International Court of Justice (ICJ), and argued that the United States acted in violation of international law. Not surprisingly, the United States utilized its veto power in the UN Security Council and blocked the vote on the matter. France and

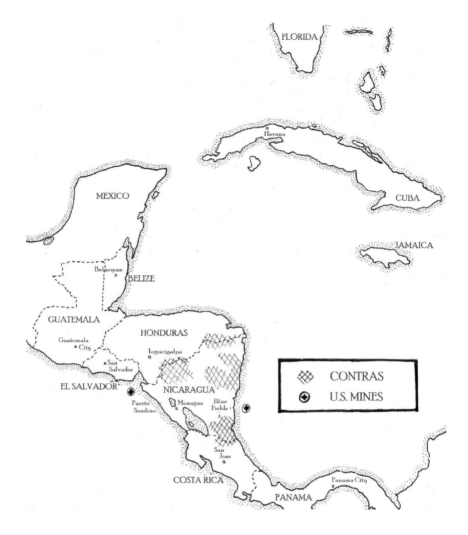

Figure 4.1. Harbor mines. *Source*: Alexander Marris.

the Netherlands were the most vocal supporters of a UN proposal to "condemn the mining of Nicaraguan ports."[3] The ICJ moved forward in the process of hearing Nicaragua's case and over the course of the next two years, the Reagan administration ignored the proceedings.

The year 1984 marked the beginning of a transition in the United States' conduct of the Cold War, and the mining operation was evidence of this shift. During 1984, the administration advanced a reconceptualization of foreign policy and of the Cold War. This rethinking was cumulative and brought on largely in response to the spike in acts of terrorism during 1983. The mining operation represented an escalation of hostilities against Nicaragua, a sovereign and internationally recognized nation. The goal of the program was to establish a blockade of Nicaragua by targeting oil tankers and discouraging other countries from sending vessels into Nicaragua's ports. This accelerated anti-Sandinista policy focused first on crippling the country economically. This intensified phase began with this illegal naval blockade and a year later with the enacting of unilateral economic sanctions against the Sandinista government and, eventually, with the overt pursuit of a military overthrow of the Nicaraguan government. The United States mining directly violated Nicaragua's international rights as a sovereign state. Regardless of a technical state of peace, the Reagan administration over the next three years developed an offensive strategy that tore down the practice of containment and further challenged the accepted norms of international behavior. The mining was the first step in this change.[4]

The mining of Nicaragua's harbors, however, also demonstrated that Congress and the American public were not ready for a more aggressive United States. The controversy that the operation inspired both nationally and internationally meant that the atmosphere required for the acceptance of a US offensive war directed against Nicaragua was not yet present. The administration lacked the political capital required to justify a war of regime change in Nicaragua. In response, the Reagan administration, first, developed the policy framework for an offensive against leftists and state sponsors of terrorism, and, second, advanced a public education campaign designed to gain support and congressional authorization for its war. In 1984, the administration resorted to a thorough speaking campaign designed to shape the attitudes of Americans. In the aftermath of the mining, members of the State Department used public speeches as a first step designed to promote a more aggressive approach with Nicaragua.

As in 1982, when journalists revealed the secret Contra support program, the White House at first denied direct responsibility for the mining, and argued that the problem rested entirely with the leftist leadership in Nicaragua that allegedly encouraged the independent action of guerrilla counterrevolutionary forces. On March 21, the White House released a statement that categorically denied allegations issued by the Soviet Union and Nicaragua of its involvement in the mining operations.[5] In a matter of days, however, the media again fully exposed the nature of US involvement, and the administration struggled to defend itself.

The revelations of the mining of Nicaragua's ports infuriated members of Congress on both sides of the isle. House Speaker Thomas ("Tip") O'Neill (D) summed up the feelings of many of those opposed to US activity with the Contras, claiming, "I have contended that the Reagan Administration's secret war against Nicaragua was morally indefensible. Today it is clear that it is legally indefensible as well."[6] As from 1982 to 1983, when the Boland

Amendment was first developed, many considered the Reagan Administration's actions illegal. Even Republican Barry Goldwater remarked that the mining was "an act violating international law . . . an act of war."[7] The crisis over the mining of Nicaragua's ports intensified the debate over policy, and memories of Vietnam resurfaced. Many Americans recognized what journalist Philip Taubman of the *New York Times* reported in April 1984 that, "The last time the United States openly mined foreign harbors was in 1972, when President Nixon ordered the mining of all North Vietnamese ports to prevent the flow of arms and supplies."[8] The Reagan administration's action challenged the accepted norms of international behavior by violating the sovereignty of Nicaragua and the result was a storm of controversy.

Angered by the mining Americans went to the streets to voice their displeasure with the administration's tactics. In April, protestors forced Henry Kissinger, whom Reagan appointed to chair a problem solving committee on Central America and had defended the mining, to cancel a speech at Tufts University. The demonstrators carried caricatures "linking Kissinger to U.S. policies in Vietnam, Cambodia, Chile, and Central America."[9] Nine months later the Veterans of Foreign Wars post in Santa Cruz, California, came out in public opposition to Reagan's policy and promoted instead a policy of

Figure 4.2.   Secretary Shultz and National Security Adviser Robert McFarlane brief President Reagan, January 4, 1985. *Source:* **Ronald Reagan Presidential Library.**

"nonintervention and self-determination in Central America." Spokesperson Dean Metcalf claimed, "Everybody knows somebody who died for nothing in Vietnam."[10] Metcalf hoped the nation could learn the right lesson from Vietnam. A week later, several hundred protestors gathered outside the federal building in Los Angeles. Max Inglett, a Vietnam veteran, exclaimed, "We want to be certain that another Vietnam does not happen again in El Salvador."[11] Inglett was part of a small demonstration, but the *Gallup Poll* suggested that public concern was strong nationally: from 1984 to 1985, 58 percent of persons polled feared a Vietnam-like escalation in Central America and felt that the United States should "stay out completely."[12] Political activism and poll figures reflected the widespread national debate about Central America. The Reagan administration struggled to win the debate, in part, because it still hinged on the difficult legacy of Vietnam.

It was not only Nicaragua and the Soviet Union that complained about the US-led mining of another sovereign nation. Great Britain condemned the act, France offered minesweepers to assist the Sandinista leadership in clearing their ports, and the Canadian Prime Minister Pierre Trudeau, recently nominated for the Nobel Peace Prize, referred to the action as "an act of international terrorism and . . . an act of war no different."[13] At this moment, the world, Congress, and the American public appeared poised to stop the Reagan administration. However, the situation with Nicaragua was in flux, and the escalation of international terrorism factored significantly in the upcoming course of events.

In the summer of 1984, George Shultz led the administration's growing public education campaign on Nicaragua and terrorism. The effort relied on public speaking and was designed to create a climate of fear and urgency and convince Americans that a military offensive was necessary to address a world transformed by a terrorism crisis perpetrated by the forces of leftism. Shultz was Alexander Haig's replacement and overtime he developed a positive reputation among his colleagues. Shultz was intelligent and experienced. He was an economist by trade, taught at MIT, and Reagan's cabinet was the fourth administration in his distinguished career. Historians often regard Shultz as a moderate whose diplomatic efforts were integral to improved relations with the Soviet Union. His opposition to the hostage for weapons scandal with Iran is often regarded as evidence of his pragmatism. George Shultz, however, was also a primary advocate for a policy based on the use of preemptive and preventative war as vehicle for overt regime change of the government of Nicaragua. Relative to the idea of forcible regime change in Nicaragua there was little difference between hardliners and moderates in the Reagan administration. With the exception of a few outliers that opposed the policy against Nicaragua many moderates and hardliners in the administration agreed on the idea of using force against the government of Nicaragua.

During the months following the mining controversy, Secretary of State George Shultz took the lead in establishing the groundwork for what eventually became known as the Reagan offensive. On April 3, he spoke before the Trilateral Commission in Washington, DC. He titled his speech, "Power and Diplomacy in the 1980s." Shultz spoke about American ideals and of the interconnection between power and diplomacy. He exclaimed that the Cold War in the 1980s was different. The primary concern was the threat from small-scale conflict in the developing world. State sponsored terrorism was, he testified, a new theme in the world. He insisted that "Terrorism, particularly state sponsored terrorism, is already a contemporary weapon directed at America's interest, America's values, and American allies." Shultz constructed a new image of threat in the world that linked the radical aims of communists and terrorists. The Secretary believed that this Cold War was different, and involved a new kind of threat from leftism. [14]

Shultz eagerly sought to change the minds of the people, but his words were not purely rhetoric. The Secretary spoke of a shift in US foreign policy. President Reagan signed the most significant counterterrorism directive to date on the same day that Shultz spoke before the Trilateral Commission. In response to the escalation of international terrorism and a rise in urban violence in El Salvador the administration composed "National Security Decision Directive 138: Combatting Terrorism." This directive established the principle that the United States prepared to take active measures to address the issue of international terrorism. The document emphasized the emergent problem posed by state sponsors of international terrorism. The administration believed that, "International terrorist movements and some of those which enjoy state sponsorship [were] receiving guidance directly or indirectly from the Soviet Union." The Reagan administration formally adopted a position that the world was in a transition phase, and that the old Cold War status quo was changing. There was a new threat, international terrorism, allegedly driven by a Soviet-inspired radicalism. The goal of this conspiratorial coalition presented "a common problem for all democratic nations." In the directive, the Reagan administration pledged that it would "work intensively with others to eliminate the threat of terrorism to our way of life." Further, the administration insisted, "States that practice terrorism or actively support it will not be allowed to do so without consequence. . . . Acts of state-sponsored and organized terrorism should be appropriately exposed and condemned in every available forum." The emergent issue of state sponsorship of terrorism was changing the Cold War as well as outlining a new course for the future of US policy. [15]

NSDD-138 established a two-phased program overseen by the secretary of state, secretary of defense, the director of the CIA, and the treasury secretary. The head of the Terrorist Incident Working Group (TIWG), Robert Oakley, oversaw the implementation of this program over the course of the following year. The central initiatives were to expand intelligence and cooperation to combat terrorism, but also to, "Develop a full range of options for dealing directly with terrorism, both at the threat stage and after such acts are carried out." According to NSDD-138, the program incorporated the use of "sanctions [and] continue[d] improvements in the U.S. capability to conduct military operations to counter terrorism." The authors sought most to, "develop a military strategy that is supportive of an active, preventative program to combat state-sponsored terrorism [and] develop a broad range of defensive measures to protect military forces, dependents, and facilities worldwide." In response to the terrorism crisis that emerged in 1983 the United States developed a policy for a new offensive war on terrorism. The mining was the first test of this new aggressive policy against leftists. [16]

This idea of international terrorism as shaped by Shultz and the Reagan administration was broad and applied to not only Middle Eastern organizations and states, but also to communist and Marxist-revolutionary states. The administration constructed terrorists and communists as mutual allies. Not all terrorists were communists, but all communists by the mid-1980s, allegedly, sought the export of terrorism throughout the world. In this respect, the administration presented the threat and consequences posed by Cuba, Nicaragua, and the Soviet Union as effectively the same as those posed by terrorist organizations and states like the PLO, Libya, and Iran. Terrorism was a new way of defining the enemies of the United States. The idea of international terrorism and subsequent events allowed the administration to characterize the role of Nicaragua in El Salvador as criminal. Many in the administration insisted that this behavior required an aggressive military oriented approach that pressed the accepted norms of international behavior.

In 1984, the State Department also took a major step toward reconstructing the meaning of terrorism in such a way as to delegitimize leftist revolutions across the developing world. The State Department created an enlarged catalogue of actions that it considered terrorist in nature, and by contrast it created a stringent definition of insurgency. According to the State Department, a legitimate insurgency was a group in which, "Its members wear a uniform [and] operates in the open." Further, according to the document, "Its (insurgency) methods are military [and] its targets are military, both tactical and strategic, and its legitimate operations are governed by the international rules of armed conflict." Lastly, for the United States to recognize a revolutionary or guerrilla movement as a legitimate insurgency rather than a terrorist threat, "Its primary interests [must] relate to one country." [17]

Effectively, no insurgency at any time previous or since fell into the administration's new definition. As an almost universal rule of insurgency combatants did not wear uniforms, operated as guerrillas, acted across national borders, possessed transnational links, and engaged in a wide array of violence. The United States formally characterized the FMLN in El Salvador as a terrorist army with a membership numbering 7,500. The FMLN was actually a revolutionary insurgency, but this number placed the FMLN among the largest terrorist groups in the world. The Reagan administration catalogued and discussed the FMLN at length in *Terrorist Group Profiles,* a publication, for which, Vice President Bush provided an eloquent introduction. Of course, Nicaragua and Cuba the administration deemed as its primary state sponsors. Obviously, the Contras did not fall into the State Department definition of insurgency either, and the Reagan administration, of course, did not admit to this contradiction. In defending the Contras, Bush insisted that, "Freedom fighters . . . seek to adhere to international law and civilized standards of conduct."[18] The Reagan administration expanded the definition of terrorism to exclusively justify aggressive actions against insurgent groups and nations at odds with the United States.

In Central America, the conflict between Nicaragua, the Contras, and El Salvador was increasingly violent. On May 30, 1984, a bomb exploded at a press conference in Costa Rica held by Eden Pastora. Pastora was an enigmatic Nicaraguan that initially fought with the Sandinistas but turned his sympathies toward the Contra resistance following the consolidation of Sandinista power. US intelligence confirmed that the bombing was coordinated by the Sandinistas and the Spanish terror group ETA. Three were killed in the attack and twenty-eight were wounded, Pastora included.[19] Shortly following this event leftist guerrillas kidnapped Eduardo Vides Casanova, the Salvadoran defense minister's brother.[20] The Reagan administration knew the close relationship between the Sandinistas and the Salvadoran revolutionaries and these events further enhanced the administration's growing opinion that Nicaragua served as a base for the forces of international terrorism in the region. These events, however, did not provide the kind of catalyst necessary to create the atmosphere for a US offensive war of regime change primarily because US citizens were not the target of the strikes. Such events barely made headlines in the United States. These were minor incidents that did not target Americans and fell far off the radar of the public and Congress in the United States.

NSDD-138 leaked to the press, and in the wake of the mining controversy, this resulted in further criticism and suspicion about the intentions of the United States. The *Wall Street Journal* accurately reported that the administration considered the use of "preventive strikes against international terrorist groups."[21] Together, the mining and the report demonstrated that the Reagan administration was beginning an offensive as part of a new policy direction. This caused controversy and brought significant opposition to the hardline approach called for in NSDD-138. The leaked details and the controversy of the mining meant that the offensive envisioned by top officials in the Reagan administration had to wait, the country was not ready. Following the controversy surrounding the mining of Nicaragua's harbors the Reagan administration did two things: first, it actively argued for the need for an offensive approach against state sponsors, and, second, policy makers moved cautiously with legal actions that presented little likelihood of drawing controversy. [22]

A comprehensive counterterrorism policy document sent from National Security Advisor Robert McFarlane to Attorney General Edwin Meese affirmed the administration's cautious approach following the mining fiasco. McFarlane acknowledged that the controversy surrounding the mining and the leaks of NSDD-138 had caused the administration to move with caution and to deemphasize the unilateral preemptive military option. In prefacing his delivery of the materials pertaining to US terrorism policy, he noted, "We have sought to minimize the attention placed on preemptive covert activities in order to preclude adverse reactions which could constrain our options." While the operational directive for US terrorism policy in 1984 was grounded in taking active measures against state sponsors the controversy moved the focus to improved intelligence and it "explicitly rule[d] out responding in kind, recognizing that this would hurt an open society far more than it would hurt terrorists." After the revelations of the mining of Nicaragua's ports and of NSDD-138, the pressure was on the administration and the NSC felt it apparent that it was not the time to pursue offensive military options. NSDD-138 was a "lame duck" directive, it established principals but those which the administration felt unable to act on. [23]

Because of the controversy surrounding the aggressive activities of the United States, particularly in Central America, the administration emphasized its public speaking campaign. The purpose was to sell the new US strategy, the Reagan offensive, to the media, the public and Congress. Throughout 1984 the administration remained cautious about the application of aggressive military options to the terrorism strategy, but top officials like George Shultz, and President Reagan spoke frequently about the urgency of the terrorism crisis. Their goal was to convince Congress and the public of the need for the active measures called for by NSDD-138.

The primary aim of the Reagan administration's educational campaign in 1984 was to convince Congress and the public that Nicaragua was a state sponsor of international terrorism, and that only aggressive hardline policies were appropriate to deal with this threat. The United States' first step was simple, it accused the Sandinistas of being the ones involved in illegal international terrorist acts. On May 9, 1984, Reagan announced to the world that this threat factored into US motivations in Central America. Speaking in a televised address from the oval office the President reiterated the well-known theme of communist conspiracy abroad. He proclaimed that "the Soviet Union and its surrogates move[d] to establish control over Vietnam, Laos, Cambodia, Angola, Ethiopia, South Yemen, Afghanistan and recently, closer to home, in Nicaragua and El Salvador." [24] In building on George Shultz's description of the new Cold War, Reagan connected Nicaragua to not only the Soviet bloc but also to a global terrorist network rooted in the Middle East. He insisted that the PLO and Libya were supplying the Sandinistas and helping that government drive a "reign of terror" in Central America.[25] According to Reagan, leftist terrorists carried out a new kind of offensive war.

On June 24, 1984, George Shultz outlined his model for the use of preventative war at a speech at the second conference on International Terrorism held at the Jonathan Institute. The conference at the Jonathan Institute was significant, in part, because it demonstrated the crystallization of the flawed notion that international terrorism was primarily a problem associated with leftist revolution. Claire Sterling's book, *The Terrorism Network*, influenced the United States in this respect, but so too had the leadership in Israel. Israel was at the forefront when it came to addressing terrorism with hardline measures. This, of course, was associated with its conflict over Palestine. The Israeli's promoted the use of aggressive counterterror operations. The most well-known such case was Operation Entebbe in 1976. The operation came after an airline hijacking conducted by Palestinian militants took passengers to Uganda where dictator Idi Amin offered sanctuary. The militants, ultimately, released all non-Israeli passengers and then hoped to use the remaining Israelis to force the government to exchange Palestinian prisoners captured in campaigns in the ongoing conflict. However, the Israeli government sent an attack force and raided Uganda freeing the hostages. The only Israeli commando that died was the brother of Benjamin Netanyahu, Jonathan. Benjamin Netanyahu soon developed into a leading proponent of the idea that international terrorism was a leftist phenomenon targeting the West, and which hardline measures of preemption and regime change were among potential appropriate responses. Netanyahu oversaw the Jonathan Institute and the conference in 1984 largely conferred the idea of a global internationally connected leftist terror network that threatened the civilized world. Of the participants, none was as significant as George Shultz, and, in all likelihood, none were as eager to embark on a new hardline approach against terror groups and state sponsors of terrorism.[26]

At the Jonathan Institute conference Secretary Shultz embraced the hardline approach of Israel. The Secretary described the new terror threat and the appropriate US response. The Secretary spoke of the development of a new and dangerous threat, that of "state-sponsored terrorism." He remarked, "In the past five years more states have joined the ranks of what we might call the 'League of Terror,' as full-fledged sponsors and supporters of indiscriminate-and not so indiscriminate-murder."[27] These state sponsors made international terrorism more dangerous and viable because it provided safe-havens, arms, and global access. Shultz insisted that terrorism was a fundamental threat to democracy. Regardless of the type of terrorism, whether perpetrated by communists or Islamic militants, it posed a legitimate threat to the most basic of American values. Because terrorism sought to achieve political ends by creating an atmosphere of fear, it was "a threat to the democracies."[28] Likewise, Shultz argued, "If freedom and democracy are the targets of terrorism, it is clear that totalitarianism is its ally."[29] The Reagan administration constructed a perspective of the world in which communism and terrorism were naturally aligned. Shultz insisted that this assault on the free world by radical leftists warranted a new US position in the world, an aggressive and offensive posture. Over the next two years, no conflict demonstrated this new direction more than relations with Nicaragua.

Due to its struggles with the PLO, Lebanon, and Syria, Israel was a leading power in addressing terrorism and the audience at the Jonathan Institute was strongly pro-Israel and receptive to Shultz's calls for a military offensive against state sponsors of terrorism. He declared that the United States must, "Go beyond passive defense to consider means of active prevention, preemption, and retaliation. Our goal must be to prevent and deter future terrorist acts." The secretary insisted that the administration "will need the flexibility to respond to terrorist attacks in a variety of ways, at times and places of our own choosing." Schultz argued for a freer hand in military actions, the support of the public, cooperation from the international community and a strengthening of intelligence. While the United States remained in a cautious position, Shultz's statements changed the discussion and portended the future of US counterterrorism policy.[30]

As the summer of 1984 ended, the United States named, for the coming year, those states that had "repeatedly provided support for acts of international terrorism."[31] The states listed as repeat offenders were Iran, Syria, Libya, Cuba, and South Yemen, and the consequences were economic and trade sanctions. Despite the directive for active measures, such as unilateral and preemptive attacks, the United States continued to proceed with caution. As the controversy over the mining of Nicaragua's ports and the information in NSDD-138 revealed, Congress and the public remained skeptical of offensive action.

While Nicaragua was not yet on the United States' formal state terrorism list, this did not mean that the Sandinista government did not remain a target of the allegation. The Reagan administration built its case against Nicaragua and increased military pressure despite Congress' ban on support to the Contras. It seems that the United States intended to escalate the conflict through third party support and use this to implicate the Sandinistas as the government increased its own military operations and capabilities in response to the US-led proxy war. The administration alleged Sandinista involvement in the assassination of Somoza, and the attempted assassination of Eden Pastora. The administration made a case that the Sandinistas provided "ideological and material support" for terrorist groups throughout the region and particularly in El Salvador. It insisted that government supported urban terrorist groups like the Clara Elizabeth Ramirez Front (CERF). CERF was responsible for the 1983 murder of US Navy Lieutenant Commander Schau-felberger outside of the Central American University in San Salvador. In 1984, the group had killed two US embassy employees in El Salvador and had fired machine guns on the outside of the building in San Salvador. In addition to the allegation of support for urban terrorism in El Salvador, the administration continued to press its case against Nicaragua that the Sandi-nistas provided safe haven and support for international terror groups from the PLO, ETA, the Red Brigades, the Argentine Montoneros and the Uru-guayan Tupamaros. The Reagan administration developed its argument for preemptive regime change in Nicaragua. [32]

George Shultz argued that military force was the best option for address-ing the problem of state sponsorship of terrorism. This contention, that the threat posed by state sponsors was such that it required a hardline military response that disregarded the sovereign rights of alleged states, was an area of concern for the leadership in the State Department's Office of Counterter-rorism. In 1984 a quiet disagreement between George Shultz and the Office of Counterterrorism seemed to emerge. On August 15, 1984, the Director for the Office of Counterterrorism, Robert Sayre, spoke before the Foreign Poli-cy Association in New York City. Sayre's speech reiterated several key points. First, he insisted that state sponsors linked to the Soviet Union facili-tated international terrorism, and in large part, were Marxist-Leninist in or-ientation. The agents of terrorism, he asserted, were directing the war against the United States and the democracies of the world. Unlike Shultz, however, Sayre argued that "Combatting terrorism is essentially a police and not a military matter." In his speech, the director argued that intelligence, law, and cooperation were the best measures for addressing the emergent issue of international terrorism. Whereas Shultz insisted that state terrorism was a criminal act that required the United States to take military action that disre-garded sovereign rights, Sayre insisted that legal means and international justice was the most effective tool at the administration's disposal. This was the beginning of a significant fissure between the Reagan administration and the Office of Counterterrorism over the issue of state sponsorship and the proper response to this problem. [33]

In addition to the outlook proposed by Sayre, there was also concern from Congress over the proposed new direction. On September 27, 1984, Con-gress released a report that expressed concern over the proposed military offensive implied by NSDD-138 and Shultz. The report, prepared by the Congressional Research Service, highlighted a number of issues raised by the possibility of an active military offensive against state sponsors and terrorist groups. Some of the areas of concern were related to how the War Powers Resolution applied to the new doctrine and how Congress would oversee the new approach. Since the mining of Nicaragua's harbors and the leaks of NSDD-138 Congress was concerned over the prospect of a new military offensive to combat the forces of international terrorism.[34] Given the Contra aid program, and the mining operation, Congress had every reason to fear the potential next steps of the Reagan administration with Nicaragua.

One month later, speaking in New York City before the Park Avenue Synagogue, George Shultz again promoted the administration's ideas for a military oriented approach. His statements further identified a subtle divide between his thinking and top officials in the Office of Counterterrorism on this subject. The Secretary outlined the emergence of radical leftism, an alliance of tyrannical states that facilitated low-intensity covert war against the United States and the Western democracies. Terrorism, as the use of force against innocent civilians to achieve a political goal, he insisted was a key tool of these radical leftists. Whereas the Director of the Office of Counterterrorism Robert Sayre presented only a short list of state sponsors, Shultz expanded it to include Nicaragua. The secretary insisted that "Libya and the PLO provide arms and training to the communists in Central America. . . . Cuba and Nicaragua, in particular, used narcotics smugglers to funnel guns and money to terrorists in Colombia." According to Shultz, Nicaragua was a part of a dangerous and unpredictable problem that represented a new and dangerous Cold War. Unlike Sayre, who insisted that the legal system provided the best arena for combating terrorism, Shultz proposed that military force was the first and primary way to deal with radical states like Nicaragua. He argued that, "To combat it, we must be willing to use military force." The secretary praised Israel for its cutting edge and aggressive military approach, and further he implied that terrorism represented a gray area in terms of international law. The consequence of this was that the United States needed to take offensive military action. While the administration waited for the right catalyst for its new offensive, Shultz claimed that the most important thing was to convince the public of the value of "combating terrorism with overt power."[35]

The fearsome rhetoric that emanated from the White House and State Department following the revelations of the mining of Nicaragua's ports portended a new kind of Cold War. The new conflict was, for the first time, on the American mainland and Reagan insisted that it involved a more devious and insidious threat from a united communist-terrorist brand of leftism. The enemy in this new Cold War allegedly targeted civilians and used shock and deception to undermine the American way of life.

There is no better example of the pop-culture resonance of the administration's language in 1984 than the blockbuster Hollywood hit film, *Red Dawn.* Patrick Swayze starred in the film and it brought Reagan's nightmarish fears to life on the silver screen. The movie depicted a first time invasion by the forces of radical leftism. On the surface the plot appeared little more than a movie about the Soviet Union attacking the United States, but half-way through the film the true details of the events are un-earthed as Swayze's guerrilla band of high school students, "Wolverines," rescued a downed US pilot. Sitting in front of a campfire during winter months in the Rocky Mountain West the Captain informed the group of what transpired. His description was of a Nicaraguan and Cuban force that staged an invasion by hijacking civilian airliners flying across the US-Mexican border. The producers brought to life the concern that the White House and State Department peppered the American people with at this time. This was the danger of a communist-terrorist offensive that was allegedly emergent in Nicaragua. The administration described a Cold War enemy that targeted civilians, hijacked planes, and used terrorist deception to attack and undermine cherished American values of freedom and democracy.[36]

Four years later, in 1988, the comedy film *The Naked Gun* also revealed the pop-culture resonance of the administration's description of a new communist-terrorist Cold War. The film starred the American comedian Leslie Nielson, who played Lieutenant Frank Drebin of Police Squad. Drebin tended to bungle things, but despite his incompetence he was consistently successful in defeating the villains. In the opening scene, the key elements of the Reagan administration's new Cold War sat around a table in Beirut, Lebanon. The participants included Fidel Castro, Mikhail Gorbachev, Muammar Qaddafi, the Ayatollah Khomeini, an individual that was most likely a depiction of Nicaragua's Minister of Interior Tomas Borge and others of the administration's alleged band of communist-terrorist state sponsors. Together the group argued about their next act of terrorist violence against the United States. After the Ayatollah insisted that they must conduct an act of terrorism that would "show America, the great Satan, as but a paper tiger," Frank Drebin, disguised as a waiter burned the Ayatollah's hand with a teapot and began to single handedly beat up the communist-terrorist leaders. At the end of the debacle one of the characters asked, "who are you" to which Nielsen responded "Lt. Frank Drebin, Police Squad, and don't ever let me catch you guys in America!" While the scene was from a ridiculous comedy, the image conjured up by the authors mirrored the speeches and statements of the Reagan administration during the 1980s when it pledged that the United States faced a new more aggressive enemy, a communist-terrorist alliance of radicals. Films like *Red Dawn* and *The Naked Gun* were evidence that the way in which Americans understood the Cold War was considerably different during the 1980s than in previous decades. Whether taken seriously or comically, the Reagan administration intentionally sought to build anxiety over the issue of terrorism in the United States. Fear and concern, it seems to have believed, was critical to gaining a mandate for the conduct of a new aggressive foreign policy that challenged the norms of international law and state sovereignty.[37]

As Ronald Reagan ran a stunningly successful campaign over Walter Mondale in the presidential election of 1984, US newspapers published a

CIA training manual that revealed that the US ally, the Contras, utilized acts that could only be defined as terrorism. The manual directed the guerrillas in the methods of assassination. The guerrillas were encouraged to infiltrate small villages controlled by the Sandinistas and assassinate its leaders. To make matters even more complicated for the Reagan administration, an anonymous Contra leader came out shortly after the revelations and insisted that the guerrillas goal was the overthrow of the Nicaraguan government rather than contain it, as was the official reason provided by the White House and State Department at this time. The training manual added further controversy to the United States policy toward Nicaragua and sent the Reagan administration back peddling yet again as it attempted to deny that there was a concerted policy of regime change or assassination promoted by the White House or State Department. Reagan dismissed the manual as produced by underlings of the CIA, and swept into office for a second term in one of the most thorough landslides in the country's history.[38]

Did the CIA guidebook, though, provide evidence that the Reagan administration was already pursuing a formal policy of regime change in Nicaragua? The answer to this question is, no. In *America's First War on Terrorism* Political Scientist David C. Wills did an excellent job of documenting the discontinuity of the Reagan cabinet. Wills demonstrates that Reagan's managerial style often allowed the individuals directly involved with a particular incident to handle it on their own accord. This loose organizational style created certain discontinuities in US counterterrorism strategy. While the CIA manual appeared to confirm that the United States was involved in supporting guerrillas that fought for the mission of regime change there was still no evidence to suggest that the administration, as yet, adopted a formal policy to alter the government of Nicaragua. As Wills demonstrates, it was entirely conceivable that CIA operatives and Contra guerrillas operated in a manner inconsistent with official administration policy and that Reagan knew little of the matter as the president generally failed to maintain tight control over his subordinates.[39] However, regardless of whether the Reagan administration sought regime change at this moment or not, the assassination manual and its ardent attempt to support the Contras demonstrated that the United States was itself a state sponsor of terrorism. While it struggled to promote its own war on terrorism the United States supported a group of anti-leftist guerrillas originally organized by Argentina's state terror program.

The revelations of the CIA assassination guidebook provided confirmation that the Contras used tactics that critics interpreted as acts of terrorism. However, the Reagan administration's understanding of terrorism was less concerned with the nature of the violence itself as much as the ideological and anti-American purpose of such acts. The year 1984 was a transition time. It was a moment in which the Reagan administration built the philosophical and rhetorical groundwork for an offensive war on terrorism that developed amid a further escalation of a terrorism crisis in the coming year. In 1984, the administration constructed the image of an enemy that was international, monolithic, and unpredictable. Its understanding of terrorism blurred the distinction between criminal and revolutionary.

Beginning with the controversy over its Contra aid program the administration brought its argument to the people frequently and created a dialogue designed to delegitimize the Nicaraguan government and justify a policy of military force that clearly violated the sovereign rights of the small Central American nation. The ability of the administration to communicate its opinion was integral to creating support for a new more aggressive policy with Nicaragua in subsequent years. The campaign was an important tool for marginalizing the opposition's narrative in Congress, which tended to fight administration policy in Central America by evoking the memory of Vietnam and comparing actions in Central America to the previous failure of Cold War containment policy. International terrorism proved a key tool in the debate over Nicaragua and, used as propaganda, it helped mobilized a military offensive that hinted at a new era of US hegemony.

Beginning in 1983, the escalation of a terrorism crisis extended a refashioning of the Cold War and a re-definition of the Nicaraguan conflict by the Reagan administration. Terrorism is an old form of warfare that involves targeting non-combatants through assassination, bombings, shootings, kidnappings, and so on, in pursuit of some form of political objective. During 1983, the conflict in El Salvador escalated and in the process, terrorism, both rightist and leftist, developed as a significant problem in an increasingly brutal conflict. Initially, Ambassador Thomas Pickering and Vice President George H. W. Bush emphatically condemned all forms of terrorism in Central America. However, despite these initial statements, during 1984 the Reagan administration led by Alexander Haig's replacement as Secretary of State, George Shultz, reconstructed the meaning of terrorism. What were the causes and solutions to the terrorism problem? According to the Reagan administration, the cause was an offensive by the forces of leftism, and the solution was the pursuit of an offensive policy that relied on military force against alleged state sponsors of terrorism like Nicaragua. Following the mining incident, the Reagan administration acted cautiously, but it used the period to explain its philosophical reevaluation of the Cold War and form the basis for an offensive against Nicaragua.

NOTES

1. John F. Burns, "Moscow Holds U.S. Responsible for Mines off Nicaragua's Ports: Moscow Blames U.S. in Nicaragua," *New York Times*, March 22, 1984, http://ntserver1.wsulibs.wsu.edu:2184/docview/424916709?accountid=14902.

2. Philip Taubman, "Latin Debate Refocused," *New York Times*, April 9, 1984, http://ntserver1.wsulibs.wsu.edu:2184/docview/424935498?accountid=14902.

3. "U.S. Vetoes U.N. Bid to Condemn Mining of Nicaragua Ports," *New York Times*, April 5, 1984, http://ntserver1.wsulibs.wsu.edu:2184/docview/424948184?accountid=14902.

4. Memorandum for Robert C. McFarlane from Oliver North and Constantine Menges, "Special Activities in Nicaragua," March 2, 1984, in Kornbluh and Byrne, *The Iran-Contra Scandal*, 19.

5. Burns, "Moscow Holds U.S. Responsible for Mines off Nicaragua's Ports."

6. Philip Taubman, "House to Block Aid for Rebels O'Neill Asserts," *New York Times*, April 10, 1984, http://ntserver1.wsulibs.wsu.edu:2184/docview/424940890?accountid=14902.

7. "Illegal, Deceptive and Dumb," *New York Times*, April 11, 1984, http://ntserver1.wsulibs.wsu.edu:2184/docview/424938472?accountid=14902.

8. Taubman, "Latin Debate Refocused."

9. Ross Gelbspan, "Kissinger Cancels Tufts Talk Because of Protest," *Boston Globe*, April 3, 1984, http://ntserver1.wsulibs.wsu.edu:2184/docview/294249465?accountid=14902.

10. "Santa Cruz VFW Post Rips U.S. Policy," *San Francisco Chronicle*, January 15, 1985, http://ntserver1.wsulibs.wsu.edu:2184/docview/301878145?accountid=14902.

11. Patricia Hurtado, "Eight Arrests Made at Downtown Federal Building 200 Protest U.S. Policy in Latin America," *Los Angeles Times*, January 22, 1985, http://ntserver1.wsulibs.wsu.edu:2184/docview/292020880?accountid=14902.

12. *The Gallup Poll* (Wilmington, Del.: Scholarly Resources Inc., 1986), 70–72.

13. Memo from US Canadian Embassy to Secretary of State, "Trudeau Condemns Mining of Nicaragua's Harbors," April 12, 1984, *The Digital National Security Archive* (Ann Arbor: Proquest, 2012), NI02056, http://gateway.proquest.com/openurl?url_ver=Z39.882004&res_dat=xri:dnsa&rft_dat=xri:dnsa:article:CNI02056.

14. Memo from McFarlane to Meese, "Background Material on Terrorism," August 15, 1984, *The Digital National Security Archive* (Ann Arbor: Proquest, 2012), TE00715, http://gateway.proquest.com/openurl?url_ver=Z39.88-2004&res_dat=xri:dnsa&rft_dat=xri:dnsa:article:CTE00715.

15. "National Security Decision Directive 138: Combatting Terrorism, April 3, 1984," Folder "Combatting Terrorism Task Force, Folder 1 of 7," Box 2, OA/ID 19849, Donald P. Gregg: Task Force on Terrorism, George Bush Vice Presidential Records.

16. "National Security Decision Directive 138: Combatting Terrorism, April 3, 1984," George Bush Vice Presidential Records.

17. Memo from McFarlane to Meese, "Background Material on Terrorism," August 15, 1984, *The Digital National Security Archive*.

18. "Terrorist Group Profiles," November 1988, viii, *The Digital National Security Archive* (Ann Arbor: Proquest, 2012), TE00967, http://gateway.proquest.com/openurl?url_ver=Z39.882004&res_dat=xri:dnsa&rft_dat=xri:dnsa:article:CTE00967.

19. Bureau of Diplomatic Security, US Department of State, "Lethal Terrorist Actions Against Americans 1973–1986," in Friedlander, *Terrorism*, 215.

20. "Phony Newsman Suspected in Latin Bombing," *Philadelphia Daily News*, June 5, 1984, http://ntserver1.wsulibs.wsu.edu:2184/docview/428739356?accountid=14902.

21. Robert S. Greenberger, "White House Seeks to Broaden Authority to Thwart Growing Terrorism Threat," *Wall Street Journal*, April 27, 1984, http://ntserver1.wsulibs.wsu.edu:2184/docview/397960222?accountid=14902.

22. Memo from McFarlane to Meese, "Background Material on Terrorism," August 15, 1984, *The Digital National Security Archive*.

23. Memo from McFarlane to Meese, "Background Material on Terrorism," August 15, 1984, *The Digital National Security Archive*.

24. "Transcript of President Reagan's Speech on Central America Policy," *New York Times*, May 10, 1984, http://ntserver1.wsulibs.wsu.edu:2184/docview/122499282?accountid=14902.

25. Steven Weisman, "Reagan Predicts Loss of El Salvador if U.S. Ceases Aid: Goes on TV with Appeal Says the 'Freedom Fighters' Opposing the Sandinistas Also Require Support Reagan Warns of a Rebel Victory in Salvador," *New York Times*, May 10, 1984, http://ntserver1.wsulibs.wsu.edu:2184/docview/122490530?accountid=14902.

26. Benjamin Netanyahu, *Terrorism: How the West Can Win* (New York: Farrar, Straus, Giroux, 1986).

27. George Shultz, "Terrorism: The Challenge to the Democracies," June 24, 1984, in Steven Anzovin, *Terrorism* (New York: H. W. Wilson, 1986), 50.

28. Shultz, "Terrorism: The Challenge to the Democracies," in Anzovin, *Terrorism*, 51.

29. Shultz, "Terrorism: The Challenge to the Democracies," in Anzovin, *Terrorism*, 54.

30. "Excerpts from Schultz's Address on International Terrorism," *New York Times*, October 26, 1984, http://ntserver1.wsulibs.wsu.edu:2184/docview/425213685?accountid=14902.

31. Memo from McFarlane to Meese, "Background Material on Terrorism," August 15, 1984, *Digital National Security Archive*.

32. "Patterns of Global Terrorism, 1984," Folder "Vice President's Task Force on Combatting Terrorism Statistics 2 of 2," George Bush Vice Presidential Records, Task Force on Combatting Terrorism, General Office Files: Subject Files, OA/ID 15394, George Bush Presidential Library.

33. Robert Sayre, "International Terrorism: A Long Twilight Struggle, August 15, 1984," Folder "Terrorism Material, 2 of 4," Box 3/1, Donald P. Gregg: George H. W. Bush Vice Presidential Records, National Security Affairs, Task Force on Terrorism Files, OA/ID 19850 and 19851, George Bush Presidential Library.

34. "Anti-Terrorist Activities: Issues Raised by the Reagan Administration's Proposals, Sept. 27, 1984," Folder "Terrorism 3 of 4," Box 2, Donald P. Gregg: George H. W. Bush Vice Presidential Records, National Security Affairs, Task Force on Terrorism Files, OA/ID 19851, George Bush Presidential Library.

35. George Shultz, "Terrorism and the Modern World, October 24, 1984," Folder "Terrorism Material, 2 of 4," Box 3/1, Donald P. Gregg: George H. W. Bush Vice Presidential Records, National Security Affairs, Task Force on Terrorism Files, OA/ID 19850 and 19851, George Bush Presidential Library.

36. Kevin Reynolds, *Red Dawn*, DVD, directed by John Milius (1984: MGM).

37. Jerry Zucker and Jim Abrahams, *The Naked Gun: From the Files of Police Squad*, DVD, directed David Zucker (1988: Paramount).

38. Hedrick Smith, "CIA Manual: A Policy is Undermined," *New York Times*, October 30, 1984, http://ntserver1.wsulibs.wsu.edu:2184/docview/425209111?accountid=14902.

39. David C. Wills, *America's First War on Terrorism: Counterterrorism Policy During the Reagan Administration* (New York: Rowman & Littlefield, 2003).

Chapter Five

The Terrorist and the Freedom Fighter

On December 14, 1984, Deputy Director for Intelligence Robert Gates wrote a memo to CIA Director William Casey concerning the situation in Nicaragua. The Deputy Director was at the beginning of an impressive career that ultimately took him to prominence in both the George W. Bush and Barak Obama cabinets. Long before he became one of the architects of the United States' war on terrorism in the aftermath of 2001, he advocated the offensive overthrow of the Nicaraguan government. Gates believed that the United States' policy of using the Contras to contain Nicaragua from supporting the insurgency in El Salvador was doomed to fail. Like so many members of Congress that had discussed the issue, Gates evoked the legacy of Vietnam as a lesson that the Reagan administration needed to follow. He wrote, "Those who forget the past are condemned to repeat it." For Gates the Vietnam War was a mistake, but not because the United States' grand designs of Cold War national security policy were misplaced. Instead, it showed the shortcomings of a policy of containment. Gates feared that the United States was in danger of receiving a significant blow by the forces of the communist-terrorist left. He insisted that the United States had to stop this development in Nicaragua by taking offensive measures that went beyond containment, and could bring about the overthrow of the Nicaraguan government. The first step, according to Gates, was the imposition of strict economic sanctions that would devastate the strength of the Nicaraguan government and society and make it vulnerable to an escalation of war by the Contras and even the possible exacting of direct US attacks on the small Central American state.[1]

Gates' memo to William Casey was one example that suggested that at the beginning of Reagan's second term the administration moved closer to deploying an offensive policy of regime change against Nicaragua. The administration, increasingly, targeted the Sandinistas in statements and threats.

Previously, operational directives and statements expressed an objective of containing Nicaragua by intercepting weapons shipments and using guerrilla violence to prevent the Sandinistas from undermining neighboring governments. The administration's statements at the beginning of 1985 suggested that this objective changed. At the beginning of Reagan's second term, it was clear that the goal of the administration was to force the alteration of the government of Nicaragua. In 1985, the Sandinistas faced an ultimatum on its government, either capitulate or face an escalation of hostilities. Several scholars have documented this moment, the outset of Reagan's second term, as the beginning of the Reagan offensive.[2]

The Reagan offensive was the strategic component of the Reagan doctrine: a US policy in the developing world that involved supporting insurgencies capable of either overthrowing unfriendly governments or forcing them to democratize on a basis acceptable to the United States. In the grand scheme of the Cold War, this represented a departure from containment and a pursuit of offensive tactics designed to undermine vulnerable leftist regimes. The policy was directed specifically at Nicaragua. It began with an ultimatum that the Sandinistas must include the Contras in a new democratic government or face regime change. Some scholars date the beginning of this policy to Reagan's second inaugural address while others like former Reagan administration official, Robert Kagan, suggest that this was developed over a number of years prior to the beginning of the second term. Regardless of which is correct, the second term marked the point in which the Reagan administration consciously adopted a policy of regime change in Nicaragua.[3]

While there is little question as to the fact of this shift from containment to offensive in the developing world, scholars have failed to explain the degree to which terrorism factored into the Reagan offensive. The emergence of a terrorism crisis in the 1980s provided a vehicle for the construction and justification of this offensive strategy. The escalation of terrorist violence encouraged policy makers to redefine the Cold War and the threat allegedly posed by countries like Nicaragua. Top officials like George Shultz described a deterioration of national security that resulted from an expanded Cold War offensive by radical leftists. The alleged offensive was in the developing world and terrorism, the administration argued, was the primary weapon of this expanded global enemy. The Reagan offensive was not simply the pursuit of the "rollback" of communism, it was also marked the creation of a new offensive war on terrorism.

Terrorism caused a change in US-Nicaraguan relations. It allowed the administration to redefine what the conflict was about by using terrorism as a propaganda tool capable of delegitimizing the Sandinista leadership while simultaneously legitimizing the Contras. Over time, the dialogue that the Sandinistas were a criminal and illegitimate government challenged the criticism that the administration pursued a flawed containment strategy, had oversimplified the causes of the Nicaraguan Revolution, and exaggerated the threat posed by the Sandinistas. Terrorism proved a powerful rhetoric that, when combined with international events, was capable of creating a heightened sense of fear and urgency within Congress and the public that could justify a more offensive approach. Because of the regulatory role played by Congress in the US-Contra War the Reagan administration relied on propaganda to sell the conflict to the people of the United States. In 1985, the administration redoubled an intensive effort to manipulate the perception of the conflict with a thorough and invasive propaganda effort. It sought to shape the dialogue over Nicaragua by incorporating the allegation of state sponsorship of terrorism into a renewed call for congressional funding for the Contras.

Responding to the administration's renewed call for congressional support for the Contras at the beginning of Reagan's second term, the Office of Public Diplomacy intensified a propaganda campaign designed to change the argument over Nicaragua. The key to this involved promoting a dialogue that unfairly demonized the Sandinistas and glorified its enemy, the Contras. A new and integral part of this campaign involved the allegation that Nicaragua under the Sandinistas was a state sponsor of terrorism. This public education program coordinated public speeches, op-ed pieces in newspapers and magazines, personal phone calls by Reagan to members of Congress, as well as attempts to contact news media outlets and manipulate the coverage of the Nicaraguan conflict, all of which the administration designed to reconstruct the image of both the Sandinistas and the Contras. In 1985, the propaganda campaign sought to use terrorism to redefine the Sandinistas as a criminal state and the Contras as freedom fighters. The allegation of terrorism helped demonize the Sandinistas while it simultaneously uplifted the Contras and, the administration hoped, would facilitate congressional support. During the spring of 1985, the administration bombarded Congress and the public with a refined justification for its hardline approach toward the Sandinistas.

Knowing the importance of public and Congressional support amid the original legislative battles surrounding the Boland restrictions, the administration created National Security Decision Directive number 77 (NSDD-77), entitled "Management of Public Diplomacy Relative to National Security." The document, signed on January 14, 1983, outlined the creation of a "special planning group . . . responsible for the overall planning, direction, and coordination and monitoring of implementation of public diplomacy activities."[4] This body produced an intensive propaganda program to win support for the Reagan administration's policy. The group developed speeches, prepared statements, and lobbied the news media in an attempt to address public and congressional opposition. Activities included not just speeches that emphasized the wide regional threat that communism represented in Central America, but also pressuring US media corporations like CBS and the *New*

York Times to report the conflict in a light more favorable to the administration.[5] This program was thorough and integral to the pursuit of congressional support for lethal aid to the Contras.

Here, I will refer to propaganda and public diplomacy interchangeably. In this case, the two terms both refer to efforts that involve shaping the perception of international affairs, but public diplomacy refers to a more thorough effort that extends beyond spoken or published information. However, in this case both terms I use to describe the Reagan administration's attempt to manipulate public perceptions about the nature of US policy with Nicaragua. Historian Justin Hart traced the origins of public diplomacy in US history back to the late 1930s. The purpose of public diplomacy, he suggests, "encompasses an incredibly broad set of initiatives designed to shape the image of the United States in the world."[6] The difficulty of the Reagan administration in the conflict in Central America caused the Executive Branch to reinvigorate this practice in the hope that it could better shape the dialogue and likewise its prosecution of the conflict.

The Reagan administration's public diplomacy campaign was a lasting consequence of the influence of the Vietnam War on the United States during the 1980s. That divisive and widely opposed conflict in Southeast Asia resulted in a heightened concern from the public and lawmakers alike with the role of the United States in the world. Concerned about the unjust application of American power, Congress and the American public were not enthusiastic about the use of force abroad and were particularly critical of such applications of power in the developing world for the expressed purposes of fighting the grand threat of communism. As a result of the Vietnam War, Americans criticized the application of power abroad, and Congress felt it a fundamental responsibility to act as an oversight body for the Reagan administration's Central American policy. For this reason, the Reagan administration sought to communicate its side of the story to the American people. Because the administration selected a course in clear violation of traditional norms of sovereignty, international law, and recognition of human rights it told the story through misinformation and propaganda.

Public diplomacy was an integral part of the Reagan administration's Central American policy. The primary goal was to create public support by providing the kind of information that could help the Reagan administration's position while avoiding information that might undermine its initiatives in the region. Public diplomacy was a way of telling the story the White House's way and encouraging increased support for the policy primarily by demonizing its enemy, the Sandinistas.

In early 1985, Washington officials recognized that attempts to convince the American people of the need for a military oriented war on terrorism were falling short. According to a Roper poll in February, "67 percent opposed using military force in efforts to preempt terrorist actions if innocent lives were threatened, and 51 percent opposed using military force even to retaliate after a terrorist attack, if innocent lives were at risk." Both the public and the media supported efforts to improve intelligence, and embassy and personnel security, but "significant doubts remain[ed] about preemption and retaliation, principally on the grounds of effectiveness, danger to innocent lives, and the risk of undercutting Western moral values and legal concepts." The Counterterrorism Public Diplomacy Working Group recognized that broad public support for the development of the administration's war on terrorism and escalation against Nicaragua was unlikely. For this reason, it focused its initiatives on convincing moderate members of Congress to support actions like the renewal of aid for the Contras and to embolden supporters by communicating through sympathetic agencies and publications like *American Legion* and *Commentary*.[7]

On March 12, 1985, the Office of Public Diplomacy produced a confidential directive titled "Support for the White House Educational Campaign." The directive outlined the Reagan administration's propaganda effort designed to gain support for the Nicaraguan Contras and bring about the collapse of the Nicaraguan government. The action plan proposed a campaign that catered to Congress, interest groups, and the media and it hinged on the construction of a false dichotomy, the terrorist and the freedom fighter. The goal of the effort was to depict the Sandinistas as criminals whose connections were not only to the Soviet/communist bloc but also to agents of international terrorism that were involved in poisoning the youth of the United States with its involvement in the illegal drug trade, racism, and totalitarianism. By contrast, the directive sought to humanize the Contras. The administration ignored evidence of Contra involvement in human rights abuses and drug trafficking. Instead, it presented the guerillas as freedom fighters and underdogs, similar to the revolutionary founders of the United States, and that offered a legitimate democratic alternative in Nicaragua. A few weeks later, and in continuing administration attempts to humanize the Contras, Reagan insisted that, "They are the moral equal of our founding fathers and the brave men and women of the [World War II] French Resistance."[8] The administration hoped this language could sway Congress to support a call for aid to the Contras and for the authorization of a policy of regime change in Nicaragua.[9]

One of the principal goals of the propaganda surrounding terrorism involves an intentional effort to panic the public and a create fear capable of justifying the administration's desired initiatives. President Reagan and Secretary Shultz both took a lead role in the educational campaign. In February, Reagan announced that his administration supported the forced alteration of the Sandinista regime. He insisted that the only way that Daniel Ortega and the Sandinistas could prevent the pursuit of this US-directed offensive policy was to allow the Contras into the government and to democratize in a manner that was acceptable to the United States.[10] Similarly, George Shultz threatened that if the Congress refused this most recent attempt at aid for the Contras that it could be necessary to use US troops in the region. Shultz warned that, "If we do not take the appropriate steps now to pressure the Sandinistas to live up to their past promises, then we may find later, when we can no longer avoid acting, that the stakes will be higher and the cost greater." Like Reagan, Shultz openly acknowledged that the administration sought a regime change in Nicaragua, and one that he insisted inherently required some kind of military force. Shultz hoped Congress would allow the Contras to apply the necessary force, but threatened that force was necessary. He insisted, "Whether it [a democratization of the government] is achieved through . . . unilateral actions by the Sandinistas alone or in concert with their domestic opponents, or through the collapse of the Sandinista regime, is immaterial to us." Shultz was certain that "they will not modify" unless the United States and its allies apply military force.[11] The United States leadership encouraged fear over Nicaragua and its solution was simple: either the people support its war or American boys will have to fight in a much bigger and more dangerous conflict.

In 1985, the Reagan administration appointed Robert Oakley as the new Director of the Office of Counterterrorism. Robert Oakley was a foreign service veteran. His service included ambassador to Somalia, and Zaire. He served in the United States embassy in Saigon during the Vietnam War, and the United States mission to the UN. He was an experienced diplomat of nearly thirty years. Oakley replaced Robert Sayre and took a lead role in vocalizing the administration's policy with the Sandinistas. In March, he spoke to Congress on the issue of combating terrorism. Speaking before the Subcommittee on Arms Control, International Security and Science and the Subcommittee on International Operations of the Committee on Foreign Relations on March 5, and then to the Committee on Foreign Relations and the Judiciary Committee on March 15, Oakley gave his own view of the developing US counterterrorism strategy. In both speeches, he backed Shultz and Reagan for providing the leadership necessary to create the public awareness that a war on terrorism required. Like Shultz, the new director built a case against Nicaragua. He asserted that Nicaragua posed a security threat because of continued support and assistance to international terror groups, the El Salvadoran insurgents, and its involvement in the new danger of narco-terrorism that emerged particularly in Latin America.[12]

Despite Oakley's tough talk on Nicaragua, however, he also moved to clarify the volatile statements made by Shultz several months earlier. The year ahead demonstrated that Oakley was not in full agreement with the administration's attempt to use propaganda to panic the American people. In fact, counter to the administration's efforts, Oakley sought to avoid arousing the fears of the people. Knowing the controversy that swirled around the issue of offensive military measures, Oakley was, like his predecessor Robert Sayre, more cautious about military options. The Director tried to lighten Shultz's comments. He insisted that Shultz was simply warning state sponsors that the United States did not rule out the use of preemptive military force. However, Oakley insisted, "While use of force presents one variation of such additional activities, we should recognize that there are other active measures." The Director placed the military option as lowest on the list of options mentioned on March 15. Unlike Shultz, who was emphatic about the necessity of force, Oakley expressed caution. He argued, "We must recognize that in many cases the disadvantages of military action from the global perspective might outweigh the advantages . . . rather in most circumstances other sorts of actions might be more appropriate than a military response." In a further elaboration on Shultz's earlier statements, Oakley addressed the Secretary's comment about the efficacy of Israel's military oriented strategy by insisting that "even key Israeli anti-terrorist experts have acknowledged . . . that the use of force cannot, by itself, solve the terrorist problem." While Oakley spoke in deference and respect of George Shultz, his comments represented the continued development of a subtle divide between officials in the Office of Counterterrorism and those in the State Department leadership and the NSC over the development of a military offensive against alleged state sponsors of terrorism like Nicaragua.[13]

Oakley's statements came amid a flurry of controversy at the outset of 1985. Following the mining of Nicaragua's harbors, the leaks of NSDD-138 and Shultz's suggestive statements that a use of force was in the minds of top officials in Washington, the American public and Congress were concerned about what the administration might do next. In 1985, a swirl of controversial comments emerged relating to the issue of international terrorism throughout the world and the intentions of the Reagan administration. The administration's efforts to use terrorism to change the dialogue over Nicaragua and the growing relevance of the terrorism problem increased the public discussion of the topic.

The Reagan administration's public diplomacy efforts on the issue of terrorism turned a significant amount of attention to Nicaragua and the administration's allegation that the Sandinista government was a significant part of the new problem of state sponsorship of international terrorism. On March 3, the *Miami Herald* reported that the Sandinistas represented a haven for terrorists groups from throughout the world, from the PLO to the Red Brigades. On March 24, the *Washington Post* reported that the Reagan administration had Green Berets involved in training Honduran counterterrorism forces. Such reports raised concerns about the United States' intentions. Administration officials defended the Honduran operations as designed to assist the Honduran government in internal events like hijackings and hostage taking, but critics in Congress were concerned that the program was part of the administration's attempts to support the Contras in its guerrilla war against the Nicaraguan government. In early 1985, and despite any preponderance of evidence, the Reagan administration's public diplomacy efforts as well as press and media coverage moved Nicaragua to the center of the conversation over state sponsorship of international terrorism. [14]

In terms of the Sandinistas and the Contras, the Reagan administration's public diplomacy efforts had two goals: first, to criminalize the Sandinistas, and, second, to uplift the image and legitimacy of the Contras. The administration sought to change prevailing perceptions about the United States' proxy ally. The Contras did not represent a united front. The individual leaders vied for power amongst themselves and for the support of the United States. The members of these groups were to a significant degree ex-members of Somoza's armed forces, and were involved in brutal acts of assassination, sabotage, and drug trafficking. In 1985 the public diplomacy effort did two things in respect to these guerrillas: first, the administration created a new political organization, and, second, it peppered the public with one of the most visible propaganda symbols in United States international relations history, the freedom fighter. [15]

In 1985, the Reagan administration created the United Nicaraguan Organization (UNO). Arturo Cruz, Alfonso Robelo, and Adolfo Calero made up the leadership of this body. The administration hoped that UNO might demonstrate that the Contras were a unified political organization and an alternative to the Sandinistas. In reality, UNO was not a unified organization. The leadership often disagreed with one another, and this led to its collapse only two years later. Calero, the leader of the most powerful group of guerrillas, the FDN, was often accused by Robelo and Cruz of bullying and using them as mere figureheads. The three leaders were Nicaraguan businessmen and political leaders before the Nicaraguan Revolution. Both Robelo and Cruz defected from original positions in the FSLN political apparatus, and played a significant role in the anti-government resistance. Calero, however, possessed the most political capital. In 1984, he was selected as the candidate to represent the guerrillas in an election in Nicaragua that Ortega announced as a possible way of undermining the United States war policy. Calero intended to run, but pulled out before the election amid pressure from the United States, which sought a solution through military pressure. [16] Calero played a critical role for the Contras not only as a political figure, but as the individual primarily responsible for the acquisition and use of covert funds from the United States. [17]

The process of legitimizing the Contras involved making the guerrillas appear as democrats bound to ideals of human rights, fair government, and international law. This was a monumental task for the Reagan administration, and involved an outright denial of the significance and scale of atrocities committed by the guerrillas. That spring two reports, one from *Americas*

Watch and the other by acclaimed human rights lawyer and one time New York State Assistant Attorney General, Reed Brody, documented a consistent use of violence against civilians by the Contras. The two reports relied on firsthand accounts of violence against civilians conducted by the Contras.[18] One of the most vivid depictions was of a Contra-led robbery of a truck carrying coffee harvesters. Witnesses accused the US-backed guerrillas of executing non-combatants. Some of the victims had their throats cut, others were shot, and even more shocking was testimony that the Contras burned the remaining survivors alive after locking them in the back of a farm truck.[19] Amid the administration's call for aid to the Contras, these reports provided a damning allegation of inhumanity on the part of the US ally.

Regardless of the scathing reports of crimes against humanity in early 1985, the administration increased its efforts to humanize the Contras. Shortly after the creation of UNO, the Office of Public Diplomacy arranged for guerrilla leaders to meet with major news media outlets like *USA Today* and assert its democratic position. In conjunction with these meetings, George Shultz in a press conference acknowledged that the Contras record on human rights was not pristine, but insisted that these were limited in scope and did not reflect a systemic problem or frequent aspect of the administration's ally or efforts. Instead, Shultz dismissed the reports as anomalies designed by those seeking to discredit the Reagan administration's pursuit of funding for the Contras. The administration continued to insist that the Contras were democrats, turned away by the totalitarian shift of the Nicaraguan Revolution, and were the equivalent of even the United States' founding fathers.[20]

There was little basis of reality in characterizing the guerrillas as freedom fighters. The Contras were militants involved in a dirty proxy war. These surrogate forces conducted assassinations, sabotage operations against civilian targets, and were connected to drug smuggling to the United States. Despite the visibility of these actions, the Reagan administration deployed propaganda, the freedom fighter, to create a false image of the Nicaraguan conflict. The administration used this characterization to define similar guerrilla movements throughout the world, none of which reflected the virtuous praise that the term referenced.

Freedom fighter was a charged term used to counter allegations that the United States supported terrorists, and that it used terrorism as tactic against leftists. This construct was the result of the development of a US war on terror. Vice President George H. W. Bush summarized this distinction in an essay that he wrote in 1986 titled "The Terrorism Dilemma."[21] According to Bush, "The phrase, one man's freedom fighter is another man's terrorist . . . misses a very significant point, and that is the concept of innocence. With terrorism there is no sense of innocent victim. . . . With terrorists there are no laws of war, non-combatants or neutrals . . . freedom fighters . . . have a sense of rules, order or codes."[22] Bush insisted that terrorists were those that attacked the United States' cherished ideological values of democracy and justice. The difference between the two for the majority in the administration was not in specific actions, but rather in the political and ideological motives involved. Formed in the background of the Cold War, terrorists, like communists, the Reagan administration considered a threat and enemy because the objective was to undermine America's values of capitalist democracy. The ends of radical leftists were the anti-thesis of the goals of the United States. In contrast, the freedom fighter's ends were a friendly relationship with America, and this justified the means taken. The administration cloaked a calculated Cold War realism in the eloquent rhetoric of the freedom fighter, and used the language of terrorism as a weapon against its enemies. The nature of actual acts committed by either was far less relevant because the administration defined terrorism exclusively as an act perpetrated by leftists.

The other part of the administration's efforts to shape the dialogue over Nicaragua and convince Congress to support its hardline strategy involved vilifying the Sandinistas as not just agents of communism, but as criminals associated with international terrorism. Despite prior statements and suggestions the year 1985 marked the first time that a central premise of the public diplomacy campaign involved the insistence that the "FSLN [were] linked to worldwide terrorism."[23] News reports and public statements that vilified Nicaragua as a state sponsor of international terrorism came amid the Reagan administration's new drive for regime change and military support for the Contras. The new push for congressional authorization for lethal aid to the Nicaraguan Contras and the confirmation of a policy of regime change the administration formally announced on April 4, 1985, as part of an appeal to Congress by Reagan to support the Contras. The administration referred to the President's plan as his "peace proposal."[24]

Historian Cynthia Arnson, author of the book *Crossroads*, and contemporary critics regarded Reagan's April 4 peace proposal as a political trick. It asserted that if the Sandinistas accepted a signed directive, the San Jose Communique, from Contra leaders to seek democratic plurality in Nicaragua that the United States would cease to back the Contras and both parties would then enter the national political process in a democratically unified Nicaragua. The Reagan administration felt that the admission of the Contras into the political process would undermine the Sandinista leadership and result in the desired alteration of the government. The San Jose Communique, signed in March, the government of Nicaragua had already rejected as an effort by the United States to alter its government by forcing the repatriation of elements of Somoza's armed forces. Reagan's offer was, in fact, a threat to Nicaragua and a ploy to Congress. Nicaragua was to accept the Contra paramilitary organization, many of which were former members of Somoza's reviled National Guard, into the nation's democratic process. If the Sandinistas refused, the Reagan administration promised an escalation of the already on-going conflict. The proposal stated that Congress should author-ize to release $14 million for humanitarian aid to the Contras. If there were no agreement in sixty days, President Reagan would have a free hand to continue to legally distribute lethal supplies to the Contras until September 1985. The proposal was a threat to Nicaragua and a ploy that divided Con-gress, and further verified that the administration no longer sought a policy of containment, but rather an alteration of the Nicaraguan government.[25]

At no point since 1981 had the Reagan administration engaged in legiti-mate and fair negotiations with the Nicaraguan leadership. The Reagan ad-ministration did, at times, offer peace overtures to the Sandinistas. Such moves came first in 1982 and then again in 1985. However, it based these overtures on the demand that Nicaragua change its government to fit the designs of the United States. The Reagan administration insisted that Nicara-gua disarm, while facing an escalating war, and incorporate the Contra guer-rillas into a government acceptable to the United States. When the United States made peace overtures it came at a time when it pressured Nicaragua with violence from guerrillas, economic warfare, and threats of escalation. Over the course of Reagan's presidency, the administration's core position centered on the ultimatum that it would not stop the war until the Nicaraguan government met its demands in total. These were not legitimate offers for peace, but rather threatening ultimatums. It was diplomacy at the point of a gun. The United States under Reagan applied a policy with Nicaragua that relied most on the application of military and economic pressure. Following terrorist attacks in June 1985, it accused Nicaragua of behaving as a state sponsor of terrorism. The allegation came with an ultimatum: either Nicara-gua reorganize its government or face regime change.[26]

Rather than step to the table with the Sandinista leadership the Reagan administration's efforts at peace involved ultimatums on the Nicaraguan government. Either the Sandinistas complied or face an escalation of war. The administration regarded the Nicaraguan government as fundamentally opposed to the United States. Such complete concessions were the only way that Daniel Oretga's government could avoid an impending US-directed mil-itary offensive. The Nicaraguan government, however, could not maintain legitimacy by yielding to the ultimatums of the United States. This sort of direct influence and meddling in the Nicaraguan state was the very thing that the Sandinistas revolution was about, a response to US imperialism, and therefore such ultimatums were never acceptable to Daniel Ortega and the Nicaraguan leadership. Reagan's so-called "peace proposal" was, ironically, symptomatic of an escalation of a hardline strategy against Nicaragua and an example of propaganda manipulating the reality of events. Because of its alleged part as a state sponsor of terrorism in a global leftist revolution the United States accepted no trustful or direct negotiations. It was a flawed approach and it consistently resulted in more violence and a deterioration of US-Nicaraguan relations and a radicalization of the conflict.

In April, Congress went ahead with consideration of the proposal for lethal aid to the Nicaraguan Contras. By a narrow margin, the Senate passed Joint Resolution 106, the Reagan administration's peace proposal, which proposed principally that, "The Congress approves the obligation and expenditure of funds available for fiscal year 1985 for supporting, directly or indirectly, military or paramilitary operations in Nicaragua."[27] A narrow majority of the Senate was consistently supportive of the administration's proposals on the matter. The House of Representatives remained the primary legislative impediment to the Contra aid package. In the House, opponents rallied against the proposal. The White House asked for monetary support from Congress and did so in a vague manner. Many in Congress perceived this as a move to obtain a 'blank check,' and the lessons of the Vietnam War resurfaced in congressional debates as those on Capitol Hill struggled to fashion policy and control the dialogue over Nicaragua.

Opponents of the request criticized it as a dangerous proposal that brought back memories of the open-ended resolution that allowed for the unchecked escalation of the Vietnam War. One congressional representative reiterated a familiar theme by calling the administration's request for funding "a 1985 version of the Gulf of Tonkin resolution."[28] Others argued, in support of President Reagan, that if the United States failed to act it would, in language reminiscent of Vietnam, "be interpreted by our friends in the region as a sign that the US will not be able to reverse Soviet-Cuban subversion and aggression in Central America."[29] Despite efforts to build support, in part, by shifting the dialogue over Nicaragua to the issue of international terrorism the relevance of the Vietnam War remained a powerful and dominating aspect of the debate.

Besides the old Cold War rhetoric, the administration released information that it intended to further advance its case against Nicaragua for its alleged complicity as a state sponsor of international terrorism. The White House and State Department argued that agents of international terrorism from Libya, Chile, Argentina, the Spanish group ETA, and the PLO operated inside Nicaragua and with the sanction of the government. The administration insisted that Nicaragua directed terrorist acts throughout Central America. These included a 1982 Honduran airline hijacking, a power station bombing in Honduras, and the attempted assassination of Eden Pastora in Costa Rica. With urgency, the administration argued that the Sandinistas were not just communist: the Nicaraguan leadership were communist-terrorists and agents of a new and more dangerous radical leftism.[30] The public diplomacy operation continued to struggle to shape the dialogue about the conflict with Nicaragua.

On April 24, 1985, the House of Representatives formally voted to deny any extension of US support to the Contras, apparently dooming the administration's policy. Secretary of State George Shultz summed up the entire period of debate in an address to the State Department on April 25, 1985. In his speech titled "The Meaning of Vietnam," Secretary Shultz illuminated the degree to which the memory of Vietnam continued to shape the fight over Contra aid. The secretary asserted that, "Our goals in Central America are like those we had in Vietnam: democracy, economic progress, and security against aggression."[31] Shultz drew further connections between Nicaragua and North Vietnam, claiming emphatically that, "Broken promises, communist dictatorship, refugees, widened Soviet influence . . . here is your parallel between Vietnam and Central America." He continued, "Do we want another Cuba in this hemisphere? How many times must we learn the same lesson?"[32] Shultz expressed that Vietnam caused a setback for the United States in its promotion of freedom in the world. He claimed that, "America lost faith in herself [and] this must never happen again."[33] The secretary lamented over the failure to win support for the policy and the administration's persistent inability to shape the dialogue over the Nicaraguan conflict. However, despite these difficulties the battle over the United States' proxy war was not over.

Over the course of 1985 and 1986, the administration's public diplomacy campaign targeted Congress in an attempt to gain support for an offensive against Nicaragua. The Office of Public Diplomacy utilized alliances with supporters in Congress like Newt Gingrich. Gingrich was at the beginning of a long career in the United States House of Representatives, and the future Speaker of the House was already an important organizer of conservatives in the House of Representatives. Gingrich was eager, and the Reagan administration hoped to use the Georgian as a vehicle toward the achievement of support for lethal aid to the Nicaraguan Contras. According to a May 30, 1985, memorandum, the educational materials about Nicaragua the Office of Public Diplomacy planned to "feed . . . to people like Newt Gingrich to read on C-Span during the open orders and enter into the Congressional Record."[34] Gingrich, and others, acted as a liaison for the administration's anti-Sandinista educational campaign.

The Reagan administration sought to change the minds of Congress on lethal support for its proxy guerrillas. To do this meant a continuous bombardment of propaganda materials. The State Department's Office of Public Diplomacy was the primary organization responsible for the anti-Sandinista propaganda campaign. One of the primary methods used to control the dialogue over Nicaragua was the production of briefing books designed to convince Congress and the American people of the administration's position. Such materials it fed to members of Congress and supporters like Newt

Gingrich read these on the floor of the House of Representatives and submitted the materials to the daily record.

Later that summer the State Department, frustrated by a continual inability to gain the support of important swing voters in the House of Representatives, peppered Congress with materials that insisted that Nicaragua was a terrorist state and was unworthy of protections of international law and national sovereignty. Following the June attacks, the State Department published two reports that redefined the threat allegedly posed by Nicaragua. The first was released in August. The title of the first release was "The Sandinistas and Middle Eastern Radicals." The second report was released at the beginning of September and was titled "Revolution Beyond Our Borders." The central argument of these briefs was that the Sandinistas were not simply communists. The Sandinistas were also terrorists. The reports insisted that the earlier understanding that the primary threat posed by Nicaragua as a communist affiliate of the Soviet bloc was only getting at part of the equation. The other aspect of the Sandinista threat was in the alliance with radical Middle Eastern groups like the PLO and terrorist 'outlaw states' Libya and Iran. These associations implied a criminal, even crazy, element in Nicaragua. The authors argued that this association was not short term chance or convenience, but a fundamental relationship. According to the State Department, "Their [Sandinistas] ties with the Palestine Liberation Organization reached back more than ten years before the revolution in Nicaragua. Libya has given the Sandinistas both pre-and post-revolution aid . . . [and] more recently, the Sandinistas have developed closer ties with Iran."[35]

The reports recalled the Patrick Argüello and Leila Khaled story and argued that the Sandinistas had assisted the PLO in the infamous "sky-jack Sunday" in September 1970. Further as allies of individuals like Yasser Arafat the reports argued that the Sandinistas possessed sympathetic views of anti-Semitism and anti-Westernism. The document cited remarks from Nicaraguan Defense Minister Tomas Borge and Yasser Arafat in 1980. Borge allegedly stated that "Nicaragua is his (Arafat) land and the PLO cause is the cause of the Sandinistas." Likewise, the document quoted Arafat as saying that "the triumph of the Nicaraguans was the PLO's triumph."[36] According to the State Department, the Sandinistas harbored and provided sanctuary to the PLO. Through this alliance, they joined in anti-Semitic goals. The propaganda document claimed that those in leadership positions in the Nicaraguan government hijacked airlines and abetted the worst criminal elements in the world. The documents portrayed Daniel Ortega, the president of Nicaragua, as not only a communist but as a terrorist and a criminal.[37] This type of propaganda represented an attempt on the part of the Reagan administration to shape the dialogue over Nicaragua by characterizing it in such a way as to make sympathy for the Sandinistas impossible.

The Reagan administration produced numerous briefing books during 1985 and 1986 that made the allegation of state sponsorship of international terrorism a central element of the administration's suggested policy approach. Publications like "The Sandinistas and Middle Eastern Radicals" insisted on a connection between the leadership in Nicaragua and a radical terrorist network led by Libyans and Palestinians. While the administration simultaneously insisted on the illegitimacy and alleged criminal involvement of the government in Nicaragua the propaganda campaign bombarded the American people with the idea that the Contras, themselves guilty of numerous war crimes, represented freedom fighters and the only opportunity to prevent an expansion of terror and anti-Americanism in the region.[38]

As Robert Gates suggested at the beginning of the year, the US-led offensive to alter the Nicaraguan government began first with measures to undermine the economy of the Sandinista state. In May 1985, the Reagan White House could not openly deploy further military pressure in its war on terrorism against Nicaragua, but it did take a major first unilateral step against that government. By a series of executive orders derived from the International Emergency Economic Power Act, Reagan ordered a thorough economic/ trade embargo on the Nicaraguan government. Using these emergency powers the United States government barred "All imports into the United States of goods and services of Nicaraguan origin . . . all exports from the United States of goods destined for Nicaragua except those destined for the organized democratic resistance. . . . Nicaraguan air carriers from engaging in air transportation to or from points in the United States, and vessels of Nicaraguan registry from entering in United States ports." The first demand made by Reagan was that the Sandinista government must "halt its export of armed insurrection, terrorism, and subversion in neighboring countries." The administration demanded that Nicaragua had to end the military build-up, remove all Cuban and Soviet military advisors, and pursue democratic pluralism and respect for human rights.[39]

The demands attached to the sanctions regime amounted to another set of ultimatums from the United States. The Sandinista government needed to disarm, at a time when the United States supported an insurgency, and let the Contras into its government. If Daniel Ortega's government refused, the United States threatened to escalate its use of aggressive hardline measures. What was most striking about the sanctions regime was the presence of terrorism as a key justification. The enacting of unilateral sanctions on Nicaragua was a first step in an offensive policy of regime change. The administration designed the sanctions to create domestic problems for the Sandinistas that would reduce the leadership's popularity and make Nicaragua vulnerable to an increase in military pressure.[40]

The creation of a sanctions regime against Nicaragua marked an unprecedented point in US-Nicaraguan relations. Despite the failure to obtain congressional funding two significant changes were underway: first, international terrorism offered a new way of packaging policy, and, second, the Reagan administration took another step in the construction of an offensive program for dealing with alleged state sponsors of terrorism. As Robert Gates suggested in his memo to CIA Director William Casey at the outset of 1985, economic sanctions was a first step in an offensive policy of regime change. The perceived global threat of international terrorism drove a shift in US-Nicaraguan relations that assured a continued deterioration in the months ahead.

While the Reagan administration suffered a legislative setback in the spring of 1985 on its initiative to gain congressional backing for hardline measures against Nicaragua, the administration had actually taken an important step forward in the implementation of the offensive. The important step was in the realm of public diplomacy. George Shultz spoke in 1984 of the necessity of active measures to combat state sponsors of terrorism, but in 1985, the administration's public diplomacy effort pressed this significant alteration to the dialogue over the Nicaraguan conflict. It used the rhetoric of terrorism to construct a false image of reality. This deception was most visible in its construction of the idea of the terrorist and the freedom fighter, of a conflict of good versus evil. The idea of the terrorist and the freedom fighter the administration sought to convey to the American people in a myriad of ways, and represented the manner in which the problem of international terrorism was intertwined with the old paradigm of Cold War bipolarity. For the United States, terrorism was a problem associated with leftists. The term seemed to lack meaning and, instead, was more a "political contrivance" designed to justify its intervention in Nicaragua. [41]

This public diplomacy offensive did not suddenly change people's minds over Nicaragua, and during the 1980s it never created a significant majority of support for the action. Nonetheless, in the year ahead the accusation of terrorism factored into the justification for an escalation of a hardline policy with Nicaragua and encouraged swing voters in Congress to move to support the administration's Contra aid package. In the longer term, though, this development was even more significant. The new dialogue over the national security threat of terrorism harkened to a future in which this fear inducing rhetoric transformed how many Americans thought about the use of American power in the world. The conflict with Nicaragua was an early case in which the United States sought to use the criminalizing power of the allegation of state sponsorship of terrorism to justify its inclination to offensive hardline measures.

International terrorism, as the Reagan administration defined it, was an exaggeration that blurred the line between criminal and revolutionary. Nonetheless, the Reagan administration believed that this posed a unique security threat precisely because it conceived of the problem as intertwined with the bipolar world of the Cold War, and of the contest between leftists and rightists. When thinking of the Contra war one might be inclined to believe that administration comments that stated the national security concern over Nicaragua was merely a rouse, designed to distract the public from more malevolent objectives. Despite misinformation and propaganda the lead policy makers were conditioned in the Cold War, and seemed to genuinely believe that a global network of leftists was the new danger in a new era of this half-century old contest. The threat was unpredictable and carried a psychological power capable of damaging the will of the United States and its allies. In June, the danger and instability of this new world appeared in the form of a series of vicious terrorist attacks in El Salvador and in Lebanon. The attacks further demonstrated that the world was in the midst of a terrorism crisis. These events drove the crystallization of the new framework of intervention that Shultz spoke of in 1984 and led to the formation of an offensive to combat the scourge of international terrorism. The 1980s terrorism crisis led the Reagan administration to redefine how the United States dealt with sovereign states that allegedly represented an international criminal threat. Its solution was to create a policy that further challenged the accepted norms of international behavior and paved the way for the use of preemptive and offensive measures in the future.

NOTES

1. Robert Gates, Memorandum for Director of Central Intelligence Agency William Casey, "Nicaragua," December 14, 1984, in Peter Kornbluh and Malcolm Byrne, *The Iran-Contra Scandal: The Declassified History* (New York: New Press, 1993), 45.

2. Walter LaFeber, *Inevitable Revolutions: The United States in Central America*, 2nd ed. (New York: W. W. Norton, 1993); Cynthia Arnson, *Crossroads: Congress, the President, and Central America, 1976–1993*, 2nd ed. (University Park: Penn State University Press, 1993); William LeoGrande, *Our Own Backyard: The United States in Central America, 1977–1992* (London: University of North Carolina Press, 1998); Greg Grandin, *Empires Workshop: Latin America, The United States, And the Rise of the New Imperialism* (New York: Henry Holt, 2006); Robert Kagan, *A Twilight Struggle: American Power and Nicaragua, 1977–1990* (New York: Free Press, 1996).

3. Raymond W. Copson and Richard P. Cronin, "Reagan Doctrine: Assisting Anti-Marxist Guerrillas," Folder 5, Box 11, David S. Addington, Series II: Chron Files, 1987–1988, Ronald Reagan Presidential Library.

4. National Security Council, "Management of Public Diplomacy Relative to National Security," in Simpson, *National Security Directives of the Reagan and Bush Administrations*, 265–267.

5. Shultz to Reagan, April 15, 1984, in Peter Kornbluh and Malcolm Byrne, *The Iran-Contra Scandal: The Declassified History* (New York: New Press, 1993), 35.

6. Justin Hart, *Empire of Ideas: The Origins of Public Diplomacy and the Transformation of US Foreign Policy* (New York: Oxford University Press 2013), 1.

7. "Public Affairs Strategy and Action Plan: Domestic Public Affairs Working Group, Interagency Counterterrorism Public Diplomacy Working Group," Folder "Combatting Terrorism Department of State Report, 1985 1 of 2," Box 1, Richard L. Canas, Files: George H. W. Bush Presidential Records, Subject Files, OA/ID CF01573, George Bush Presidential Library.

8. George Skelton, "President Reiterates Firm Backing for Contras," *Los Angeles Times*, March 2, 1985, http://ntserver1.wsulibs.wsu.edu:2184/docview/292041598?accountid=14902.

9. Daniel Jacobowitz, "Public Diplomacy Action Plan: Support for the White House Educational Campaign," March 12, 1985, in Peter Kornbluh and Malcolm Byrne, *The Iran-Contra Scandal: The Declassified History* (New York: New Press, 1993), 22–29.

10. Jack Nelson, "Reagan Warning Given Nicaragua, He Backs Removal of Leftist Regime Unless it Joins Rebels in a Democracy," *Los Angeles Times*, February 22, 1985, http://ntserver1.wsulibs.wsu.edu:2184/docview/292036155?accountid=14902.

11. Norman Kempster, "U.S. Troop Use in Nicaragua Hinted, Shultz Warns Aid Foes that if Rebels Fail, Americans May Have to Fight," *Los Angeles Times*, February 23, 1985, http://ntserver1.wsulibs.wsu.edu:2184/docview/292042705?accountid=14902.

12. Robert Oakley, "Statement Before the Subcommittee on Arms Control, International Security and Science and the Subcommittee on International Operations of the Committee on Foreign Relations, March 5, 1985," Folder "Terrorism Material, 1 of 4," Box 3/1, Donald P. Gregg: George H. W. Bush Vice Presidential Records, National Security Affairs, Task Force on Terrorism Files, OA/ID 19850 and 19851, George Bush Presidential Library; Robert Oakley, "Statement Before the Committee on Foreign Relations and the Judiciary Committee, March 15, 1985," Folder "Terrorism Material, 1 of 4," Box 3/1, Donald P. Gregg: George H. W. Bush Vice Presidential Records, National Security Affairs, Task Force on Terrorism Files, OA/ID 19850 and 19851, George Bush Presidential Library.

13. Oakley, "Statement Before the Committee on Foreign Relations and the Judiciary Committee, March 15, 1985," George Bush Presidential Library.

14. Press Clippings, Folder "Terrorism Material, 1 of 4," Box 3/1, Donald P. Gregg: George H. W. Bush Vice Presidential Records, National Security Affairs, Task Force on Terrorism Files, OA/ID 19850 and 19851, George Bush Presidential Library.

15. Robert Owen, Memorandum to Oliver North, "Overall Perspective," March 17, 1986, in Peter Kornbluh and Malcolm Byrne, *The Iran-Contra Scandal: The Declassified History* (New York: New Press, 1993), 53.

16. Copson and Cronin, "Reagan Doctrine: Assisting Anti-Marxist Guerrillas," 1987–1988, Ronald Reagan Presidential Library.

17. Owen, Memorandum to Oliver North, "Overall Perspective," in Kornbluh and Byrne, *The Iran-Contra Scandal*, 53.

18. *Human Rights in Nicaragua: Reagan, Rhetoric and Reality* (New York: Americas Watch, 1985).

19. Larry Rohter, "Nicaragua Rebels Accused of Abuses," *New York Times*, March 7, 1985, http://ntserver1.wsulibs.wsu.edu:2184/docview/425358009?accountid=14902.

20. Joel Brinkley, "Nicaraguan Rebels Seeking Inquiry Into Abuse Charges," *New York Times*, March 8, 1985, http://ntserver1.wsulibs.wsu.edu:2184/docview/425354124?accountid=14902.

21. George Bush, "The Terrorism Dilemma," Folder "Terrorism" (5 of 6) OA/ID 19849, Box 1, Donald P. Gregg: Task Force on Terrorism Files, George Bush Presidential Library.

22. Bush, "The Terrorism Dilemma," George Bush Presidential Library.

23. Jacobowitz, "Public Diplomacy Action Plan: Support for the White House Educational Campaign," in Kornbluh and Byrne, *The Iran-Contra Scandal*, 22–29.

24. Briefing Material, "President Reagan's April 4 Peace Initiative on Central America," April 4, 1985, *The Digital National Security Archive* (Ann Arbor: Proquest, 2012), NI02421, http://gateway.proquest.com/openurl?url_ver=Z39.88–2004&res_dat=xri:dnsa&rft_dat=xri:dnsa:article:CNI02421.

25. Briefing Material, "President Reagan's April 4 Peace Initiative on Central America," April 4, 1985, *The Digital National Security Archive*.

26. National Security Council, "National Security Security Decision Directive on Cuba and Central America," in Simpson, *National Security Decision Directives of the Reagan and Bush Administrations*, 53–54.

27. 99 Cong. Rec. S8916 (1985).

28. 99 Cong. Rec. S8916 (1985).

29. 99 Cong. Rec. S8911 (1985).

30. Briefing Material, "President Reagan's April 4 Peace Initiative on Central America," April 4, 1985, *The Digital National Security Archive*.

31. 99 Cong. Rec. 9751 (1985).

32. 99 Cong. Rec. 9751 (1985).

33. 99 Cong. Rec. 9751 (1985).

34. Daniel Jacobwitz, Memorandum for Otto Reich, "Duties of TDY (Psychological Operations) Military Personnel," May 30, 1985, in Kornbluh and Byrne, *The Iran-Contra Scandal*, 31.

35. State Department Report, *The Sandinistas and Middle Eastern Radicals*, Folder "The Sandinistas and Middle Eastern Radicals," Box 16, David S. Addington Files, Ronald Reagan Presidential Library.

36. State Department Report, *The Sandinistas and Middle Eastern Radicals*, Ronald Reagan Presidential Library.

37. State Department Report, *Revolution Beyond Our Borders: Sandinista Intervention in Central America*, Folder "Revolution Beyond Our Borders," Box 15, David S. Addington Files 1987–1988, Ronald Reagan Presidential Library.

38. State Department Report, *The Sandinistas and Middle Eastern Radicals*, Ronald Reagan Presidential Library.

39. "Economic Sanctions Against Nicaragua," May 1, 1985, *The Digital National Security Archive* (Ann Arbor: Proquest, 2012), NIO2463, http://gateway.proquest.com/openurl?url_ver=Z39.88–2004&res_dat=xri:dnsa&rft_dat=xri:dnsa:article:CNI02463.

40. Gates, Memorandum for Director of Central Intelligence Agency William Casey, "Nicaragua," in Kornbluh and Byrne, *The Iran-Contra Scandal*, 45.

41. Paul Thomas Chamberlin, *The Global Offensive: The United States, the Palestinian Liberation Organization, and the Making of the Post-Cold War Order* (New York: Oxford University Press, 2012), 9.

Chapter Six

Outlaw States

It was July 8, 1985, President Ronald Reagan, a charming orator, looked out at the audience at the American Bar Association. Only weeks prior Reagan adorned four flag draped coffins with purple hearts to honor those American Marines killed in El Salvador. The mood was serious, and Reagan understood the gravity of the moment. He prepared to utter the words of a speech that signified the emergence of the Reagan offense and of a new model for the use of hardline power in the world. The President opened his speech by labeling five states as part of "a confederation of terror states" and a "new version of murder inc." that had attacked the United States and its allies with "outright acts of war." Reagan listed Nicaragua, Cuba, Libya, Iran, and North Korea as the heart of world terrorism. These states, he insisted, were "outlaw states."[1] As a culmination of ideas expressed by Shultz in 1984, Reagan acknowledged that the Cold War had changed, and that Americans should fear the activity of criminal leftist regimes that sought to use terrorism against the United States' allies and interests.

Reagan's outlaw states speech came in the aftermath of a series of terror attacks in June 1985. In El Salvador, four US servicemen were shot at an outdoor café in San Salvador. In the Mediterranean, Palestinian hijackers took TWA flight 847 from Athens, Greece, to Beirut, Lebanon. The United States mourned the death of US citizens in both events. These attacks represented a peak moment in a terrorism crisis and presented a unique national security problem for the Reagan administration. The threat was unpredictable and often directed at civilian targets that were difficult to defend. Likewise, while sporadic terrorist violence was unlikely to have any significant effect on the military capabilities of the United States, it did pose a unique psychological threat to United States citizens and its allies. This period marked the crystallization of a shift in US foreign relations.

Throughout the previous year Secretary of State George Shultz insisted that the United States needed to develop a way to deter and defeat state sponsors of international terrorism. States like Nicaragua, Libya, and Cuba the administration insisted, were the glue that allowed terrorists to operate throughout the world, and Shultz argued that the United States needed to adopt aggressive offensive measures to preempt Radical-Left states allegedly dedicated to undermining the United States. In 1984, NSDD-138 had proposed that the Reagan administration should assert an offensive policy against state sponsors of terrorism. However, the controversy with that directive coupled with the illegal mining of Nicaragua's harbors made it impossible to implement the most controversial aspects of the directive. In June of 1985, however, events that symbolized a mounting terrorism crisis compelled the Reagan administration to press the opportunity to put its offensive war on terrorism into action.

On June 20, the day after the killings in El Salvador, Congress met to discuss the crisis and it offered Reagan's allies an opportunity to voice the administration's hardline opinions. The tone of discussion was markedly different from the previous debates held earlier that month about humanitarian aid to the Contras. Representatives Bob Dornan (R) and Newt Gingrich (R) were front and center in the renewed debate about fighting Sandinista-led Nicaragua. Dornan, a former movie star from California, issued a remark that became increasingly familiar over the next year. Dornan declared that communist-terrorists carried out 95 percent of the terrorist violence in the world. He argued that since at least 1983 Nicaragua had acted as a terrorist state. He recalled the May 1983 killing of a US advisor in El Salvador saying "communist-terrorists shot him in the face five times, as he was parking his automobile at Central American University in San Salvador." Dornan insisted that the June killings demonstrated two facts: "the operational headquarters of the Farabundo Marti Communist guerrillas [was] in Managua," and "communism spawns and sponsors 95 percent of the terrorism tearing our world apart."[2] In Congress, supporters followed the administration in insisting that terrorism and the crisis with Nicaragua was about a global communist-terrorist offensive, a conflict defined on the lines of global bipolarity.

Dornan was not alone in his conviction that the United States had to respond to these kinds of acts. Newt Gingrich, Joe Barton (R), Tobias Roth (R), and Robert Smith Walker (R) joined the Congressman to vocalize their feelings that the United States confronted a new and dangerous security threat. Reagan's allies in Congress argued that this was the unique danger caused by international terrorism, and was facilitated by the communist world. These congressional representatives implored lawmakers to be aggressive and take a hardline against this new threat. Solutions to the problem were elusive, but these members of Congress pressed for a reorganization of the intelligence community in order to learn of terror plots early and be able

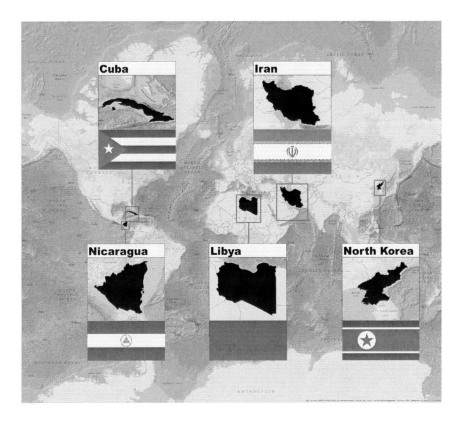

Figure 6.1. Outlaw states, 1985. *Source***: James Scanlon.**

to react to them more effectively.[3] Two days later, on June 22, President Reagan honored the Marines killed in El Salvador. His passionate speech at Andrews Air-Force base (mentioned in the introduction) demonstrated that the executive planned to address the threat of international terrorism that allegedly emanated from Nicaragua.

In late spring, the Reagan administration and Congress had achieved some minor steps toward increasing pressure on Nicaragua. In May, Reagan, by executive order, directed economic and trade sanctions on Nicaragua and in June secured from Congress $27 million in humanitarian aid for the Contras. From the perspective of lawmakers that opposed the Reagan administration's attempt to aid the Contras, the humanitarian aid that Congress allocated in June represented a step in the wrong direction, a step toward the use of American troops in a war in Central America. The language following the El Salvador killings made the Democrat opposition even more concerned. Of the worried Democrats in the House of Representatives, few were as visible as the Congressman from Washington State, Tom Foley. From Spokane, Washington, the future Speaker of the House and longtime Congressman provided leadership for those that resisted the Reagan administration's military designs on Nicaragua. On June 20, Foley proposed an amendment to the Department of Defense Authorization Act for 1986 that he hoped would guarantee that the United States could not use the $27 million in humanitarian aid as a step toward an escalation of hostile activities against Nicaragua.

The Foley Amendment was consistent with congressional action since the 1983 Boland Amendment: the main goal was to prevent the Reagan administration from conducting a US-led war in or over Nicaragua. This particular proposal declared that unless the United States was under attack (including embassies, territories, and possessions) or had declared war on Nicaragua, that "funds appropriated to the Department of Defense may not be obligated or expended for the purpose of introducing the United States Armed forces into or over Nicaragua for combat."[4] In years prior, Congress was supportive of this type of measure, but as the debate ensued following the El Salvador attack, it was clear that supporters of the administration feared that Foley's approach did not adequately consider the unique danger presented by international terrorism.

Figure 6.2.   Ronald Reagan being briefed by (from Reagan's left) George H. W. Bush, Robert McFarlane, John Poindexter, and Don Regan on the TWA Hijacking, June 18, 1985. *Source*: **Ronald Reagan Presidential Library.**

During the debate over the Foley amendment, Reagan's opponents argued that the humanitarian aid was not the real goal of the administration and its supporters. Congressman Sandy Levin (D), insisted that the executive wanted Congress to approve lethal aid for the Contras. He warned that the humanitarian aid had "opened the door to obtaining the direct military aid this administration desperately wants to fund the Contras."[5] Levin supported the Foley amendment, but following the events that June a majority of the House of Representatives were in no mood for the passage of restrictive measures. For some in the legislative branch things had changed. In her book *Crossroads*, Cynthia Arnson acknowledged that following the legislative battles of the spring and summer 1985 things did change in Congress. Arnson insists that this was due, in part, to the lack of viable policy alternatives provided by liberal Democrats in the House of Representatives. Adding to Arnson's contribution, I insist that this shift was due, in part, to the perception of a new threat, international terrorism, that altered the discussion over Nicaragua.

The events of June marked the beginning of a shift in Congress over aid to the Contras. The terrorist incidents were shocking and vivid. In El Salvador, six Americans died: two civilians and four off-duty Marines. In Beirut, one American died at the hands of gun wielding terrorists that presented demands with bags over their heads through American news media. While the administration had yet to secure congressional approval for lethal aid to the Contras, the attack in El Salvador and the TWA hijacking together catalyzed the development of a shift in Congress on the issue of terrorism. Supporters of the Reagan administration deployed a passionate call to action, and Congress began to take steps toward acceptance of greater support for the Contras and authorization of a more active program to combat international terrorism.

The opponents of the Foley Amendment included John McCain (R), Dick Cheney (R), Newt Gingrich, Bob Dornan, and others from the Republican and Democrat party. These critics were primarily concerned with limiting the power of the Commander in Chief to act when necessary. Duncan Lee Hunter (R) of California proposed a hypothetical scenario in which hijackers took an airline to Managua, Nicaragua. If no US citizens were involved, could the president take military action? Hunter insisted, "You could have hijackings of planes carrying allies of the United States. Essentially, they would find sanctuary in Managua."[6] Another insisted that the United States had to take a stand and not let the enemy know that the president would not act. Likewise, Henry Hyde (R) exclaimed that the United States was "under siege around the world by state-sponsored terrorists."[7] While Democrat opponents tried to invoke concern for a US military policy, many in Congress that day expressed a concern for the threat of international terrorism allegedly posed by states like Nicaragua. The terror attacks of that June gave the administration's argument new life.

The Foley Amendment, as originally proposed, did not have the strength to pass and opposition to it demonstrated a move away from the atmosphere present during the passage of the Boland Amendment a few years prior. Both Republicans and moderate Democrats opposed the fact that the amendment did not properly account for the threat of terrorism. Newt Gingrich exclaimed that Americans lived "in a world of terrorists."[8] There was a call for Congress to respond. What Congress ultimately did was to add an amendment a modification offered by Missouri Democrat Ike Skelton. The addition authorized the president to use military force "to respond to hijacking, kidnapping, or other acts of terrorism involving citizens of the United States or citizens of any ally of the United States."[9] John McCain (R) was among those that spoke in support of Skelton. The modified version passed with wide support. McCain and Skelton were among many in a Congress that felt that action was necessary to deal with the looming danger. From McCain's vantage, the Skelton amendment was necessary to prevent the passage of legislation that ignored the role of states like Nicaragua as a sponsor of international terrorism. While still somewhat resistant to the idea of funding the Contras with lethal material, many in the Congress did acknowledge the right of the United States to use military force for counterterrorism purposes against another sovereign nation not technically at war with the United States. After this debate, Congress went on a ten-day holiday to celebrate the nation's independence.[10]

After the Fourth of July holiday Reagan greeted Congress and the country with his outlaw states speech. In his speech to the ABA Reagan insisted that the United States planned to retool its policy to deal with terrorism. The president announced his order to form a task force to evaluate and develop US counterterrorism policy. Reagan appointed Vice President George H. W. Bush to head the task force. In addition, he suggested that the threat of international terrorism required the administration to develop a policy that was aggressive and left all options, including unilateral military interventions, on the table. Reagan's big announcement was front-page news on July 9, and it spurred a significant national debate. This was an important moment for the United States and the world.[11] The Reagan administration declared Nicaragua an illegitimate criminal state and pushed for formal authorization of aggressive actions that broke from the traditional expectations of state-to-state behavior. In the coming months, the task force determined what kind of action the United States planned for nations like Nicaragua, and began formulating a new framework of intervention against states alleged of sponsoring terrorism.

The events of June encouraged immediate reactions from the United States. Congress took some significant legislative steps to deal with the threat of alleged communist-terrorist states like Nicaragua. In passing the International Security and Development Act of 1985, Congress finalized approval for $27 million in humanitarian aid to the Contras. Lawmakers also took several important steps on international terrorism. Congress supported the use of sanctions against any nation that supported international terrorists. The body considered the expanded use of air-marshals, and increased resistance to drug trafficking in Central and South America. Congress condemned terrorism and called for greater coordination in dealing with the threat. A threat the Reagan administration defined in such a way as to make terrorism indistinguishable from revolutionary guerrilla war or drug trafficking.[12]

While Congress authorized humanitarian aid to the Contras, a majority in the House of Representatives still remained pointedly opposed to the use of military force, especially thru this transnational guerrilla group. The issue of the use of military force remained a central divergence between Congress and the Executive Branch. In July of 1985, in an act that passed with a strong majority, the House of Representatives showed that as a body it was, however, in near complete agreement with the Reagan administration on the reasons why the United States should act in the case of Nicaragua. According to the International Security and Development Act, the House accepted the Reagan administration's rationale for opposition to the Sandinistas. According to the language in the act, the Sandinista leadership was in violation of the principle of its own revolution, acted subversively toward neighboring states, created close ties with states of the radical leftists like the Soviet Union, Libya, and Cuba, and were solely responsible for escalating tensions in the region. Congress agreed with the administration on the allegations. While it still did not take the step of authorizing military force or military aid for the transnational non-state actor in the region, the Contras, it seemed to lean closer toward support of the Reagan administration's proxy war.[13]

The debate over combatting international terrorism renewed the fight on Capitol Hill over lethal funding for the Contras. Members of Congress worked alongside the administration to try and couch the war against Nicaragua in the guise of opposition to state sponsored terrorism. In this effort two of Reagan's allies in the Senate, Dick Lugar (R) and Claiborne Pell (D) sponsored the Central American Counterterrorism bill. This called for $26 million in police assistance, $1 million on the counterterrorism protection fund, and $27 million in new military assistance to the region. The counterterrorism protection fund was a proposed fund for protection of informants, and it served as incentive for those that might seek the reward money that the United States offered for the capture of terror suspects. The idea of military assistance again caused controversy on Capitol Hill. The bill proposed providing support to police forces that were allegedly involved in human rights abuses and, which, Congress had refused to fund for this reason. Positioning such requests in the context of counterterrorism, however, altered the nature of debate. Many opponents recognized this as an attempt to open an avenue for further support to the Contras beyond the already authorized humanitarian aid package. The debate on this piece of legislation continued into December, and it marked a renewed attempt since the past spring to gain new military assistance for the fight against Nicaragua.

Authorization for the Contras was highly controversial because the guerrillas acted in violation of the sovereignty of Nicaragua, Costa Rica, and Honduras, and to acknowledge open support of this was to accept a violation of the accepted norms of international behavior. There was much tough talk in Congress in late June/early July, but despite the intense deployment of the accusation of terrorism by supporters like Newt Gingrich, the consensuses in the Democrat controlled body remained that the United States should avoid the military approach, whether directly or through proxy, and continue the use of the sanctions regime which it hoped would bring the Sandinistas to the peace table and ready to negotiate a settlement with the Contras. This issue of the use of military force through the Contras remained the major disagreement between the Executive Branch and Congress.

Despite the hang up over lethal aid for the Contras, the Reagan administration directed a military escalation in reaction to the June attacks in El Salvador. As the Iran-Contra Hearings later revealed John Poindexter and Oliver North, NSC members, were already involved in funding a military escalation against Nicaragua by providing secret unauthorized funding to the Contras. The NSC created military funding for the guerrillas through private donations and provided the guerrillas with operational advice and direct assistance through the CIA and ex-military volunteers.[14] The administration, however, also took to the offensive in a more overt way. The Reagan NSC directed the El Salvadoran government, with American helicopters and weapons and with the oversight of American advisors, to attack the Revolutionary Party of Central American Workers (PRTC) an affiliate of the FMLN.[15] This group was allegedly aided by the Sandinistas and responsible for the June attack. This was designed as a major offensive against Sandinista clients operating in El Salvador.

The PRTC, according to a special State Department report in August, was a guerrilla-terrorist army that relied on urban terrorism, assassinations, kidnappings, shootings, and bombings. According to the Department of State, the Nicaraguan government was a state sponsor of this terror group. The Sandinistas, allegedly, provided training and supplied lethal materials. Nonetheless, the report suggested that, "Despite the retaliation of El Salvadoran armed forces, the success of the 19 June massacre may be accelerating a move by all elements of the guerrilla alliance toward a terrorist oriented strategy."[16] This implied a need for the United States to act. Obtaining congressional support for lethal aid to the Contras remained the primary long-term goal for the Reagan administration following the June attacks, but the

Reagan administration went ahead and sent its trained and armed allies on the offensive in Central and Eastern El Salvador. By July 11, the "assault teams" had killed twenty-five and captured ten in the pursuit of the suspected terrorists.[17]

With the precise course of US policy unknown and the strong rhetoric on Capitol Hill, there is little doubt that many Americans were already a bit wary as they read the news on July 24, 1985. The *San Francisco Chronicle* was one of many news publications throughout the country to report that the Reagan administration had threatened Nicaragua. The article revealed that the United States had planned air attacks on Nicaragua in response to killings in El Salvador. The administration insisted that the Sandinista leadership had established terrorist training camps near the capital Managua, and it was here that State Department officials argued that the attack in June originated.

The Reagan administration considered using direct military force against Nicaragua in support of the El Salvadoran offensive operations. The NSC, instead, decided to use threats while secretly escalating support for the Contra army. In the summer of 1985, these actions created a heightened tension between the United States and Nicaragua. Earlier that July the Nicaraguan government recovered an American radar buoy near Bluefields and reported an escalation of Contra activity as well as military operations in neighboring El Salvador. The Reagan administration was sending a stern message to the Sandinista leadership. The United States ambassador to Nicaragua, Harry Bergold, warned Nicaragua that if the United States linked the Sandinista leadership to future terrorist acts the Reagan administration would order air attacks on the country.[18] Rather than seek legitimate discussions with Nicaragua, the United States, again, turned to threats and military pressure.

In the weeks following Reagan's "outlaw states" speech, there was apprehension in the United States. Reports centered to a significant degree on the question of whether or not the newly formed Task Force to Combat Terrorism would create a policy based on the offensive application of military force. Some journalists insisted that Reagan preferred the use of military force.[19] Other reports speculated that Bush, the head of the new task force, was likely to take a more cautious approach to the terrorism crisis.[20] Adding to the unknown, Abraham Sofaer, the State Department's legal adviser, went on record and argued for the legal right of the United States to take preemptive military action against states like Nicaragua and praised the potential deterrent effect of such methods.[21] Further, George Shultz, the most adamant high level Reagan administration official in favor of a military oriented counterterrorism strategy, pressed for clarification on the presidential ban on assassinations in the case of terrorism. Shultz defined International terrorists as criminals, rather than political/military actors, that were engaged in an illegal war against the United States. The ban on assassination, originally

signed by Gerald Ford and renewed by Reagan in 1981, the Secretary implied, needed clarification in order to open up military options for the United
States when dealing with terrorists and state sponsors.[22] Not long after this a
classified dispute between the Office of Counterterrorism and the NSC
erupted over a proposal for kidnapping operations within other sovereign
nations, even close allies like France. The head of the Office of Counterterrorism Robert Oakley grew increasingly concerned as such actions threatened the very principal of national sovereignty as well as positive relationships with allies.[23] While the task force was in its formation stages, these
were likely the issues that engaged citizens contemplated as they wondered if
the United States might attack Nicaragua or another one of those alleged
outlaw states.

The United States had addressed the threat of terrorism before, but the
response following the El Salvador killings, and the hijacking of TWA 847
represented the most advanced move taken by the United States to date.
Rather than patching up an existing problem by creating a law here and a law
there, the Reagan administration ordered a thorough reevaluation of the nation's foreign policy conducted by the Task Force to Combat Terrorism. The
task force was a cabinet wide review group that prepared to review the crisis
and consider the most effective ways of combatting this threat. This process
established the model for US interaction with state sponsors of terrorism. It
began on July 20, 1985, with President Reagan's signing of National Security Decision Directive 179 (NSDD 179). This short NSC document operated
as the modus operandi of the task force.[24]

As yet, scholars have neglected the role of George H. W. Bush's Task
Force to Combat Terrorism in the development of the Reagan offensive. A
significant reason for the absence of scholarship pertaining to the task force
is due primarily to the declassification of many documents relating to this
body. A majority of the documents relating to the Task Force to Combat
Terrorism received declassification only in the twenty-first century. The terrorism task force is important for understanding the Reagan administration's
reaction to the terrorism crisis of the 1980s and for the development of the
Reagan offensive in Central America and elsewhere. Some scholars, writing
before the availability of many documents, suggested that the task force was
little more than a consensual reiteration of US policy.[25] Recently available
documents, however, demonstrate that the work of the task force was intri-
cate and important to the development of the Reagan administration's
counterterrorism approach.

The headquarters for the task force were located just to the North of the
White House in the historic district of Lafayette Square. 730 Jackson Place
was the nerve center for the operation.[26] The offices were equipped with the
most sensitive and top-secret communication mechanisms. Headquarters included secure phone lines and safes for classified material.[27] Vice President

Bush's Task Force to Combat Terrorism involved senior officials from all pertinent departments and agencies. The Central Intelligence Agency (CIA), the State Department, Department of Defense, the National Security Council (NSC), the White House, the Joint Chiefs of Staff (JCS) the Federal Bureau of Investigation (FBI), Office of Budget and Management (OBM) as well as Departments of Transportation, Treasury, and Justice were part of this task force. This was the most thorough effort made at combatting terrorism yet.[28]

The group combined three distinct parts: the working group, the senior review group, and the research and analysis group. The working group and research and analysis group were responsible for conducting the investigative and written elements of the process. By contrast, the senior review group acted as oversight. The senior review group's job was to keep the task force on track and make key decisions for the final report. The organization was not bi-partisan. While Democrats did participate in the process, the task force derived from Reagan's cabinet.[29]

The appointment of Vice President George H. W. Bush to head the task force was a clear sign that this was a serious step by the administration. Bush carried significant insight and influence in the making of policy. Having served the United States with distinction during World War II and as the Director of the CIA in the late 1970s, the Vice President was uniquely in tune with the motor of policy. The administration appointed Bush because he understood how foreign policy worked and what was required to address the unique threat of terrorism. The Vice President, however, was not the acting director of the group, rather, this job fell to the executive director, retired navy admiral James Holloway III.

Admiral Holloway, a personal choice of Bush, was also distinguished for his prior service to the nation. In 1978, Holloway was the chief of naval operations. He remained active after retirement, and his participation in the investigation of the Iran hostage situation made him an ideal candidate for the position of executive director in the terrorism task force. Both Bush and Holloway played important roles in directing the shape of US terrorism policy.

The initial stages of the task force lasted for about six weeks. During this time, officials received appointments and began the research and background work in preparation for the beginning of the administration's counterterrorism program review, which began in September. The central purpose of the task force was, first, to evaluate the problem and consider solutions and, second, to better understand the public perception of the terrorism problem and to take steps to shape the way in which the problem was presented and perceived by Congress, the American public, and the international community. These first two goals occurred simultaneously, and together climaxed in the development of a new policy framework. December 20, 1985, was the deadline to have the final report ready for approval by Vice President Bush and President Reagan. [30]

The task force's senior review group met for the first time on Wednesday, September 11, 1985. The meeting began at 9:00 am and lasted for an hour. The purpose was to bring together the chief members of the administration and consider essential objectives. The meeting began with opening remarks from Executive Director James Holloway III. The first steps in this inaugural meeting were basic in nature. The Reagan administration did not have a formal definition of international terrorism, and so Holloway began the meeting by outlining the particular issue. International terrorism, he asserted, was the usage of criminal actions to "intimidate or coerce a civilian population, to influence the policy of a government by intimidation or coercion or to affect the conduct of a government by assassination or kidnapping." Further, this threat occurred outside the boundaries of the United States and involved the need for states and territories to provide sanctuary and support. International terrorism was, like terrorism in general, "The calculated, criminal use or threat of violence for political purposes to intimidate a target audience beyond the immediate victims." The phenomenon, it was assumed, was primarily an extension of the global Cold War and conducted by affiliates of radical leftists against the United States and the democracies of the world. The task force agreed that terrorism, whether in Nicaragua or Lebanon, was part of a global communist-terrorist offensive. This outlook formed the basis of the work of the task force. [31]

The second meeting of the Senior Review Group was held on September 18. This was the first time that the heads of all pertinent agencies and departments attended: Secretary of State George Shultz, Director of the Office of Counterterrorism and Emergency Planning Robert Oakley, Secretary of Defense Caspar Weinberger, Head of the Joint Chiefs of Staff John Wickman, Deputy Director of the CIA John McMahon, Director of the FBI Judge William Webster, and Attorney General Edwin Meese joined Vice President George H. W. Bush and Executive Director Holloway in the Roosevelt Room at 10:30 am. There were a number of members of the White House at the meeting: in addition to the Vice President, Deputy Assistant to the President for National Security Affairs John Poindexter, Staff Member for the Office of National Security Affairs Oliver North, and Chief of Staff Craig Fuller joined this executive meeting of the President's cabinet. [32] This was the first time that these high-ranking officials provided direct insight to the task force on the course of US counterterrorism policy. [33]

Vice President Bush opened the meeting and made key points about how the task force should define terrorism and what this new security crisis meant to US policy. Bush knew that only with congressional support could the United States take the more aggressive actions that both he and Shultz believed the threat demanded. He also understood that international terrorism provided the possibility of achieving congressional support for more broad offensive measures against the nation's enemies. Furthermore, he understood that terrorism was a powerful rhetorical weapon that might help swing the debate over Contra aid in the administration's favor. The evidence for this is found, first, in his opening remarks at this inclusive meeting. The Vice President insisted that, "Once the President approves the recommendations of this task force this congressional support affords a real opportunity to package legislation under anti-terrorism that will stand a good chance of passage." Bush implied that this new threat introduced a tool that could allow for the authorization from Congress of a more aggressive foreign policy. The attainment of lethal aid for the Contras was of central importance to the task force and the Reagan administration, and this provided a potential avenue to the achievement of this funding. In his opening remarks at this closed-door meeting, Bush acknowledged that international terrorism changed the game and made the attainment of these goals possible. Terrorism implied an illegitimacy of targeted states that in the post-Vietnam period allegations of communism did not.[34]

Members present at the meeting agreed that what made this new threat unique, thereby requiring a new approach, was that it was internationally connected. Domestic terrorism or terrorism within a country at war, had occurred for many years and in virtually every major conflict. According to the members present, the international character and its role in a global anti-American offensive made this threat new and unique. The acts involved state supported transnational criminal agents. They targeted citizens, soldiers, and world leaders through a network of loosely connected state sponsors. Secretary of State Shultz provided a suggestion for defining terrorism in such a manner as to help facilitate the goals of regime change in places like Nicaragua. First, he insisted, "The international aspect of terrorism is the essence of the matter. . . . The terrorist connections are international." Next, Shultz suggested broadening the dimensions of what represented international terrorism by incorporating the illegal drug trade into the catalogue of international terrorism. The allegation of Sandinista involvement in drug trafficking, so-called "narco-terrorism," could enhance the administration's call for military escalation. Shultz argued, "There is a definite connection with illicit drugs as a source of financing activities." Defining terrorism loosely was a key component to the inclusion of Nicaragua in this war on terrorism. The decision by the task force to define the problem broadly provided an increased justification for war against the Sandinistas.[35] The task force took steps to use terrorism as a tool that justified aggression against enemies on the fringe of what might legitimately be considered part of the crisis over international terrorism.

At the meeting, the task force considered the use of active measures in combatting international terrorism. The members present debated whether offensive actions against or within sovereign states might violate norms of international law. This issue pertained to applications of force against sovereign states not technically at war with the United States. Shultz, a leading advocate of an offensive approach, suggested that international law should not impede the United States' attempts to fight terrorism. He insisted that, "We often torture ourselves with these moral dilemmas of justice when we forget the victims and the consequences of the incident." The Secretary implied that the threat was new, and the United States needed to respond aggressively and if necessary without the impediment of "moral dilemmas of justice." It was clear from this meeting that unilateral military action, aid to transnational guerrilla forces, and other preventative and preemptive measures were all on the table as potentially acceptable options for dealing with outlaw states.[36]

For many in the Reagan administration, international terrorism justified the use of hardline measures that challenged the norms of sovereignty and international law. Over the course of the next year George Shultz and George H. W. Bush led the way in explaining the new aggressive, unilateral, and preemptive approach that the United States adopted in 1985–1986. In May 1986, *American Legion* published an interview with the Vice President titled, "A Warning to Terrorists: We Will Protect Our Citizens." In the interview Bush insisted that, "If there is evidence that a nation is mounting or intends to conduct an act of terrorism against this country the United States will take measures to protect its citizens, property, and interests." Bush continued, "U.S. military counter-terrorists forces are well equipped, superbly trained and highly capable of responding." The Vice President's first emphasis was on the use of force, and while he did acknowledge that, "There are also other ways besides force to battle terrorism," he nonetheless positioned force as primary and lamented that, "Unfortunately, multilateral sanctions [on state sponsors of terrorism] are difficult to organize, and even then may not be effective." Bush spoke publically in favor of the hardline considerations suggested behind closed doors by the terrorism task force.

In the interview for *American Legion* Bush insisted that Nicaragua was, contrary to popular perspective, a serious terrorist threat. Bush insisted,

> While we usually associate terrorism with the Middle East, a very serious problem exists much closer to our borders. More terrorist acts were directed at U.S. citizens in Latin America last year than any other region. Both Nicaragua and Cuba have been implicated in this activity. Our support for the Contra cause against the Sandinistas is, in part, to ensure that we are not going to have a terrorist beachhead right in our own hemisphere.

George H. W. Bush led the way in advocating an aggressive preemptive counterterrorist campaign against Sandinista-led Nicaragua. In Central

America, the United States used the Contras to fight the increased threat from state sponsors of terrorism.[37]

Perhaps, at first glance, it seems strange that George H. W. Bush and George Shultz promoted an aggressive unilateral offensive against state sponsors of terrorism while simultaneously leading the United States toward greater cooperation and coexistence with the Soviet Union and Mikhail Gorbachev. Despite assertions by some of the complicity of the Soviet Union in terrorism, by the second term this perspective on terrorism appeared to change in light of greater cooperation between Gorbachev and the Reagan administration. Bush and Shultz understood the late 1980s as a time of transition. During Reagan's second term the United States pursued greater cooperation with the Soviet Union, but in doing this it also escalated its offensive counterterrorism war. Bush and Shultz believed that terrorism threatened both the Soviet Union and the United States. In *American Legion*, the Vice President insisted that increased diplomacy with the Soviet Union "indicates a developing consensus among all nations, including the Soviets, that terrorism is unacceptable international behavior." Bush and Shultz, the leaders of policy, pursued a greater coexistence with the Soviet Union while simultaneously constructing an aggressive counterterror war against Nicaragua and others alleged of facilitating the new threat of international terrorism.[38]

Several days after the September 18 meeting, Admiral Holloway led an envoy to Great Britain, Ambassador Edward Peck and Robert Earl to Central and South America, Dave Cole to Italy, and Dave McNunn to the Middle East. The purpose was to visit the places most urgently threatened by international terrorism. Ambassador Peck's group visited the two places considered most at risk by Nicaraguan backed terrorism, El Salvador, and Colombia.[39] On this trip, the task force members met with heads of state, military officials, and businessmen that were involved in projects like the Colombian oil pipeline.[40] NSC members John Poindexter and Charles Allen both adamantly opposed Peck's visit to San Salvador. The situation in El Salvador remained very dangerous and the two feared that urban terrorists with affiliation to the FMLN and to the Sandinistas might target the envoy as reprisals for the US-backed El Salvador offensive in July. Their concern was not without warrant. Ambassador Thomas Pickering had two attempts on his life thwarted by the United States and the El Salvadoran government a year earlier.[41] Peck, however, insisted, "The trip [was] necessary to insure that the final report has a proper assessment of the terrorist threat worldwide [and] El Salvador is a particularly important country to visit because of the ongoing terrorist activity."[42] The administration took the terrorism crisis seriously and intended to create a complete understanding of the situation and a coherent framework of intervention in response.

On October 7, 1985, international events again reminded the world of the danger. The world watched as terrorists with links to the PLO hijacked the cruise ship Achille Lauro in the Mediterranean. In the course of the events a Jewish-American man, Leon Klinghoffer, died and the hijackers threw his body over the side.[43] In response, President Reagan ordered fighter planes to intercept an Egyptian passenger airline that carried four of the Palestinian hijackers attempting to escape to safe havens. The action forced the plane to land in Italy and the authorities arrested the hijackers. The widow of Klinghoffer praised Reagan, and was "glad the president did something."[44] Egyptian president Hosni Mubarak was, however, not pleased. Mubarak accused the United States as having conducted "an act of piracy" against an Egyptian aircraft.[45] In the midst of these events, the task force worked on as planned. The atmosphere was so tense that the Deputy Director for Counterterrorism Parker Borg recalled that, "There seemed to be hijackings or terrorist incidents almost continuously."[46]

During late September and throughout October 1985 the situation with Nicaragua did not improve. The Sandinistas continued to pursue a case against the United States at the Hague International Court of Justice (ICJ) in Holland. Daniel Ortega countered the United States' claim that he was an agent of terrorism by labeling the United States a state sponsor of terrorism. The Reagan administration refused to participate at the ICJ and Ortega had a world stage. However, Oretga made several diplomatic errors. In the middle of October, the Sandinista leadership placed restrictions on civil liberties in Nicaragua. The restrictions involved shutting down some media outlets, religious groups, and political parties.[47] President Daniel Ortega justified the actions as necessary to focus on the conflict with the Contras. The Reagan administration was constantly searching for hard evidential reasons to demand an escalation of hostilities against the Sandinistas and Ortega either did not understand this or believed that the Reagan administration was undeterred in its will to attack Nicaragua. Ortega's first mistake during these critical moments when US aid to the Contras was still uncertain was traveling to Moscow after the rejection by Congress of lethal funds to the Contras the previous spring. The Sandinista's crack down on civil liberties played further into the hands of the Reagan administration.

Following Ortega's announcement to restrict freedom of press, speech and assembly in the middle of October, other circumstances further damaged the position of the Sandinista leadership in the eyes of the United States Congress. In Early September, guerrillas kidnapped Ines Guadalupe, the daughter of Jose Napoleon Duarte, the president of El Salvador. On November 1, after the release of his daughter, President Duarte declared publically that Nicaragua was responsible for the terrorist act. In a passionate speech to the National Press Club he exclaimed that, "In Central America, in my own country, countless persons from all walks of life, and in the case of my family . . . would not have been victims of merciless violence of the terrorists if terrorists did not have the support, direction, approval and timely protection of the terrorist dictatorship in Nicaragua."[48] Duarte affirmed the position of the Reagan administration, and the United States' criminal allegations against the Sandinistas resonated.

Throughout November, tension continued to rise and investigative journalism fueled the rumor mill. On November 3, Bob Woodward, the iconic investigative journalist for the *Washington Post*, published an article that suggested that the Reagan NSC planned to begin a new covert war against Libya. Woodward argued that the Reagan administration intended to replicate the surrogate counterterrorism war in Nicaragua in the territory of other alleged "outlaw states."[49] The following day tension with Nicaragua increased further as a US SR-71 Blackbird overflew Cuba. The Cuban air defenses unsuccessfully fired on the plane. The last time that such an engagement occurred over the island of Cuba was during the Cuban Missile Crisis when Cuban air defenses brought down a U-2 spy plane. The SR-71 spent nearly an hour over Cuban airspace. The result was outrage from the Cuban and Nicaraguan governments, but the intelligence added more fuel to the administration's argument. The Reagan administration alleged that it identified Soviet and Bulgarian military equipment being unloaded and prepared for shipment. The administration insisted that it was destined for Nicaragua and from there to El Salvador. The intelligence also included evidence of Soviet made tanks allegedly going to Nicaragua. These assertions came two weeks after Daniel Ortega had pledged to defeat the Contras in a matter of weeks.[50] A few days later, the Sandinista government detained fourteen Nicaraguans working at the United States embassy in Managua for questioning. These new intelligence revelations and the reactions of the Sandinista leadership provided fuel for the Reagan administration already involved in the construction of an offensive framework for intervention and diligently attempting to use rhetoric to criminalize the Nicaraguan government.

That same week in November, only one month since the United States task force team had visited, a horror unfolded in Colombia. Neither Colombia nor the United States were ready for what happened on November 7. The Colombian group, April 19 Movement (M-19), attacked the Colombian Supreme Court. The terrorists took hostages and a twenty-five-hour siege unfolded in downtown Bogota. The deadlock was broken when military and police forces stormed the building. The results were shocking: eighty-nine lay dead. The dead included Alfonso Reyes, the head of the Supreme Court, and six other judges.[51] The United States investigated the tragic event and a month later insisted that Nicaragua had helped facilitate the actions of the M-19 faction. The Reagan administration exaggerated the role of the Sandinistas in the attack. The link was only the presence of several small arms of Nicaraguan origin that were involved in the attack.[52] Nonetheless, eager to use any evidence it could in an elaborate propaganda campaign, this event provided yet another justification for the Reagan administration to demand that Congress allow aggressive action against Nicaragua, the alleged terrorist state.

While the situation in the Americas and the world escalated, the task force continued with its work. The group appealed to the best and brightest minds in American foreign policy. Members of the task force working group conducted interviews with dozens of specialists. The list of those scheduled for interview included Henry Kissinger, Bob Woodward, Zbigniew Brzezinski, Alexander Haig, and many others from groups as wide ranging as Interpol and the Department of Defense. Through this process, the task force hoped to gain a broad spectrum of insight on the terrorism issue and develop an efficient way of combatting the problem.

While the task force sought a thorough understanding of the terrorism issue, the principle architects seemed to have already accepted a desired approach. The group sought an approach that placed military measures at the center and utilized proxy war and regime change as a solution to the problem of state sponsored terrorism. Not surprisingly, Henry Kissinger, the hardline national security specialist from the Nixon and Ford eras, was one of the most highly admired by the task force. Many members of Reagan's cabinet felt admiration for Kissinger's advocacy of realism in foreign policy.

In order to ensure the image of balance the task force also interviewed the more critical Brzezinski. Carter's former national security advisor fundamentally rejected the administration's interpretation of terrorism as a phenomenon related to global bipolarity. Brzezinski suggested to the task force that the United States should not wage a military oriented war on terrorism. He believed that the issue of terrorism was regional and local. A grand strategy, he argued, was an ineffectual route.[53]

The final report of the task force proved that it ignored Brzezinski's opinion. Brzezinski's outlook, though, provided a potent insight into a fundamental flaw of the Reagan administration's policy on terrorism and with Nicaragua. Brzezinski warned that the administration's insistence on interpreting the terrorism crisis from the stand point of Cold War global bipolarity was flawed and dangerous because it simplified matters that involved complicated local and regional factors. The Cold War outlook exaggerated the threat and oversimplified the causes of revolution and conflict by reducing it to designs of world communism and radicalism. The administration's insistence that international terrorism was a symptom of global bipolarity, a struggle against leftism, encouraged war and slowed the peace process. This outlook had, as early as 1981, encouraged the pursuit of a military oriented strategy that created tension with Nicaragua and increased the deterioration of that situation rather than promoting solutions. The administration's perspective in the wake of the terrorism crisis further escalated tension with Nicaragua.

In contrast to Brzezinski's views, the final report of the task force would show that it shared ideas with Henry Kissinger. Kissinger was intimately involved in the United States' work in Central America. In 1984, he headed a team, appointed by President Reagan, which went to Central America and reported on the details of and solutions to the violence in the region. Kissinger was on the top of the list for consultations on the issue of international terrorism, and on November 11, the task force got its chance. Nixon's former secretary of state interpreted events through the lens of super power competition. Terrorism and communism, he insisted, were connected and the United States needed to respond aggressively. Terrorism was a different kind of threat, it was criminal, and Kissinger argued that the United States should use force when necessary and never negotiate with terrorists. He argued that, "Innocent lives must, and will be sacrificed in pursuit of this higher purpose."[54] His aggressive hardline national security approach embodied the leanings of many in the task force.

Vice President Bush knew that achieving the goal of a more active and effective counterterrorism policy required not only the support of Congress, but also the United States public. Terrorism was a powerful rhetorical weapon that provided a new opportunity to control the attitudes of the American public and the dialogue over the conflict in Nicaragua. The task force considered public opinion extensively, the members were aware that prior to the TWA-847 hijacking and the killings in El Salvador that a Roper Poll found that 78 percent of Americans saw terrorism as "one of the most serious problems facing the United States government today."[55] The task force also understood that a Washington Post-ABC news poll found 80 percent in favor of the Reagan administration's response to the Achille Lauro hijacking.[56] The task force also understood the potentially negative impact of public opinion and dissent from the experience with the Vietnam War. The group sought to understand and manipulate the attitude of the public by shaping the dialogue over terrorism and Nicaragua.

In early November, the task force contracted a research group, *Populus Incorporated*, to conduct a scientific review of attitudes about terrorism and US policy. There were 106 news reading subjects aged from eighteen to sixty-four. The individuals selected came from a varied spectrum in terms of political ideology and geographical location. The surveyed individuals came from Iowa, Southern California, Texas, New York, and Connecticut. The report noted that Americans saw terrorism as a danger that threatened US prestige in the world. A consensus was that the administration needed to address international terrorism, and that the United States should not back down to terrorists and must do anything necessary to protect innocent lives. The task force's consensus on the final report was that, "Americans will welcome actions which are swift, proactive, and even aggressive." The key, the report implied, was that counterterrorist actions needed to be relatively quick with few casualties. From the perspective of the task force, this gave authorization from the public to conduct a more aggressive policy against state sponsors of terrorism. The report indicated that the American people supported covert/surrogate actions, like those in Central America, and quick strike missions for rescue or retaliation.[57]

During the twentieth century, technology changed alongside the growth of an increasingly internationally involved United States. Technology revolutionized many things and among these was news journalism. The Vietnam War embodied this change. The United States increasingly involved in a far off region of the developing world and fighting for global influence was covered by modern television media in a surprising contrast to the sterilized news reels seen in movie theaters in years before. The result was a sometimes adversarial relationship between the executive branch and the media. During Vietnam, Presidents Kennedy, Johnson, and Nixon all sought to prevent the media from fully disclosing the reality of US military involvement in Vietnam. Following the exposure a US combat role in Vietnam John F. Kennedy sought the demotion of *New York Times* journalist David Halberstam. Following Moraley Safer's exposure of the village burnings at Cam Ne in 1965, Lyndon Johnson launched a tirade against CBS news, at one point exclaiming over the telephone to CBS president Frank Stanton, "Are you trying to fuck me!" Johnson implied that Safer was a communist and that CBS had "shat on the American flag."[58] For Richard Nixon the release of the *Pentagon Papers* in 1971 was but one of many perceived reasons for Nixon's obsession with the meddling of the media. Vietnam established an adversarial relationship between the executive and the media in matters of foreign policy.

After Vietnam many in the policy establishment took it as a given that the media had somehow undermined the United States' war effort, and none more than those in Ronald Reagan's cabinet. Because the United States was more internationally engaged than at any other time during the late Cold War, and because video and recording technology revolutionized how the media functioned, attempting to control media was considered a vital component of US foreign policy during the 1980s.[59]

The public diplomacy effort focused not only on public opinion, and influencing Congress, but also on the role of the media. The media was one of the primary groups that the administration hoped to influence. The media, perhaps more than the White House itself, influenced the public perception of the terrorism crisis and US policy. The task force hoped for greater cooperation from the media in reporting terrorist events and US counterterrorism activity.

On November 23, Admiral Holloway and Vice President Bush convened a meeting of senior news media executives. The task force hoped a cooperative and sympathetic media could report news on terrorism and US policy in a manner less harmful to the position of the United States. The meeting was held at 10 am at the vice president's personal residence. Since the terrorist events of the past summer, the administration was increasingly critical of the media. In particular, many Republicans and Democrats in Congress considered the coverage of the TWA-847 hijackings problematic. The media televised the events on that runway in Beirut and provided the hostage takers with a 'news conference' to propose demands. George H. W. Bush knew that if the United States responded more aggressively to terrorist acts and to alleged state sponsors like Nicaragua and Libya, the manner in which the media covered such events determined how many Americans perceived of such offensive actions. The task force hoped that if it could create an alliance with media leaders to report terrorist acts and US responses in a manner sympathetic to the administration's position that it would significantly assist its efforts to shape the dialogue over the terrorism crisis. In the wake of Vietnam the administration hoped to change the relationship between the executive and the media.

The participants at the meeting between the task force and media executives included: Ben Bradlee of the *Washington Post*, Ed Turner of CNN, Shelby Coffey of *U.S. News & World Report*, Ron Cohen of *United Press International*, Jack Smith of ABC, George Watson of CBS, Bob McFarland of NBC, Bill Kovach of the *New York Times*, Ann Blackman of *Time*, Morton Kondrake of *Newsweek*, and Charles Lewis of the *Associated Press*. Bush and Holloway hoped to find these senior media executives in a mood to cooperate. However, from the beginning of the meeting it was clear that these media representatives understood the meeting as an attempt by the administration to control news reporting in service of its own ends. Before the meeting commenced, CBS clarified its position that, "The shape and content of the news must not be calibrated to serve the administration or any other entity." This statement set the tone for the meeting. [60]

The meeting did not begin well. Ben Bradlee of the *Washington Post* expressed immediate frustration. He exclaimed, "Why you guys always trashing the press?" At the outset of the meeting, the task force attempted to shape the dialogue. Initially, Admiral Holloway proposed a hypothetical of how potentially damaging media coverage of a Delta Force rescue operation might be, but the media executives denied the relevance of the point and turned the task force's idea around. Ed Turner from CNN insisted that "hypotheticals don't work." Morton Kondracke of *Newsweek* reminded the task force that there is an agreement among journalists to avoid reporting things that might endanger troops or civilians in the field. The media members established the tone for the remainder of the hour and a half meeting. The executives proposed that, contrary to the assumptions of Bush and Holloway, that television media coverage had saved the lives of those involved in the TWA hijacking rather than putting the hostages at risk. Ben Bradlee suggested that television put pressure on the situation and forced the parties involved to a resolution. After the meeting, the minutes acknowledged, "The task force should have thought this through."[61]

Throughout the meeting, either Vice President Bush or Admiral Holloway proposed various scenarios as if the conclusions were self-evident, but each time the media executives responded with a rebuttal. After the failure of the first hypothetical, Admiral Holloway resorted to a suggestion about the fragile and naïve nature of the America public by insisting that, "People see the media treatment of a terrorist incident as *Dallas*."[62] The media members immediately disagreed, and again Kondrake contended that publicity helped solve terrorist incidents. At this point Holloway backed down and acknowledged that there was no evidence to disprove the position taken by Kondrake, Bradlee, and others. Vice President Bush expressed his frustration. Bush seemed to feel as though the group was bickering over a self-evident truth and he insisted that there existed a common attitude in the United States over the media. He described the attitude as one of "frustration." According to Bush, the careless role that the media played in issues that involved the lives and credibility of the United States frustrated many Americans. However, Charles Lewis of the *Associated Press* insisted that the task force's concern with the media was not self-evident. He insisted that an important job of the media was to put pressure on the president and force him to do his job effectively. Throughout the meeting, the media leaders turned the tables on the task force and frustration on the administration's side was evident.[63]

By the end of the meeting, the task force and the media executives simply did not see eye to eye. The media representatives disagreed that the reporting of the United States' free media was a problem. The media executives argued that in many cases, like the TWA hijacking, free media helped rather than hurt the situation. As the meeting closed, Admiral Holloway summed up the main points. Holloway, likely with a certain degree of emotional exhaustion, concluded that the meeting demonstrated that, "There will be media coverage of future terrorist incidents, the coverage will not be controlled by the government, the press has its own guidelines, and the government must rely on press judgment."[64] Having entered the discussion in the hope that the press would agree to some set of guidelines, like pledging not to broadcast terrorist incidents live, the task force members were frustrated. The task force wanted to influence the debate over terrorism in order to empower its actions, but the United States' independent media resisted.

The meeting's final remarks testified to the task force's failure. Kondrake spoke last for the media and again put the onus on the administration. He insisted that, "The important lesson was that the national leadership must not get rattled [by press pressure]." At this moment NSC advisor, former CIA operative and friend of Bush's, Don Gregg, caused shock and outrage from the press when he exclaimed that, "There was little terrorism in countries with a controlled press!" Gregg's remark showed disdain for the First Amendment and visibly shocked the media members present. If the United States were to conduct an offensive against nations like Nicaragua, it would do so without the cooperation of the media. [65]

The strong stand taken by the media during the 1980s represented the final moments in which a free and investigative journalism network functioned in the United States. Tom Fenton's popular book *Bad News* demonstrates that after the 1980s journalism was corporatized and increasingly brought under control of the power establishment in the United States. Today cable news companies have commodified the news as a paid-for product. Rather than informing, the big cable news magnates sell the story that it believes its audience wishes to hear. Likewise, in areas of foreign policy journalists are largely brought to cower to the leadership on issues deemed in the interest of national security. In many cases journalists are strongly censored and in others the reduction of foreign posts means that journalists must simply rely on secondhand reports from the present administration or other agencies. In the area of foreign policy, investigative journalism is largely defanged today, and while the Reagan administration failed to fully achieve this, its effort in the fall of 1985 marked an important trend toward a less effective investigative journalism in the United States. [66]

From September to November, the task force used the information obtained from the foreign visits, consultations, meetings with members of Congress and the press, as well as public opinion polls to develop forty-five issue papers. Decisions made on these issues created the basis for the final report of the task force. The papers each presented a topic that the task force considered in developing the final report, which was due for completion by December 20. The issues ranged from the definition of terrorism and of national policy, as well as to specific issues like extradition treaties, border control, airport and port security, intelligence sharing, and types of military responses. [67]

An important and interesting topic in these papers was the push to define terrorism broadly and exclusively as a crime rather than as a political act connected to insurgency, civil war, and revolution. The United States had never acknowledged terrorism itself as a crime. Instead, the crime was hijacking, kidnapping, robbery, and so on. The modern concept of terrorism developed rapidly in the months following June 1985 and part of this development was to construct terrorism as a unique crime that was, somehow, more heinous, treasonous and conspiratorial, and to use the accusation as a weapon against the administration's enemies, in this case the Sandinistas. This carried consequences for the nation-states that the United States alleged were state sponsors of terrorism. [68]

Despite the absence of a formal war, the allegation of criminality on the nation-state level coincided with the United States position that on the grounds of national security it possessed the right to take active measures to isolate and ultimately eliminate the threat presented by an alleged outlaw state. The United States defined revolutionary nations like Nicaragua as terrorist, it blurred the distinction between revolutionary and terrorist. During 1985, the Reagan administration unjustly alleged that the Sandinista government was a criminal state sponsor of international terrorism in Central and South America. The reconstructing of Nicaragua as, not only a communist state, but also a terrorist state, provided an important justification for the United States to move more aggressively in the coming year.

The Reagan administration's war on terrorism against Nicaragua began most earnestly in 1985 with preparatory actions designed to create a more accepting atmosphere for an offensive. Following the terrorist attacks of June the administration reacted and began the formulation of a coherent policy designed to oppose what officials perceived as a conspiratorial global communist-terrorist offensive. The United States labeled Nicaragua an "outlaw state" and worked with its supporters in Congress to shape the dialogue over the Sandinistas. The administration escalated tension by openly spying on and threatening Nicaragua as well as backing military operations against the PRTC in El Salvador. The administration positioned terrorism at the center of the conversation and Congress responded with support for economic sanctions and greater agreement over the nature of the Nicaraguan threat. The United States' actions following the June attacks were not limited to public denunciations and reactionary measures. The development of the Task Force to Combat Terrorism represented a concerted effort to develop a lasting policy strategy to combat states that the United States alleged supported terrorist acts. In 1986 the task force's policy would go into action against Nicaragua. Measures taken in the six months following the attacks of June 1985 amounted to preparations for an offensive counterterrorism operation that specifically targeted Nicaragua in the coming year.

NOTES

1. Bernard Weinraub, "President Accuses 5 'Outlaw States' of World Terror," *New York Times,* July 9, 1985, http://search.proquest.com/docview/425474442?accountid=14902.
2. 131 Cong. Rec. H4552 (daily ed. June 20, 1985) (statement of Congressman Dornan).
3. 131 Cong. Rec. H4552 (daily ed. June 20, 1985).
4. 131 Cong. Rec. H4552 (daily ed. June 20, 1985) (summary of Foley Amendment).
5. 131 Cong. Rec. H4552 (daily ed. June 20, 1985) (statement of Congressman Levine).
6. 131 Cong. Rec. H4552 (daily ed. June 20, 1985) (statement of Congressman Hunter).
7. 131 Cong. Rec. H4552 (daily ed. June 20, 1985) (statement of Congressman Hyde).
8. 131 Cong. Rec. H4552 (daily ed. June 20, 1985) (statement of Congressman Gingrich).
9. 131 Cong. Rec. H4552 (daily ed. June 20, 1985) (summary of Skelton Amendment).
10. 131 Cong. Rec. H4552 (daily ed. June 20, 1985).
11. Weinraub, "President Accuses 5 'Outlaw States' of World Terror."
12. 131 Cong. Rec. H5541 (daily ed. July 11, 1985).
13. 131 Cong. Rec. H5541 (daily ed. July 11, 1985).

14. "Nicaraguan Rebels Getting Advice from White House on Operations," *New York Times*, August 8, 1985, http://search.proquest.com/docview/111164138?accountid=14902.

15. Special Analysis, "El Salvador: Tracking Down Terrorists," July 11, 1985, *Digital National Security Archive* (Ann Arbor: Proquest 2012), EL00151.

16. "El Salvador: Tracking Down Terrorists," August 13, 1985, *Digital National Security Archive*.

17. Special Analysis, "El Salvador: Tracking Down Terrorists," July 11, 1985, *Digital National Security Archive*.

18. "US Considered Surgical Raid on Nicaragua Base," *San Francisco Chronicle*, July 24, 1985, http://search.proquest.com/docview/301914590?accountid=14902.

19. "Reagan Reportedly Favors Force to Combat Terrorism," *Houston Chronicle*, July 12, 1985, http://search.proquest.com/docview/295084311?accountid=14902.

20. "Bush Recommends Caution When Striking Back at Terrorists," *San Francisco Chronicle*, July 12, 1985, http://search.proquest.com/docview/301924218?accountid=14902.

21. Curtis Sitomer, "Lawmakers Stress International Cooperation to Combat Terrorism," *The Christian Science Monitor*, July 16, 1985, http://search.proquest.com/docview/1400449442?accountid=14902.

22. Doyle McManus, "Assassination Ban May Not Apply in Anti-Terror Raids," *Los Angeles Times*, July 13, 1985, http://search.proquest.com/docview/292116773?accountid=14902.

23. Robert Oakley, interview by Charles Stuart Kennedy and Thomas Stern, The Association for Diplomatic Studies and Training, *Foreign Affairs Oral History Project.*

24. National Security Decision Directive 179, July 20, 1985, Folder "VP Task Force on Combatting Terrorism 1st Meeting with Senior Review Group," Box 32, Oliver North Files, Ronald Reagan Presidential Library.

25. David C. Wills, *The First War on Terrorism: Counterterrorism Policy During the Reagan Administration* (Oxford: Rowman & Littlefield, 2003).

26. Memo, Admiral Holloway to Staff, September 4, 1985, Folder "VP Task Force on Combatting Terrorism 1st Meeting with Senior Review Group," Box 32, Oliver North Files, Ronald Reagan Presidential Library.

27. Memo, Admiral Holloway to Staff, September 4, 1985, Ronald Reagan Presidential Library.

28. Memo, Office of the Vice President to Task Force, Folder "VP Task Force on Combatting Terrorism 1st Meeting with Senior Review Group," Box 32, Oliver North Files, Ronald Reagan Presidential Library.

29. Memo, Admiral Holloway to Staff, September 4, 1985, Ronald Reagan Presidential Library.

30. Memo, Admiral Holloway to Staff, September 9, 1985, Folder "VP Task Force on Combatting Terrorism 1st Meeting with Senior Review Group," Box 32, Oliver North Files, Ronald Reagan Presidential Library.

31. Meeting itinerary, Agenda for Task Force on Combatting Terrorism Senior Review Group, September 11, 1985, Folder "VP Task Force on Combatting Terrorism 1st Meeting with Senior Review Group," Box 32, Oliver North Files, Ronald Reagan Presidential Library.

32. List of Participants for the Second Meeting of the Vice President's Task Force on Combatting Terrorism, September 18, 1985, Folder "Second Meeting With Task Force Principles," Box 32, Oliver North Files, Ronald Reagan Presidential Library.

33. Memo, Admiral Holloway, Minutes of the Second Task Force meeting, September 19, 1985, Folder "Second Meeting With Task Force Principles," Box 32, Oliver North Files, Ronald Reagan Presidential Library.

34. Memo, Admiral Holloway, Minutes of the Second Task Force meeting, September 19, 1985, Ronald Reagan Presidential Library.

35. Memo, Admiral Holloway, Minutes of the Second Task Force meeting, September 19, 1985, Ronald Reagan Presidential Library.

36. Memo, Admiral Holloway, Minutes of the Second Task Force meeting, September 19, 1985, Ronald Reagan Presidential Library.

37. Interview with George H. W. Bush, "A Warning to the Terrorists: We Will Protect Our Citizens," *American Legion Magazine*, May 21, 1986, Folder 3 of 3, OA/ID 19849, Donald,

Gregg P. Files, subject files, George H. W. Bush Vice Presidential Records, National Security Affairs, Office Of, Holloway's Terrorism Review, OA/ID 19863-010.

38. Interview with George H. W. Bush, "A Warning to the Terrorists: We Will Protect Our Citizens," May 21, 1986, Donald, Gregg P. Files, subject files.

39. Diplomatic Missions, International Consultations, September 11, 1985, Folder "VP Task Force on Combatting Terrorism 1st Meeting with Senior Review Group," Box 32, Oliver North Files, Ronald Reagan Presidential Library.

40. Memo, "Terrorism Task Force Working Group's Trip to Bogota," October 1985, Folder "Incoming 10/16/1985- Classified" Box 32, Oliver North Files, Ronald Reagan Presidential Library.

41. Wills, *The First War on Terrorism*.

42. "Proposed Terrorism Task Force Visit to San Salvador," Folder "Terrorism" (4 of 9), Box 2 OA/ID 19849, Donald P. Gregg Files: George Bush Vice Presidential Records, National Security Affairs, George Bush Presidential Library.

43. George James, "For 15 Achille Lauro Passengers, Cruise Ends in Newark," *New York Times*, October 13, 1985, http://search.proquest.com/docview/111307085?accountid=14902.

44. James, "For 15 Achille Lauro Passengers, Cruise Ends in Newark."

45. "Mubarak Denounces Interception of Airliner by the US as Piracy," *New York Times*, October 13, 1985, http://search.proquest.com/docview/111296660?accountid=14902.

46. Parker Borg, interview by Charles Stuart Kennedy, *Foreign Affairs Oral History Project*, Association for Diplomatic Studies and Training, August 12, 2002.

47. William Long, "Liberty Tested in Nicaragua, Opposition Surviving Despite Sandinista Curbs," *Los Angeles Times*, October 21, 1985, http://search.proquest.com/docview/2921825 88?accountid=14902.

48. GM Boyd, "Duarte says Nicaragua helps terrorists," *New York Times*, November 1, 1985, http://ntserver1.wsulibs.wsu.edu:2184/docview/425699509?accountid=14902.

49. Bob Woodward, "Reagan plans covert scheme to undermine Khadafy," *Toronto Star*, November 3, 1985, http://ntserver1.wsulibs.wsu.edu:2184/docview/435363963?accountid=14902.

50. KNT News Service, "Rocket Shot Misses US Spy Plane Boats in Cuba Loading Arms for Nicaragua," *Orlando Sentinel*, November 5, 1985, http://ntserver1.wsulibs.wsu.edu:2184/docview/276707217?accountid=14902.

51. William Long, "Colombia Storms Court; 7 judges Among 89 Dead," *Newsday*, November 8, 1985, http://ntserver1.wsulibs.wsu.edu:2184/docview/285335049?accountid=14902.

52. "State Support for International Terrorism," May 1986, Folder "Terrorism Info-General (3 of 4)," Box CPC-1, FBI 098, Craig P. Coy: Files, Ronald Reagan Presidential Library.

53. Meeting with Brzezinski, Folder "Brzezinski Meeting with Vice President, 11/19/1985," Box 32, Oliver North Files, Ronald Reagan Presidential Library.

54. Meeting with Henry Kissinger, Folder "Meeting with Kissinger, Tuesday November 11, 1985," Box 32, Oliver North Files, Ronald Reagan Presidential Library.

55. "Background Information, Public Opinion Survey," Folder "VP Task Force Meeting with Selected Media, November 23, 1985," Box 32/34, Oliver North Files, Ronald Reagan Presidential Library.

56. "Background Information, Public Opinion Survey," Ronald Reagan Presidential Library.

57. "Terrorism, View Point of the American People," Folder "National Security Council Meeting, January 7, 1986, Vice President's Task Force on Combatting Terrorism," Box 32/34, Oliver North Files, Ronald Reagan Presidential Library.

58. Chester Pach Jr., "And That's the Way It Was: The Vietnam War on the Network Nightly News," in David Fabrber, *The Sixties: From Memory to History* (Chapel Hill: University of North Carolina Press, 1994), 102–104.

59. Pach, "And That's the Way It Was," 90–118.

60. "Memorandum for the Record: Vice President's Meeting with the Media, November 25, 1985," Folder "VP Task Force Meeting with Selected Media, November 23, 1985," Box 32/34, Oliver North Files, Ronald Reagan Presidential Library.

61. "Memorandum for the Record: Vice President's Meeting with the Media, November 25, 1985," Ronald Reagan Presidential Library.

62. "Memorandum for the Record: Vice President's Meeting with the Media, November 25, 1985," Ronald Reagan Presidential Library. Holloway referenced the popular television series *Dallas* and implied that the American people could not tell the difference between TV and media coverage of terrorism.

63. "Memorandum for the Record: Vice President's Meeting with the Media, November 25, 1985," Ronald Reagan Presidential Library.

64. "Memorandum for the Record: Vice President's Meeting with the Media, November 25, 1985," Ronald Reagan Presidential Library.

65. "Memorandum for the Record: Vice President's Meeting with the Media, November 25, 1985," Ronald Reagan Presidential Library.

66. Tom Fenton, *Bad News: The Decline of Reporting, the Business of News, and the Danger to Us All"* (New York: Harper Collins, 2005).

67. Issue Papers, Folder "Senior Review Group Meeting Nov 7, 1985 (Folder 1 of 3)," Box 32, Oliver North Files, Ronald Reagan Presidential Library.

68. Issue Papers, Folder "Senior Review Group Meeting Nov 7, 1985 (Folder 1 of 3)," Ronald Reagan Presidential Library.

Chapter Seven

A War on Terrorism

It was Monday, December 2, 1985, and tension was high between the United States and Nicaragua. Despite a congressional ban on lethal support to the Contras the administration's private funding program for the guerrillas had yielded some dividends. The Contra army numbered over 10,000 and operated deep inside Nicaraguan territory. On December 2, the guerrillas were on operations near Mulukuku. The area was a lightly populated jungle region located near the geographic center of Nicaragua. The guerrillas moved through the countryside about eighty-five miles northeast of Managua, and around seventy-five miles south of the Honduran border. Nicaraguan government forces were on alert and in pursuit of the insurgents in Soviet supplied Mi-8 helicopters.[1] The Contras spotted one of the helicopters and with a surface to air missile (SAM) fired and destroyed the craft. This was the first time that the Contras employed SAM technology, and the first time that the Nicaraguan government admitted to the loss of a military helicopter. All fourteen members of the crew died, and the guerrillas reported that at least one of the dead was a Cuban officer.[2]

There was an immediate reaction when news of the attack reached Washington. On December 5, Assistant Secretary of State for Inter-American Affairs Elliot Abrams insisted that the Cuban officer flying with the crew was further evidence of Cuba's involvement in fighting the Contras. Abrams feared that, "We may be seeing Cubans move into a combat role on the mainland."[3] The following day Secretary of State George Shultz congratulated the Contras for shooting the Mi-8 down. He insisted that Nicaragua was a repressive state and the administration knew that there was a "relationship of that government to terrorism in the region."[4] Shultz referred to evidence that Nicaragua helped facilitate the M-19 attack on the Colombian Supreme Court a month earlier as well as the killing of several Americans in a café in

San Salvador the previous June. The secretary made it known that the Reagan administration intended to push hard for congressional authorization of military support for the Contras. At the dawn of 1986, the United States was poised to launch an offensive.

In December of 1985, the final proposal of the task force outlined a framework for offensive intervention to counter the threat from international terrorism. Whereas a cloud of increasing opposition and controversy limited the implementation of the 1984 directive NSDD-138, the report of the task force came at the height of a 1980s terrorism crisis and represented an operational directive for offensive hardline action against alleged state sponsors of terrorism. Nicaragua and Libya made up the top of the list. The proposal, which culminated in NSDD-207 and superseded NSDD-138, outlined a three-fold strategy for combating these states. The policy was based on hardline measures that included diplomatic non-negotiation, economic and trade sanctions, and a complete spectrum of military force options. These were designed to pressure Nicaragua into either voluntarily altering its government to the designs of the United States or to bring about the collapse of the regime. The proposal of the task force created a new framework of intervention that encouraged diplomatic isolation, economic ruin, and increased war in order to alter the government of Nicaragua. The task force called for an aggressive hardline war on terrorism that was capable of deterring the threat posed by alleged state sponsors of terrorism, and Nicaragua was a primary target.

Since the beginning of the Reagan administration, the purpose of diplomacy with Nicaragua was to isolate the leadership by presenting it with ultimatums and an increasingly powerful propaganda that by 1985 hinged less on the rhetoric of communism and far more on the criminalizing accusation of terrorism. The administration's public diplomacy campaign utilized the language of terrorism as a primary method of shaping the dialogue over Nicaragua. In this process, however, the task force insisted on a broad definition of terrorism that extended its application to the administration's enemies in the developing world whether or not the state merited the accusation. The public diplomacy campaign maximized the damning rhetorical power of terrorism in such a way as to criminalize the Sandinistas while simultaneously distancing the actions of its ally, the so-called freedom fighters, from the concept.

The thrust of the proposal of the task force was an array of military force options designed to address the problem of terrorism and particularly state sponsored terrorism. Economic measures were already an established method dating back to the Carter administration, but the task force's proposal insisted that military pressure promised greater effectiveness. However, two outspoken officials in the Office of Counterterrorism, Parker Borg and Robert Oakley, contested the militaristic thrust of the proposal. The insistence on a military oriented strategy in the task force's report alarmed these two individuals and both argued, instead, for a multilateral diplomatic approach. These high-ranking members of the Office of Counterterrorism pleaded with their counterparts to back away from a policy that emphasized a military offensive against nations like Nicaragua. There were many hardliners and pragmatists within the Reagan administration. However, Oakley and Borg stood out for two reasons: first, the Reagan offensive was, in part, a product of a reevaluation of US counterterrorism strategy, and second, the position of Oakley and Borg as the top officials in the Department of State's Office of Counterterrorism made their criticisms to the program significant. Borg and Oakley's positions within the Task Force to Combat Terrorism make them the most significant opponents of a dangerously aggressive US strategy, and examples of individuals that attempted to shift the course away from the military option.

By no means do I intend to imply that no other opposition existed within the administration's cabinet, but only that Borg and Oakley represented a visible and vocal opposition from key counterterrorism specialists that provided a clear alternative to the course proposed. Their status as top counterterrorism specialists make their opposition to a military oriented framework of intervention a potent lesson that suggests that other avenues were available, but ignored. In the end, their opposition was futile and the United States continued the descent into another troubling chapter in US–Central American relations.

During 1986, the United States directed an offensive war on terrorism at two states, Nicaragua and Libya, both of which the administration vilified with the accusation of terrorism and conducted invasive hardline actions against. This study is concerned particularly with Nicaragua, but US action against the Sandinistas was part of a broad counterterrorism offensive that targeted alleged state sponsors that the administration insisted were part of a new Cold War offensive against the United States. The Reagan offensive against Nicaragua was more than a war against communism: it was also a war on terrorism. Declassified government documents located at the Ronald Reagan Presidential Library and at the George Bush Presidential Library form the basis of the content in this chapter. The release dates for these documents range from 2006 to 2012 and they provide convincing evidence that at the beginning of 1986 the terrorism task force created an offensive framework for action against states alleged of sponsoring terrorism. In 1986, the administration launched the Reagan offensive, the United States' first modern war on terrorism.

As 1985 neared to a close, the world seemed engulfed by a terrorism crisis. Incidents of international terrorism were at an all-time high: hijackings, bombings, shootings, and kidnappings occurred on a monthly basis in Europe, Latin America, and the Middle East. After ranking members of the

Reagan administration publically alleged that Nicaragua was a state sponsor of international terrorism in July of 1985 the Sandinista leadership resisted the overt hostility of the Reagan administration and responded in kind. Nicaraguan President Daniel Ortega accused Washington of state sanctioned terrorism. On December 6, Ortega gave a press conference in which he argued that the United States had supplied the SAM missile that brought the Mi-8 helicopter down a few days earlier. He insisted that the Reagan administration was "stimulating a wave of international terrorism and leaving the way open for anybody to use truly dangerous weapons." Ortega threatened Washington when he stated that the use of the SAM had "opened the floodgates." He implied that Nicaragua might provide similar weapons to its paramilitary allies fighting in El Salvador. As he spoke, a crowd marched on the United States embassy in Managua, chanting, "Yankees, here no one surrenders." Tension between the United States and Nicaragua escalated.[5]

The following day a Soviet-made Lada car crashed in Honduras, and when the police searched the vehicle, they found it loaded with weapons. The contents included 7,000 rounds of ammunition, 21 grenades, 86 blasting caps, 12 radios, and 39 "code booklets" that the Department of State alleged were for terrorist communication with its headquarters in Nicaragua.[6] This incident, from the perspective of officials in Washington, was further evidence of the Sandinista role in aiding subversive elements in neighboring countries. In December 1985, as tension grew, the United States and Nicaragua angrily blamed one another for the escalating violence.

The administration's policy with Nicaragua was to use diplomatic, military, and economic pressure to force the Sandinistas either to give into the wishes of the United States or to react in a manner that escalated tension and justified a further expansion of the administration's hardline strategy and overthrow of the government. The response of the Nicaraguan government to US allegations and pressure in the fall of 1985 enhanced Washington's argument that the Sandinistas were a threat. The regime had increased military aid from the USSR, Libya, and Cuba. Ortega resorted to firebrand rhetoric in response to US claims and, despite a plea from eighty members of the United States Congress, refused to relax restrictions placed on civil liberties.[7] These choices by the Sandinista leadership played into the hands of the Reagan administration, and helped open the door to an intensification of hostilities between the two nations.

While the atmosphere worsened amid escalating hostilities and allegations of state terrorism, the international community took some important first steps on the issue. The same day that Shultz spoke suggestively about escalating hostilities against the government of Nicaragua, the UN passed a landmark resolution. The UN recognized an act of international terrorism as a crime. The resolution "unequivocally condemns, as criminal, all acts, methods and practices of terrorism wherever and by whoever committed, including those that jeopardize friendly relations among states and their security."[8] Cuba voted against the resolution, Iran abstained, but Nicaragua and other nations that the United States had alleged were state sponsors of international terrorism voted for the measure. Nicaragua and Libya argued that the UN should have specifically singled out the United States for conducting state terrorism.[9] In the days following, the Organization of American States (OAS), a Washington, DC, headquartered league of American nations that included virtually every nation in the hemisphere from Nicaragua to Brazil, passed a similar resolution that outlined "torture and terrorism as international crimes."[10] In the process, the Organization of American States labeled Nicaragua a human rights violator. As 1985 neared to a close, the United States was not alone in its concern over terrorism. The international community also recognized terrorism as a global problem.

Meanwhile, the task force revised its report, which was due for completion by December 20. The proposal formally outlined the Reagan administration's counterterrorism policy. George H. W. Bush insisted that once signed the document represented "the gospel" for the future of US counterterrorism policy.[11] Despite these bold assertions there was controversy among the members of the task force. Ambassador at Large for Counterterrorism, Robert Oakley, sent a critical letter to Executive Director James Holloway. Oakley was the head of the Office of Counterterrorism, which was located in the Department of State. During 1985, Oakley gave numerous speeches on the emergent issue of international terrorism.[12] The Ambassador was not dismissive of the issue of international terrorism. The divide between Oakley and figures like Bush and Shultz, however, was with the role of the military and the intentional exaggeration of the threat of terrorism to the people. Oakley believed in a multilateral diplomatic approach that the United States could undertake without panicking the public. He acknowledged the potential role of the military in counterterrorism strategy, but his own understanding as a diplomat was that force was only for use as a last resort. While Oakley praised the overall process and the move to get serious on the issue of terrorism, his three-page letter to Holloway was a stinging critique of the final report.

Oakley was primarily upset over the final report's reliance on the usage of active military measures. He argued that the administration framed the issue of international terrorism incorrectly, as though the use of military measures was a solution to the problem. The ambassador exclaimed, "The report and issue papers taken as a whole convey a very clear impression that there is a solution to international terrorism and that it lies primarily in the better use of active measures by the United States government. In my judgment, this is as erroneous a conclusion as it is dangerous."[13] Oakley argued that the task force was getting it all wrong. He was concerned that the report over-emphasized the credibility of military measures and threatened to ramp up public and congressional sentiments by overstating the significance of the terrorism threat. Oakley believed in a multilateral diplomatic approach that the United States could undertake without panicking the public.

On December 10, following up Oakley's letter to Holloway, the Deputy Director for Counterterrorism, Parker Borg, also sent a letter to the members of the task force assailing the approach suggested in the report. Borg was also a diplomat. He was well known for his service in Southeast Asia during the Vietnam War and to African nations Zaire and Mali.

Parker Borg and Robert Oakley did not know each other before working together in the Office of Counterterrorism. In a 2002 interview for the Association of Diplomatic Studies and Training's *Foreign Affairs Oral History Project*, Borg recollected the moment that Oakley called him and offered him the position as Deputy Director. Borg responded to Oakley's invitation, "I don't know if I have the recent experience that qualifies me for counterterrorism," and to this Oakley responded with levity, "Well neither do I, but I want you to be my deputy."[14] Like Oakley, Borg was a diplomat and preferred to approach the terrorism problem with non-military means. In 2002, Borg explained that he and Oakley had disagreed with the majority opinion in the task force on several key points.

Led by Shultz and Bush the task force report considered terrorism a problem that was uniquely connected to the Cold War and leftism, and included Marxist-revolutionaries like the Sandinistas and even drug traffickers.[15] The definition of terrorism adopted by the task force was loose and made to apply to a broad grouping of enemies associated with leftism. The statements made by Bush and Shultz at the September 18 meeting of the task force suggested that this was to facilitate the aggressive offensive policy designed to carry out the Reagan doctrine. Borg and Oakley both disagreed that the terrorism crisis was necessarily rooted in the Cold War. Parker Borg insisted there was a difference between terrorism and the actions brought on by revolutionary warfare. For this reason, Borg recalled that the Office of Counterterrorism "declined . . . to consider the various groups in Central America, the Sandinistas or El Salvador groups . . . as being terrorists per-se."[16] The Office of Counterterrorism directly resisted lumping revolutionary factions as part of the terrorism problem. The definition offered by Borg and Oakley was more specific and nuanced. This outlook, however, was doomed from the start as it ran counter to the attempts of the task force, and most significantly of Shultz and Bush, to use a loose definition of terrorism as a way of carrying out the Reagan doctrine, particularly in Central America.

The report shocked Borg. He complained that, "The report reflects a certain bias toward activist military responses to the terrorism problem which is dangerous and overly simplistic." He pointed out three specific flaws in the draft. Borg argued that the report represented a dangerous shift in US policy. He exclaimed that, "Military options are given unwarranted prominence

[and] do not accord with this country's policies or practices." According to Borg, and Oakley for that matter, the draft of the report also gave little attention to the real solution, which was multilateral and diplomatic. Borg was concerned that the task force decided to "avoid a precise definition of terrorism." This loose definition allowed the United States greater freedom to use military force in the name of counterterrorism and in the place of its choosing rather than only when warranted of the charge. Borg feared that if such information leaked, "The Soviets will have a field day with it." He further warned that the openly militaristic approach "will be disastrous for the United States if such a concept becomes known publicly." Finally, he regarded the draft as sloppy and carelessly composed. Together, the leadership in the Office of Counterterrorism agreed that the task force should rewrite the report. Borg doubted that it had the time to do such a thorough rewrite. He suggested that it request an extension from Bush of at least a month.[17]

When he received Borg's stinging memorandum NSC and task force official Bob Earl provided extensive comments directed toward the Deputy Director. Earl's thoughts on Borg's reservations to the report represented the opinion of the majority faction in the task force. Earl disagreed on the issue of military deterrence and the role of diplomacy. He insisted that "diplomatic is not the proper focus." Earl responded to the concerns of the Office of Counterterrorism by insisting that "we [the United States] gotta be up first" and take on the forces of the radical leftism. He argued that Borg's attitude was a "subjective judgment" and that his faction was "too defensive." In his view, and in that of the majority of the task force, it was time for the United States to go on the offensive. As far as Earl was concerned, the Reagan offensive was a go.[18]

The same day that Borg's concerned memo went out, December 10, Secretary of State George Shultz spoke to the Pilgrims Society in London. Shultz reiterated, though not necessarily intentionally, the position taken by Earl. The secretary argued that with communist-terrorists states like Nicaragua the problem and the solution were military. He insisted that, "Only when they see the futility of their military 'solutions' and the resolve of opposing strength will real compromise become possible." Shultz pressed for the United States to support the Contras, he argued that, "The immediate problem [was], regrettably, openly military . . . a Nicaraguan attempt to subvert neighboring countries, and Cuban combatants using Soviet weapons in Nicaragua. Diplomacy is unlikely to work, unless there is effective resistance." Shultz insisted that Nicaragua posed a national security threat as a state sponsor of international terrorism, and that the best course of action for the United States was the type of "covert action" offered by support of the Contras.[19]

Since 1984, Shultz was a primary proponent of the adoption of offensive hardline measures to deal with Nicaragua and other states alleged of sponsoring terrorism. Aspects of such a policy were legally dubious and in direct violation of Nicaragua's sovereignty. The administration's legal specialists prepared the administration's defense and so verified the challenge to international law posed by a policy of preemptive regime change perpetrated on an internationally recognized sovereign nation. The administration's legal office argued several times over the previous two years that such an approach the United States could justify, loosely, under the right to self-defense.[20] Such an argument was a weak one. The Reagan administration exaggerated the threat and oversimplified the causes of terrorism in the world. The Sandinistas were not a significant threat to the United States. It was true that Nicaragua received arms and aid from the Soviet Union, Cuba and Libya, and that the Sandinistas had a substantial military that worried neighboring states. However, these developments, most likely, were not because the Nicaraguans were part of a grand plot by global leftists to destroy freedom and undermine the United States. Instead, Nicaragua reacted to a long legacy of US imperialism and exploitation and the more recent hostility of the Reagan administration, which through the CIA and the Contras had made war on the Sandinistas since the beginning of Reagan's presidency.

The positions of both Parker Borg and Robert Oakley represented a minority opinion. These two top officials in the State Department's counterterrorism office correctly criticized the administration for exaggerating and oversimplifying the terrorism threat. Borg believed it was incorrect to equate guerrilla insurgency and leftist revolutionary states with the terrorism problem. Likewise, Oakley did accept that there was an issue with leftists and terrorism, but he did not accept that the two were mutually exclusive or that all revolutionary leftists were terrorists.[21] Borg and other members of the Office of Counterterrorism believed that the administration was misconstruing the scope of the terrorism crisis.[22] The administration was intentionally panicking the public. Regardless of their positions as terrorism specialists, their views regarding the administration's war on terrorism and hardline policy against Nicaragua were in vain because the administration's top figures did not agree. Shultz proposed that a military course of action was the best form of deterrent against state sponsors of terrorism. Others like Attorney General Edwin Meese supported Shultz and labeled Nicaragua a "terrorist country club" and part of an international conspiracy to undermine the Western world.[23] To the dismay of Borg and Oakley, the leadership argued that this was not a time for diplomacy but rather a time for military action against Nicaragua. The Reagan administration was committed to a policy of regime change.

As a capstone to its call for military escalation and regime change in Nicaragua, President Reagan spoke to the nation. At 12:06 pm on December 14, 1985, President Reagan gave a radio address to the nation. Speaking from the Oval Office, he began the speech as he often did, "My fellow

Americans." In the speech, he ushered a call for the increased use of force against Nicaragua. In his grandfather-like tone, he explained to the American people that a Sandinista crackdown on civil liberties was evidence of domestic human rights abuses. Enhancing allegations that linked the Nicaraguan government to anti-western terror groups, the president alleged the repression of Christians by the Islamist-friendly Sandinistas. Reagan lamented the present danger of "Nicaragua transformed into an international aggressor nation, a base for subversion and terror." He insisted that Nicaragua was a sanctuary for radical terrorist groups and communist bloc members. Further, Reagan argued, as Shultz had already done, that Nicaragua helped facilitate the M-19 attack on the Colombian Supreme Court and the June killings in San Salvador. The president urged support for the Contras exclaiming that, "If Nicaragua can get material support from communist states and terrorist regimes and prop up a hated communist dictatorship, should not the forces fighting for liberation, now numbering 20,000, be entitled to more effective help in their struggle for freedom?" These so-called freedom fighters were the primary offensive weapon that the administration employed to attack communist-terrorist states across the developing world from Central America to Afghanistan and to Africa.[24]

Not surprisingly, Reagan's speech was not a fair description of reality. The speech like those made by George Shultz was part of a propaganda offensive that involved the use of rhetoric designed to manipulate the meaning of the conflict. Because the Cold War model of national security grounded the administration's counterterrorism approach policy makers believed that negotiation with communist-terrorists was futile. Terrorism resulted in an increased understanding of the danger and urgency of the Cold War and this factored centrally into the renewed offensive push against Nicaragua. However, because the administration defined the terrorism problem from the standpoint of global bipolarity, the problem was oversimplified, and any pursuit of fair diplomacy was ignored from the beginning. The support for M-19 that the administration alleged was actually the presence of a handful of small arms that originated in Nicaragua, and there was no evidence to suggest that the Sandinista government played any direct role in planning the attack.[25] Blinded by its acceptance of a global struggle against leftism the leadership in the Reagan administration sought any means to pursue its war of regime change. As propaganda and a powerful rhetoric, terrorism was used to exaggerate threat and help justify the use of hardline measures by panicking the American people over the nature of threat in the world.

Despite the criticisms from Robert Oakley and Parker Borg, the task force's final report went ahead as scheduled. The statements made by Bush, Shultz, Reagan, Earl and Meese suggested that the majority in the NSC, Department of State, and the task force believed that the United States should escalate military operations against states like Nicaragua. On December 20,

1985, the task force's recommendations went to President Reagan. One month later Reagan signed "National Security Decision Directive Number 207: The National Program for Combatting Terrorism" (NSDD-207) and made the report of the task force official policy.[26] The administration implemented the new policy in the following months.

In addition to economic sanctions, the framework that the task force developed centered on several military options. These included support for insurgents, unilateral military strikes, clandestine operations of sabotage and assassination, and military and naval maneuvers designed to threaten, provoke, and/or act as a cloak for other military operations.[27] The administration re-affirmed a "no-concessions policy."[28] This meant that the United States refused to negotiate with terrorists and state sponsors, and that the alleged illegitimacy of states like Nicaragua meant that the United States would not step to the table for fair negotiations. The consequence for relations with Nicaragua was that the administration continued to refuse to seek legitimate negotiations first, and instead promoted a military oriented policy. The directive insisted that, "The U.S. government considers the practice of terrorism . . . a threat to our national security . . . and is prepared to act in concert with other nations or unilaterally when necessary to prevent or respond to terrorist acts."[29] Further, the document pledged, "States that practice terrorism or actively support it, will not be allowed to do so without consequence."[30] To deal with this threat, "The entire range of diplomatic, economic, legal, military, paramilitary, covert action, and informational assets at our disposal must be brought to bear against terrorism."[31] In order to deter and defeat the alleged state sponsors the Reagan administration asserted a hardline that included restrictive economic measures, and an entire range of military options.

The Reagan administration used the unique national security threat posed by state sponsors of terrorism to assert a policy that tested the boundaries of accepted international behavior. Despite the sovereign status of Nicaragua, and the absence of a US declaration of war, the Reagan administration pursued a policy that authorized overt proxy war within that country as well as any other state that was allegedly involved in the criminal act of international terrorism. Terrorism provoked a shift in US Cold War policy. The administration believed that the categorization of a state as a sponsor of terrorism authorized a range of offensive measures. Despite a technical status of peace, the new policy rested on measures that violated the international sovereign rights of a nation not at war with the United States. For the Reagan administration, though, this was not a violation of rights, but was behavior necessary to deal with the criminal actions of these governments. The assertion that these nations were committing crimes stood as the primary justification for a US interventionist policy. It insisted that complicity in terrorism amounted to a dismissal of international sovereign rights and an expansion of the principal of self-defense.

Because of the proposal for offensive measures against alleged criminal states, the administration remained acutely aware of the need to convince the American people of the danger. The task force created the position "Deputy Directory for Public Diplomacy" to oversee the expanded conduct of this vital element of the administration's policy that was now largely hinged on the application of the rhetoric of terrorism.[32] This was a year of controversy and war. To help prepare the American people for what lay ahead the task force published a public version of the report scheduled for release on March 6, 1986. The administration sought to sell its story to the American people.

On February 12, Robert Oakley penned another short letter of concern, this time to Bush's adviser, Donald Gregg. Oakley was concerned about the nature of the public report. He was again dismayed: the draft of the report he feared did not emphasize the need for international diplomatic cooperation, but rather the unilateral military power of the United States. Oakley spoke for the Office of Counterterrorism when he pleaded with Gregg to have Bush look over the report and revise it so that it emphasized international cooperation more and unilateral military power less. Oakley appealed to the astuteness of Vice President Bush and exclaimed, "Some of our (Office of Counterterrorism) additions put emphasis on the international angle, a point which the Vice President has frequently made and where he has been much more enlightened than others in accentuating the limitations on our unilateral capabilities."[33] This remark indicated Oakley's dissatisfaction with the majority opinion in the task force, and appealed to Bush's intelligence. As the United States stood on the precipice of a war the Office of Counterterrorism looked on dismayed at the proposed path.

At the outset of 1986, the United States was poised to focus the new counterterrorism policy at Nicaragua. The "Public Report of the Vice President's Task Force on Combatting Terrorism" explained the policy to Congress and the public. Parker Borg had argued that the only effective approach was one that addressed the situation as a global problem and not as a simplistic conspiracy against the United States, but rather one that was relevant to nations throughout the world.[34] He criticized the American-centric nature of the task force's official report, but the leadership did not acknowledge these criticisms. The public report suffered from these same maladies. While speaking at times of multilateralism, the report was American centered and considered the United States response the most critical.[35]

The public report acknowledged that the administration had reacted to an escalation of international terrorist incidents. In particular, the June TWA hijacking and the killing of six Americans in San Salvador the authors insisted had pushed the administration to act. However, while Oakley and Borg were concerned about overdramatizing the issue, the authors decided to do exactly that and, apparently, because of an intention to create a consensus for a more broad array of military action. The majority opinion in the task force wished to use the rhetoric of terrorism as a vehicle to create fear and justify a more offensive and hardline US policy. The proposal insisted that, "During the past decade, terrorists have attacked U.S. officials or installations abroad approximately once every seventeen days. In the past seventeen years, terrorists have killed as many US diplomats as were killed in the previous 180 years."[36] This statement was an intentional exaggeration of the danger of the threat. There was at this time a terrorism crisis, even critics like Parker Borg and Robert Oakley were acutely aware and concerned about this crisis. However, these two wanted to move quietly and not arouse public opinion. Later, in the 1990s Oakley praised the Clinton administration for working to counter the terrorist threat without creating a panic over the matter.[37] However, those promoting a military solution to the problem of state sponsored terrorism in the Reagan administration hoped to use propaganda surrounding terrorism to arouse the concern of Congress and the public and provide a vehicle for the pursuit of offensive measures against the enemies of the United States. The purpose of public diplomacy was to change the dialogue over Cold War conflicts like the one in Nicaragua. In order for this to work the task force wanted Congress and the American people to feel that the issue was an urgent and global offensive launched against the United States. Terrorism was a rhetorical weapon that if used correctly could criminalize an enemy and justify a strong US response. The architects of the administration's policy understood this and used the danger of terrorism as an opportunity to get people behind the Reagan offensive.

As with the classified report, the document did not acknowledge the opinions of Borg and Oakley. Both expressed a concern that the task force understood the solution to the problem primarily in military terms. Shortly after Oakley's memo to Donald Gregg in early February, Bush penned his own summation of the findings of the terrorism task force. According to Bush, both he and President Reagan "recognized that the time had come to place the emphasis on more active measures, to take the offensive against terrorists and those who support them."[38] The section in the public report titled "U.S. Policy and Response to Terrorists" further emphasized this point and showed that Borg and Oakley's concerns were secondary. The response proposed to the American people was a militaristic approach that dismissed effective diplomacy. The report insisted that terrorism was a crime perpetrated by "international criminals."[39] Tactics such as preemptive strikes and unilateral military action, both overt and covert, the task force regarded as the best methods of deterrence. According to the report, "Our principles of justice will not permit random retaliation against groups or countries. However, when perpetrators of terrorism can be identified and located, our policy is to act against terrorism . . . unilaterally when necessary to prevent or respond to terrorist acts. A successful deterrent strategy may require judicious employment of military force."[40] By and large, the task force did not heed the criticism of Borg and Oakley, but acknowledged that the unilateral military approach against a sovereign nation challenged the accepted norms of international behavior. The task force insisted that the allegation of criminality justified such actions on the grounds of the self-defense of the United States and its allies.[41]

Despite the concern of Borg and Oakley, it was not surprising that the task force did not take their advice. Secretary of State George Shultz and Vice President George H. W. Bush were leading architects of the development of the offensive against the alleged forces of international terrorism. Both of these top officials argued that the use of force was necessary to send a message and warn state sponsors. Throughout 1984 and 1985, the Secretary spoke frequently about the need for the United States to adopt active measures.[42] These measures involved non-military avenues that the Office of Counterterrorism agreed with. However, the majority in the task force also emphasized the importance of using military options as a way of deterring state sponsors.[43] Since the architects of this war on terror insisted that military force was a prerequisite to addressing the problem of state sponsorship, it was not surprising that they ignored the opinions of two wary diplomats in the Office of Counterterrorism.

Because of the dominance of hardliners in the NSC over matters of counterterrorism Robert Oakley asked Shultz to allow him to step down from his position. Shultz complied by making his post a two-year appointment allowing his term to end after 1986. Oakley's exasperation over the use of hardline and active measures to combat terrorism was due to the fact that the NSC was driving counterterrorism rather than the State Department Office of Counterterrorism. Individuals like Shultz and Bush were the top agents when it came to promoting active measures that involved preemption against state sponsors of terrorism. According to Oakley, Shultz was considered the principle figure when it came to counterterrorism. However, the actual events on the ground, the particular actions, fell on Oliver North and John Poindexter. When it came to the use of unsavory and illegal operations, North and Poindexter often cut the top leadership out of the loop and pursued counterterrorism in their own way and in a manner that they believed was consistent with the ideas of active measures that Shultz and Bush had promoted for the previous few years. It is impossible to know whether or not Shultz and Bush supported the particular measures that North undertook, but there is little question that North believed his operations were consistent with the public speeches and private statements made by Shultz as well as the ideas expressed by the task force. North's actions included, among other things, the use of terrorism to combat terrorists, kidnapping and assassination within sovereign states, and, of course, ultimately backroom dealings that eventually led to the emergence of the weapons for hostages and Contra support funding operations ultimately known as the Iran-Contra scandal. Oakley, aware of these developments, saved his career by leaving the Office of Counterterrorism. George Shultz, despite being a longtime and leading proponent of active measures of preemption and force against and within sovereign nations, was ultimately able to assert that he did not support the specific details of Iran-Contra and preserved his credibility. However, it was to a substantial extent his own rhetoric and perspective on combatting terrorism that provided the impetus for the behavior of NSC underlings like Oliver North.[44]

In the early months of 1986, the Reagan administration implemented its offensive policy against Nicaragua. The first step involved a renewal of the gritty legislative battle to obtain congressional authorization for military aid to the Contras. The administration had sought funding for these anti-Sandinista guerrillas since 1983, when the Boland restrictions were first enacted. Concerns over international terrorism and the intensified propaganda offensive designed to implicate Nicaragua as a state sponsor enhanced the renewed pursuit of this funding in 1986. On February 25, Reagan formally asked Congress to provide $100 million in funding for the Contras, the majority of which was for lethal support. According to Reagan, the aid was desperately needed because, "The Nicaraguan communists will steadily intensify their efforts to crush all opposition to their tyranny, consolidating their ability to use Nicaragua . . . as a base for further intimidating the democratic nations of Central America and spreading subversion and terrorism in our hemisphere."[45] The new policy against terrorism demanded that the United States target the most active, threatening, and vulnerable state sponsors. The Sandinista government was an ideal target for the Reagan offensive. The country was small, relatively weak, located close to the United States' border and the Panama Canal, and already immersed in a conflict with the Contras.

The rationale behind the United States' action against alleged state sponsors was that international terrorism was a war crime, and that regardless of national sovereignty, its criminal behavior warranted offensive measures and a break from the pursuit of containment. This was the central premise for the construction of the administration's new offensive framework of intervention. On March 5, Ambassador at Large and Director of the Office of Counterterrorism Robert Oakley delivered a message to the British at the US-UK Bilateral Meeting on Terrorism. The confidential statement was from Deputy Secretary of State, John Whitehead, and clearly emphasized the shift in US policy on the issue of terrorism and the Cold War. He asserted that the "USG [US government] has concluded that the past approach has not yielded adequate results, [and we] must move to [a] more active, offensive policy."[46] The statement continued, "Numbers and casualties of international terrorism demonstrate who is winning despite our intensified, defensive, containment approach."[47] Ironically, one of the stronger critics of such a policy had the responsibility for delivering the message that acknowledged the launch of Washington's offensive war on terrorism.

The following day, Vice President George H. W. Bush and Admiral James Holloway held a news conference and announced the release of the public report of the terrorism task force. Despite the looming storm of a US offensive the two gave orchestrated and cautious summations of the terrorism policy. Even though the policy directives positioned military options at the forefront, Bush and Holloway barely implied the concept of military force in their opening statements. Instead, they spoke of diplomacy, improved intelligence, extradition, and better cooperation with international allies. The public report contained these subjects, but it also placed emphasis on the importance of the application of unilateral military force.[48] When asked by members of the media on the role of the use of force, Admiral Holloway gave few specifics, but acknowledged that the task force and the administration considered the use of unilateral military force a necessary option of the new policy.[49] The press conference provided subtle evidence that the United States was preparing for an offensive.[50]

At the news conference Admiral Holloway did offer a few details that revealed specifically which government the United States directed its focus. Of all the countries and regions that the task force considered at risk or involved with international terrorism, he spoke briefly only about Latin America, specifically Nicaragua and Cuba. Admiral Holloway insisted that, "More terrorist acts were directed at U.S. citizens in Latin America last year than in any other region. Both Nicaragua and Cuba have been implicated in terrorist activity in Latin America."[51] This statement when coupled with recently declassified documents makes it clear that the White House planned to direct its counterterrorism offensive against Nicaragua. If there were any doubt that the Reagan administration positioned Nicaragua at the center of its war on terrorism this public revelation was confirmation. Of all the possible targets from Libya, to Syria, Iran, Yemen, and so on, the only one that Holloway and Bush felt worthy of mention was Nicaragua and its alleged mentor, Cuba. One of the first targets of the war on terror was Central America.

Pursuit of congressional authorization for lethal support for the Contras and the use of this guerrilla group was not the only way that the Reagan administration moved against Nicaragua. The power of surrogate guerrilla forces, like the Contras, was only one aspect of the new policy framework for the use of force against alleged state sponsors of terrorism created by the task force. The new framework included not only the use of insurgent guerrilla war, but also "conventional land maneuvers" in neighboring countries. If a friendly government bordered an offender state, the task force determined that the United States could conduct military maneuvers and construction projects "in close proximity to the offending group/state." The operations acted as "a stern warning to an offending sponsor state" and provided the potential opportunity for the conduct of "special operations against terrorist groups using exercise as a guise." This was a plan of threat, provocation, and deception. In order for this to work, though, the presence of a friendly host nation was required. Central America was the perfect location for the implementation of this style approach.[52]

The new framework of intervention that the task force constructed was a culmination of ideas that were developed over a number of years, and the concept of provocation was no different. In the context of the Reagan offensive, National Security Adviser Oliver North first offered the idea that the United States could provoke the Sandinistas and bait the government into giving the United States a justification for escalation in 1985. North, unknown to the public at the time, was involved in the clandestine funding operations of the Contras. On July 15, 1985, North submitted a secret proposal titled "U.S. Political Military Strategy for Nicaragua." The document was a detailed outline for how the United States could launch an offensive and overthrow the government of Nicaragua via the Contras. North suggested that "should the Sandinista military invade either Honduras or Costa Rica" the Reagan administration would gain much greater support for Contra aid and even "a U.S. invasion of Nicaragua." The task force incorporated this kind of thinking into its counterterrorism framework of intervention and the administration acted on it in the spring of 1986.[53]

Honduras made possible the implementation of a plan eerily reminiscent of North's suggestion the prior year. The small nation bordered Nicaragua, and was an American ally, albeit, one that was increasingly uncomfortable about the US-led conflict. In March, the United States began major conventional military maneuvers along the border of Nicaragua. These included the construction of an airstrip capable of handling military aircraft and parachute drops of Honduran troops only a matter of miles from Nicaragua's northern border. Already convinced of the need to take offensive military action against Nicaragua, the White House used the operations as a show of force. Per the implication from NSDD-207 the operations might either compel the Sandinistas to change its tune or, more likely, to respond militarily to the provocation.[54] This was a first step in initiating an offensive hardline policy designed to force the Nicaraguan government into submission on the terms of the United States.

With these operations underway, President Reagan pleaded with Congress and the American people to fund the Contras. March was full of controversy as the administration pushed Congress to authorize offensive operations against Nicaragua. At noon on March 8, President Reagan gave his weekly radio address on Nicaragua. He began, "My fellow Americans, I want to speak to you today about our request to help the Nicaraguan freedom fighters."[55] The president emphasized, as he had numerous times since 1983, that Sandinista aggression presented a national security threat directly in the United States' backyard. The language in this speech, however, reflected the growing concern over international terrorism. He insisted that the Sandinistas violated the civil liberties of the Nicaraguan people. Reagan pressed Congress for aid by arguing that, "This dictatorship now becomes more dangerous as a flood of weapons and manpower pour in from the Soviet bloc and their cold blooded allies the PLO and Libya."[56] Reagan insisted that support for the so-called freedom fighters was the only way that the United States could prevent the regional subversion allegedly directed by Nicaragua.

The following week, the public diplomacy onslaught continued. On Thursday, March 14, Reagan conducted a briefing from the White House. The next day at noon he again focused the attention of his weekly radio address to the issue of Nicaragua. These two briefs, however, were only a prelude to his appearance that weekend. On Saturday night, Reagan appeared on primetime television and his speech again insisted that Nicaragua was a terrorist threat, and a tyrannical criminal nation. Reagan pledged that military force alone could prevent the consolidation of "a second Cuba, a second Libya on the doorstep of the United States." He feared that there was little time to act because, "Gathered in Nicaragua already are thousands of Cuban military advisors, contingents of Soviet and East German and all the elements of international terror-from the PLO to Italy's Red Brigade. Why are they there? Because as Colonel Qadhafi has publically exalted: Nicaragua means a great thing, it means fighting America near its borders . . . fighting America at its doorstep."[57] Reagan hoped this hyperbolic language could build support for the offensive in Congress and the public. After two weeks of pressure, Congress did not heed the administration's plea. Shortly following this round of speeches, the Democrat controlled House of Representatives responded by again voting against the aid.

Undoubtedly, the tense atmosphere helped make this a very close vote. The legislation failed by merely twelve votes, which was closer than ever. Reagan's public diplomacy team had contracted a polling and statistics group out of McLean, Virginia, *Decision/Making/Information*, to determine what went wrong. According to the report, Reagan was successful in convincing Americans that the Sandinistas were a security threat. The allegation of terrorism had created a sense of fear and unease in the United States. Nonetheless, the press for aid to the Contras appeared to hurt, at least slightly, the administration's position. Americans did not like the Sandinistas, but they did not like the Contras either. Following the President's primetime speech, only 26 percent of those polled possessed favorable perceptions of the Contras. 52 percent of Americans believed that Nicaragua would accept Soviet nuclear missiles, and 47 percent believed that the Sandinistas backed the

PLO and Libya in its terrorism campaigns. The public diplomacy campaign successfully created fear about the alleged threat posed by Nicaragua. Most Americans, though, still thought that aid to the Contras might open the door to a Vietnam-like conflict. 61 percent of those polled agreed with the rejection of aid by the House of Representatives. Many Americans believed that the Sandinistas were a dangerous communist-terrorist threat, but they were also concerned about the potential development of US military involvement and the in-propriety of the United States' ally.[58]

Two factors figured centrally into the position of the House of Representatives and the American public on aid to the Contras. First, while the Sandinistas were allegedly involved in escalating terrorist and subversive activities throughout the region there was little recent evidence that suggested that the president's fear invoking rhetoric was accurate. At that time, the Nicaraguan government was holding talks with regional nations in pursuit of a peace proposal, and it had not been involved in any major publicized act of aggression beyond its borders in 1986. Many Americans perceived the Reagan administration as unnecessarily escalating the situation when a diplomatic solution was possible. Second, although polled Americans liked the Sandinistas less than they did the Contras, Americans held neither group highly.[59] Americans read the reports and accounts of the guerrillas involved in human rights abuses, and the public did not accept the idea that these allies were noble "freedom fighters." The Monday following Reagan's speech the PBS news program, *Frontline*, aired a report titled "Who's Running this War?" The program depicted the Contras as little more than a right-wing funded band of mercenaries comprised primarily of former members of Somoza's reviled National Guard. Members of Congress and the American public were concerned about war and the intentions of the administration's ally.[60]

Despite the failure in March, the struggle for aid to the Contras as part of the United States offensive was not over. On March 25, less than a week after the House narrowly rejected military aid to the Contras in the first round of the year's military appropriations battles, the Nicaraguan government, undoubtedly provoked by US-Honduran military maneuvers and Contra activity, invaded the territory of Honduras. The report, first released by the White House, was that the Sandinistas had unleashed a significant military offensive against rebel base areas within neighboring Honduras. Roughly 1,000 Sandinista troops were engaged in major battles as far as twenty miles inside Honduran territory. The Nicaraguan offensive began with sporadic low intensity fighting on March 17.[61] The area of the assault was a Honduran border region that jutted slightly into Nicaragua. It was a lightly populated jungle region that was only accessible by a few remote dirt roads. This was a central operational headquarters for the US-backed rebels. Reporters described the fighting as intense and casualties measured in the hundreds. The Sandinista armed forces caught the US-backed guerrillas by surprise, and

Figure 7.1.   A member of the 317th combat control team overseas parachute drops during the CABANAS 1986 operations near the Honduran-Nicaraguan border. *Source*: National Archives and Records Administration.

Sandinista soldiers breached the base perimeter. However, the recently re-supplied Contras responded effectively with an estimated death toll of 200 Sandinistas and 40 Contras.[62]

The attack was encouraged by US military maneuvers. The maneuvers that March, named CABANAS 86, were the third such operations in the past three years. BIG PINE in 1984 and CABANAS 85 preceded the 1986 maneuvers. These operations were directly connected to the United States efforts with the Contras and in supporting the government of El Salvador, and an increasing militarization of the region. The United States built six military airstrips in Honduras during this period. The airstrips were used for threatening United States military maneuvers, resupply of the Contras, the flight of drones over El Salvador to monitor guerrilla activity, and other associated activities. These operations represented an escalation of the military effort against Nicaragua. The 1986 maneuvers were the most provocative to date and involved parachute drops only a few miles from Nicaragua's borders. The operations culminated in war games simulations of a US invasion of Nicaragua. These types of operations suggested a dangerous escalation, and over the next two years Honduras launched multiple airstrikes on Sandinista armed forces in operations against Contra militants, a testament to the escalation caused by this pivotal moment from 1985 to 1986. The administration designed these operations to threaten Nicaragua and drive an escalation of the conflict. An escalation that the administration blamed on Nicaragua and provided an opportunity to further vilify the leadership and gain Congressional authorization for lethal support to the Reagan administration's proxies.[63]

According to the military options that the task force recommended to President Reagan, military maneuvers near a state was one way of putting an outlaw state on notice. For dealing with an alleged state sponsor of terrorism, the task force recommended "conventional land maneuvers [conducted] in close proximity to the offending group/state." The purpose was to issue "a stern warning to an offending sponsor state" but also as a way to conduct "special operations . . . using exercise as a guise."[64] This was, basically, the same approach suggested by Oliver North the year prior. The Reagan administration put this plan of attack into operation against Nicaragua in the spring of 1986, and provoked the Sandinistas to launch a counterattack against the Contras likely out of fear that the United States was preparing to attack Nicaragua.

After the Sandinista offensive began, US aviators flew Honduran troops to the front line. The Honduran forces did not engage in battle, but took defensive positions in case the operation expanded. Fifty US pilots used four twin-rotor Chinook and ten Huey helicopters to airlift a battalion of Honduran artillery and infantry units toward the area of fighting.[65] When the attack occurred the Reagan administration, against the opinion of the Honduran

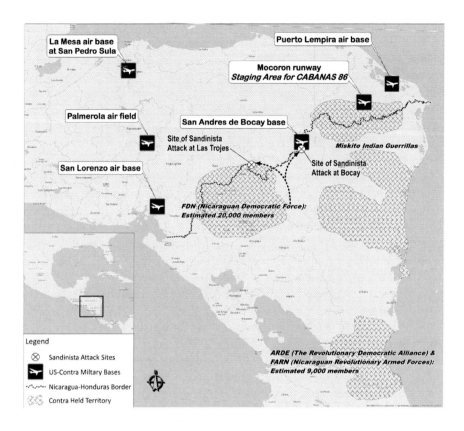

Figure 7.2.   The Nicaraguan invasion of Honduras, March 1986. *Source:* **James Scanlon.**

government, published the news and attempted to capitalize publically on the idea of Nicaraguan aggression. Top ranking, anonymous, Honduran officials confirmed to reporters that the Nicaraguan attack was not a serious threat, and that the Reagan administration encouraged the invasion and sought to use it to gain funding for the Contras.[66] While the administration denied the allegations, evidence only recently declassified from the terrorism task force suggest that the allegations were likely accurate. As part of the administration's offensive on state sponsors of terrorism the United States used provocative maneuvers near a targeted state as a way of justifying military escalation. The Reagan administration applied this approach against Nicaragua. The administration hoped that this provocation would lead to acceptance by Congress and the American people of the need for further military oriented policies and affirm the support of the Contras.

The Nicaraguan invasion left Congress dismayed. The Sandinista offensive developed just prior to the upcoming Senate vote on aid for the Contras, and some of Reagan's opponents suspected that the news report was a trumped up charge on the part of the administration. As the events unfolded, though, it was clear that the event was all too real. The Honduran government requested US support, and the Reagan administration responded by providing $20 million in emergency aid.[67] While the Government of Honduras technically denied the presence of the Contras in its territory and wanted to have little to do with Washington's operation, the government also pledged to defend the country and sought US support privately. Following this development opponents of the Reagan administration's policy lamented the turn of events. Washington State congressman, Tom Foley (D), remarked that, "I can't express my dismay enough at what's happened. . . . It was a close vote before, and this turn of events is likely to make it more difficult [to deny the president]."[68]

Shortly following the Sandinista offensive the Senate voted 53 to 47 in favor of providing military aid to the Contras. Prior to the House vote, Democrat House Speaker Thomas (Tip) O'Neill declared that his body would vote on the appropriation a second time.[69] Following the offensive, many believed that the administration had the necessary votes from moderate Democrats and Republicans in the House.[70] The military action was further proof, to many, that the administration's allegations about Nicaragua were correct. Little did they know that the events were the result of a US offensive policy against Nicaragua. Once the actions drew a Sandinista attack, the Reagan administration publicized it and sought to use it to build support for its policy of regime change.

After the Honduran raid lethal aid to the Contras received a renewed push in Congress. The Sandinista invasion seemed to prove the accuracy of the United States' claims. According to *Decision/Making/Information*, Reagan's primetime speech prior to the Honduran raid was not as widely watched as previous speeches and the president did not gain significant support for his Contra aid plan despite his intense allegations of its role as a state sponsor of international terrorism. However, after the Honduran raid the president experienced a 7 percent jump in support of his handling of the situation in Nicaragua. When asked, "Do you approve or disapprove of the way Ronald Reagan is handling the situation in Nicaragua," 46 percent of those polled said yes.[71] This represented a significant change over a two-week period and with 44 percent disapproving it marked the first time Reagan possessed a positive approval rating on the situation. Even House Speaker Tip O'Neill, the most visible opponent of support for the Contras, expressed his view of Ortega as a "bumbling, incompetent, Marxist-Leninist communist."[72] The position of the House of Representatives on aid to the Contras remained uncertain, and a majority of Americans still believed that Congress should not aid the

Contras, but the Honduran raid improved the administration's position with Congress and the public on the issue.[73]

The accusation of state sponsorship of international terrorism coupled with secretive military action against Nicaragua as part of the administration's war on terror escalated the conflict in Central America and helped build opposition to the Nicaraguan government in the United States. The new war was, however, not limited to Nicaragua. The Sandinista government was one of two states targeted by the United States in 1986: Libya was the other. Coordinated with US military maneuvers on the border of Nicaragua, the Reagan administration also provoked a Libyan attack on US naval vessels conducting maneuvers in the Gulf of Sidra, an area that Libya openly avowed as its territorial waters. Naval operations were, like conventional land maneuvers, another aspect of this war against state sponsored terrorism. According to the framework of intervention developed by the task force, "[a] naval demonstration of strength [was] useful against sponsoring states."[74]

Like the US-Honduran maneuvers, the operations in the Gulf of Sidra provoked a response from Libya. The Libyans attempted to shoot down US navy planes and the United States responded with an assault on missile sites in Libya, and on April 15, the United States followed this with a unilateral strike on that government, an attempt to assassinate Muammar Gaddafi, in response to a terrorist attack on a German discotheque frequented by US servicemen. For the first time, the United States had, in the name of counterterrorism, openly sought to assassinate the leader of another sovereign nation. Of course, Gaddafi had directed a terrorist attack against US servicemen and there existed widespread support for this action. Even Robert Oakley considered the attack justified.[75] However, in the short term Gaddafi's attack in Germany was a response to an American provocation in the Gulf of Sidra and a military engagement based on what it perceived as a blatant violation of its own sovereignty. Regardless of how much one can play a 'who started it' back and forth the reality was clear, the United States was using terrorism to fight terrorism and had set aside recognition of national sovereignty and international law in favor of preemptive hardline measures and retaliation against a state that it was not formally at war with. By no means am I defending Libya, its behavior was unacceptable. However, for the supposed leader of human rights in the world the United States should have pursued justice through legal channels. However, it was more interested in attempting to solve its problems with overt force and violations of sovereignty and international law and so it undertook overt actions of war and assassination each of which would find a lesser nation reprimanded on charges of war crimes.

In a document released in 2012, National Security advisor John Poindexter acknowledged that the Libyan strike was part of a successful operation against state sponsors of terrorism. Poindexter was integral in the illegal

Contra aid program, and acted as Oliver North's superior in the clandestine support operation. In a memo to Reagan, Poindexter acknowledged that the "unilateral military action . . . decreased terrorism at the source by putting state sponsors on notice."[76] While many Americans remained skeptical of support for the Contras, the Libyan and Nicaraguan provocations together represented a US war on terrorism. As a result, the Reagan administration, apparently facing a urgent global crisis, was in the strongest position to deliver a vital aspect of its policy, authorization of lethal aid to the Contras.

The events during the first several months of 1986 represented operational aspects of a war on terrorism. The task force outlined a policy against state sponsors that relied on the application of the entire spectrum of military options. The administration wanted to use force to deter alleged state sponsors throughout the world. The use of military maneuvers and surrogate guerrilla units was one option for deterring state sponsors. From the outset of 1986, the United States zeroed in on Nicaragua. The administration pressed for long sought congressional aid to the Contras, and further escalated hostilities against the Nicaraguan government by using provocative conventional military maneuvers and vilifying the Sandinistas with the criminalizing rhetoric of terrorism.

The pursuit of a military solution with Nicaragua in 1986 was a dangerous course of action. Despite the pleas of Parker Borg and Robert Oakley to pursue an evenhanded diplomacy that relied on better intelligence and multilateral cooperation, the United States sought a military solution. The administration did not emphasize exhausting diplomatic options first, but rather used military and naval maneuvers to provoke violence and justify its prior decision to apply a policy of force. Shortly after the United States' provocation of Nicaragua, the Central American peace talks collapsed amid heightened tension between Nicaragua and Honduras. In the United States, Congress moved toward passage of lethal support to the Contras. By the fall of 1986, the expansion of military measures led the Reagan administration into the most damaging political controversy since Watergate. Iran-Contra was only one of the problems created by the pursuit of a military offensive rather than a sound diplomacy.[77]

In order to understand the Reagan offensive one must recognize the role that the rhetoric of international terrorism and the perception that it represented a global national security threat played in making this possible. The Reagan offensive represented the United States' first modern war on terror. Bush's task force created the structure for an aggressive offensive against states that allegedly sanctioned acts of international terrorism. Parker Borg and Robert Oakley struggled to avert the implementation of a policy founded on unilateral militarism, but the majority in the administration and the task force ignored their pleas. The result was a policy that positioned military options as the key to dealing with the threat of international terrorism rather than measures that promised long-term solutions through non-military means. Despite the concerns of officials in the Office of Counterterrorism, the United States fashioned a strategy for dealing with state sponsors of international terrorism that disregarded diplomacy, cast-off the containment policy and challenged the accepted norms of international behavior by openly violating the sovereignty of a government that the international community acknowledged as legitimate.[78]

The Reagan administration was well aware that its policy of regime change in Nicaragua posed a challenge to long held principles of international law and sovereignty. The administration, however, rationalized that the threat of international terrorism meant that this old system was no longer applicable, and that the United States needed to interpret self-defense more liberally. To the Reagan administration international terrorism represented a new phase in the Cold War. It reflected an expanded threat from a loose alliance of communist and terrorist states. These agents, the administration believed, conducted a terror war against the United States and its allies throughout the developing world. Because of its geographical closeness and history within a US empire few areas were as important to officials in Washington as Central America. This development drove the Reagan administration to adopt an offensive military strategy to combat the unpredictable threat of international terrorism conducted, allegedly, from regional powers like Nicaragua. This was the Reagan offensive, but it was more than a new way of fighting the Cold War. It was built on a framework of intervention for the United States to follow in the post–Cold War world. This model rested on the idea that the United States possessed the right to define self-defense and terrorism broadly and to use this as a justification for the use of preemption and regime change of the governments of sovereign states.[79]

For officials in the Reagan administration, the unpredictable and psychological power of this new threat demanded offensive measures. As a product of the Cold War, the administration's counterterrorism policy did not reflect a multi-polar view of the world or the long-term solutions to problems of domestic inequality and violence. Rather than address local and regional divides, officials in Washington reacted to the threat from the standpoint of bipolarity and the short-term gains of military action. Many recognized that ideologically terrorists and communists possessed only loose ties, but policy makers still could not escape the tendency to affiliate the two in a grand anti-US conspiracy orchestrated by radical leftism. To justify this policy, the Reagan administration employed the language of terrorism as a rhetorical device that further undermined the credibility of the Nicaraguan government. This was the Reagan offensive, a legally dubious and aggressive military offensive, which violated national sovereignty and tested the bounds of international behavior while simultaneously using propaganda to undermine the credibility of the Nicaraguan leadership and create an atmosphere of fear and urgency in the United States that might create a willingness to accept a policy of regime change.

NOTES

1. The Mi-8 was one of the most widely produced military helicopters. Most were manufactured in the Soviet Union and like the US Huey, it served as both a troop transport and gunship. These were used widely during the late Cold War by allies of the Soviet Union.

2. "Copter Crash Kills 14, Nicaragua Says," *Los Angeles Times*, December 5, 1985, http://ntserver1.wsulibs.wsu.edu:2184/docview/292211283?accountid=14902.

3. "Shultz: Cubans Fight in Nicaragua," *Philadelphia Daily News*, December 6, 1985, http://search.proquest.com/docview/428824174?accountid=14902.

4. "Shultz: Cubans Fight in Nicaragua," *Philadelphia Daily News*, December 6, 1985.

5. W. R. Long, "Ortega Hints at US of Missiles in El Salvador," *Los Angeles Times*, December 7, 1985, http://search.proquest.com/docview/292206707?accountid=14902.

6. State and Defense Department briefing book, June 1986, Folder "The Challenge to Democracy in Central America," Box 16, David S. Addington: Files, Ronald Reagan Library.

7. Stephen Kinzer, "Nicaragua Won't End Curbs as Asked by 80 in Congress," *New York Times*, December 22, 1985, http://ntserver1.wsulibs.wsu.edu:2184/docview/425720918?accountid=14902.

8. "UN Assembly Assails Terrorism," *New York Times*, December 7, 1985, http://search.proquest/docview/425735110?accountid=14902.

9. "UN Assembly Assails Terrorism," *New York Times*, December 7, 1985.

10. "After Seven of Debate, OAS Agrees: Torture, Terrorism are International Crimes," *The Ottawa Citizen*, December 10, 1985, http://search.proquest/docview/238899557?accountid=14902.

11. Oakley to Holloway, December 6, 1985, Folder "Incoming 12/6/1985," Box 32/34, Oliver North Files, Ronald Reagan Presidential Library.

12. Oakley Speaking before the Committees on Senate Foreign Relations and Judiciary, May 15, 1985, "International Terrorism, Current Trends and the U.S. Response," Folder "Combatting Terrorism Department of State Report, 1985 1 of 2," Box 1 OA/ID CF01573, Richard L. Canas, Files: National Security Council, George Bush Presidential Library.

13. Oakley to Holloway, December 6, 1985, Ronald Reagan Presidential Library.

14. Parker Borg, interview by Charles Stuart Kennedy, *Foreign Affairs Oral History Project*, Association for Diplomatic Studies and Training, August 12, 2002.

15. Memo, Admiral Holloway, Minutes of the Second Task Force meeting September 19 1985, Folder "Second Meeting With Task Force Principles," Box 32, Oliver North Files, Ronald Reagan Presidential Library.

16. Parker Borg, interview by Charles Stuart Kennedy.

17. Memorandum, Parker Borg to the Task Force, December 10, 1985, Folder "NSDD 207 NSC Staff: Craig Coy; Robert Earl, Folder 6 of 7," Box 91956, No. 2, Counterterrorism and Narcotics Directorate NSC Records, NSC Office of, Ronald Reagan Presidential Library.

18. Memorandum, Parker Borg to the Task Force, December 10, 1985, Ronald Reagan Presidential Library.

19. "Excerpts from Shultz Remarks on Aid to Rebels," *New York Times*, December 11, 1985, http://search.proquest/docview/111233548?accountid=14902.

20. David C. Wills, *The First War on Terrorism: Counterterrorism Policy During the Reagan Administration* (Oxford: Rowman & Littlefield, 2003), 10–13.

21. Robert Oakley, interview by Charles Stuart Kennedy and Thomas Stern.

22. Parker Borg, interview by Charles Stuart Kennedy.

23. "Around the World Conspiracy of Terror Alleged by Meese," *The Globe and Mail*, December 11, 1985, http://search.proquest/docview/386224753?accountid=14902.

24. Reagan's Radio Address to the Nation, December 14, 1985, Folder "Radio Talk: Nicaragua and Tax Reform, Dec 14, 1985," Elliot/White (Folder 1 of 4), Speechwriting, Box 244, Ronald Reagan Presidential Library.

25. "State Support for International Terrorism, May 1986, Folder "Terrorism Info-General (3 of 4)," Box CPC-1, FBI 098, Craig P. Coy: Files, Ronald Reagan Presidential Library.

26. NSDD 207, January 20, 1986, Folder "Counterterrorism (8/8/1985–4/10/1986)," Vincent Cannistraro: Files, Series 2, Box 2, Ronald Reagan Presidential Library.

27. "Policy Framework for the Use of Force in Response to Terrorist Incidents," Folder "Program Review of the Vice President's Task Force on Combatting Terrorism- March-April 1987," Box 1, Carolyn Stettner: Subject Files OA/ID CF01523-004, George Bush Presidential Library.

28. NSDD 207, January 20, 1986, Ronald Reagan Presidential Library.

29. NSDD 207, January 20, 1986, Ronald Reagan Presidential Library.

30. NSDD 207, January 20, 1986, Ronald Reagan Presidential Library.

31. NSDD 207, January 20, 1986, Ronald Reagan Presidential Library.

32. State Department Status Report Recommendation 28, March 21, 1987, Folder "Folder 2" Box 91956, Counterterrorism and Narcotics: NSC Office Files, Ronald Reagan Presidential Library.

33. Robert Oakley to Donald Gregg, February 12, 1986, Folder "Terrorism- II: Terrorism Article (1 of 3)," OA/ID 19849 Box 1, Donald P. Gregg: Task Force on Terrorism Files, George Bush Presidential Library.

34. Memorandum, Parker Borg to the Task Force, December 10, 1985, Ronald Reagan Presidential Library.

35. "Public Report of the Vice President's Task Force on Combatting Terrorism, February 1986," Folder "Public Report of the Vice President's Task Force on Combatting Terrorism, February 1986," OA 18547, Box 1, Roman Popadiuk: Files, Ronald Reagan Presidential Library.

36. "Public Report of the Vice President's Task Force on Combatting Terrorism, February 1986," Ronald Reagan Presidential Library.

37. Robert Oakley, interview by Charles Stuart Kennedy and Thomas Stern.

38. George Bush, summation of the findings of the terrorism task force, February 1986, Folder "Terrorism- II: Terrorism Article (1 of 3)," OA/ID 19849 Box 1, Donald P. Gregg: Task Force on Terrorism Files, George H. W. Bush Presidential Library.

39. "Public Report of the Vice President's Task Force on Combatting Terrorism, February 1986," Ronald Reagan Presidential Library.

40. "Public Report of the Vice President's Task Force on Combatting Terrorism, February 1986," Ronald Reagan Presidential Library.

41. George H. W. Bush, Interview for *American Legion*, Folder Terrorism- II: Terrorism Article, 3 of 3, Box 1 OA/ID 19849, Donald P. Gregg Files: Task force on Terrorism File, George Bush Presidential Library.

42. George Shultz, "Terrorism: The Challenge to the Democracies," in Steven Anzovin, *Terrorism* (New York: H. W. Wilson, 1986), 50–54.

43. "Policy Framework for the Use of Force in Response to Terrorist Incidents," George Bush Presidential Library.

44. Robert Oakley, interview by Charles Kennedy and Thomas Stern.

45. 132 Cong. Rec. S1558 (daily ed. February 25, 1986) (request by President Reagan).

46. Statement By Deputy Director Whitehead at "US-UK Bilateral Meeting on Terrorism," March 5, 1986, Folder "Terrorism (folder 1)," Box 2, Vincent Canistraro: Files, Series 2, Ronald Reagan Library.

47. Statement By Deputy Director Whitehead at "US-UK Bilateral Meeting on Terrorism," March 5, 1986, Ronald Reagan Library.

48. "Public Report of the Vice President's Task Force on Combatting Terrorism, February 1986," Ronald Reagan Presidential Library.

49. Admiral James Holloway, response to press questions, March 6, 1986, Folder "Terrorism (1 of 6)," OA/ID 19849 Box 1, Donald P. Gregg: Task Force on Terrorism Files, George Bush Presidential Library.

50. George Bush, summation of the findings of the terrorism task force, February 1986, George Bush Presidential Library.

51. George Bush, summation of the findings of the terrorism task force, February 1986, George Bush Presidential Library.

52. "Policy Framework for the Use of Force in Response to Terrorist Incidents," George Bush Presidential Library.

53. Oliver North, "U.S. Political/Military Strategy for Nicaragua," July 15, 1985, in Kornbluh and Byrne, *The Iran-Contra Scandal*, 50.

54. James LeMoyne, "U.S. Army Copters Carry Hondurans to Border Region: 14 Craft with American Crews Fly a Battalion to Airstrip Near Reported Battle," *New York Times*, March 27, 1986, http://search.proquest/docview/110982768?accountid=14902.

55. "Radio Talk: Nicaragua," March 8, 1986, Folder "Radio Talk Nicaragua: March 8, 1986 (Elliot and Hayes)," Box 260, Speechwriting, Ronald Reagan Library.

56. "Radio Talk: Nicaragua," March 8, 1986, Ronald Reagan Library.

57. Reagan's Radio Address to the Nation, March 14, 1986, Folder "Address to the Nation: Aid to the Nicaraguan Freedom Fighters," March 16, 1986, Box 40, Anthony "Tony" R. Dolan: Files, 1981–1989, Ronald Reagan Library.

58. Public Opinion Report, Wirthlin to Regan, "Nicaragua and Aid to the Contras," Folder "Nicaragua and Aid to the Contras April 2, 1986," Box 12, David Chew: Files, Decision Making Information, February–March 1986, Ronald Reagan Library.

59. Public Opinion Report, Wirthlin to Regan, "Nicaragua and Aid to the Contras," February–March 1986, Ronald Reagan Library.

60. John Corry, "Frontline Examines Nicaragua's Contras," *New York Times*, March 18, 1986, http://search.proquest.com/docview/111084144?accountid=14902.

61. Stephen Kinzer, "Hondurans Meeting Amid U.S. Reports of Nicaraguan Raid," *New York Times*, March 25, 1986, http://search.proquest/docview/110965427?accountid=14902.

62. "New Honduran Airlift Raises Stakes on Border," *The Globe and Mail*, March 27, 1986, http://search.proquest/docview/386175369?accountid=14902.

63. James LeMoyne, "U.S. army units to build 6th airfield in Honduras," *New York Times*, March 3, 1986, http://search.proquest.com/docview/111072128?accountid=45760.

64. "Policy Framework for the Use of Force in Response to Terrorist Incidents," George Bush Presidential Library.

65. LeMoyne, "U.S. Army Copters Carry Hondurans to Border Region."

66. James Lemoyne, "Honduran Tells of U.S. Pressure," *New York Times*, April 3, 1986, http://search.proquest.com/docview/110973739?accountid=45760.

67. "Honduras is Given Emergency 20 Million$—Reagan Responds to Nicaragua incursion," *Seattle Times*, March 25, 1986, http://search.proquest/docview/385154422?accountid=14902.

68. Steven V. Roberts, "Lawmakers Say New Raid Will Help Cause of Contras," *New York Times*, March 26, 1986, http://search.proquest/docview/110981390?accountid=14902.

69. Leslie H. Gelb, "Aid to Contras: Congress Edges Toward Package," *New York Times*, March 29, 1986, http://search.proquest/docview/110978169?accountid=14902.

70. Roberts, "Lawmakers Say New Raid Will Help Cause of Contras."

71. Public Opinion Report, Wirthlin to Regan, "Nicaragua and Aid to the Contras," February–March 1986, Ronald Reagan Library.

72. Frederick Kempe, "Policy Test: Events in Nicaragua and Libya Aid Reagan at Least Temporarily—Big Risks Remain as Qadhafi May Step Up Terrorism, Latin Conflict May Widen—Is there any Grand Design?," *Wall Street Journal*, March 26, 1986, http://search.proquest.com/docview/397963308?accountid=14902.

73. Public Opinion Report, Wirthlin to Regan, "Nicaragua and Aid to the Contras," February–March 1986, Ronald Reagan Library.

74. "Policy Framework for the Use of Force in Response to Terrorist Incidents," George Bush Presidential Library.

75. Robert Oakley, interview by Charles Stuart Kennedy and Thomas Stern.

76. Memo, Poindexter to President Reagan, "Implementation of NSDD 207," folder "folder 3," Box 91956, Counterterrorism and Narcotics: NSC Office Records, Ronald Reagan Library.

77. "Around the World: Central American Peace Talks Collapse," *The Globe and Mail*, April 8, 1986, http://ntserver1.wsulibs.wsu.edu:2184/docview/386176399?accountid=14902.

78. Raymond W. Copson and Richard P. Cronin, "Reagan Doctrine: Assisting Anti-Marxist Guerrillas," Folder 5, Box 11, David S. Addington, Series II: Chron Files, 1987–1988, Ronald Reagan Presidential Library.

79. Copson and Cronin, "Reagan Doctrine: Assisting Anti-Marxist Guerrillas," 1987–1988, Ronald Reagan Presidential Library.

Chapter Eight

War for Peace

At 11:30 am on March 7, 1986, the White House announced that Ambassador Philip Habib was the new special envoy to Central America. Habib was a senior diplomat, and popular choice among moderate Democrats and Republicans to represent the United States' efforts in the peace process in Central America. Habib was originally a specialist in Asian affairs and played an important role in the Vietnam War during the critical year of 1968. However, Habib's defining moment was during the 1980s when he served the Reagan administration in the Middle East. In particular, he was critical in negotiating a temporary solution to the Israeli conflicts with the PLO, Lebanon, and Syria. When he was appointed special envoy to Central America most in Congress regarded him as an excellent and moderate diplomat.

Amid an escalation of tension and hostility with Nicaragua, Habib's appointment suggested that the Reagan administration was serious about negotiations.[1] Several days later, Habib boarded an airplane bound for Central America. While Congress and the White House fought over a proposal to fund the Nicaraguan Contras, and as the United States and Honduras conducted provocative military maneuvers on Nicaragua's borders, Habib met for the first time with representatives of El Salvador, Honduras, Costa Rica, and Guatemala.

Contrary to the impression of fair diplomacy, the purpose of the mission was to facilitate the administration's offensive strategy of regime change in Nicaragua. The administration hoped that Habib's visit would ensure the backing of the Central American democracies and further isolate the Sandinista leadership, as well as help gain support in the United States House of Representatives for the lethal funding of the Contras. The Reagan administration used the mission to create support among the four Central American democracies for a policy that relied on military force as the primary means to achieve peace on the United States' terms, a peace that was only acceptable when the Sandinista government yielded to the will of the United States. The support of El Salvador, Honduras, Costa Rica and Guatemala, the administration hoped, could give its aggressive policy the kind of approval necessary to solidify the strategy of using force to obtain a change of leadership in Nicaragua.

When considering the Reagan administration's involvement with Nicaragua, scholars often focus exclusively on the power of Washington neo-conservatives' intent on bending Central America to its will. However, scholars often overlook the integral role played by the leaders of the four Central American democracies. The administration wanted to alter the Sandinista government by isolating Nicaragua and escalating the conflict inside and across Nicaragua's sovereign borders. The policy represented a new framework for intervention that relied on hardline measures that included military pressure, economic sanctions, and diplomatic non-negotiation. The success of this plan, however, hinged on the support of the United States Congress and the Central American democracies. Without funding for the Contras and a continued authorization by Costa Rica and Honduras to ignore use of its territory by the Contras, the policy with Nicaragua could not succeed.

Throughout 1986 and 1987, the Reagan administration did not make securing a peaceful agreement between Nicaragua and the other Central American governments its primary objective. Instead, the purpose of its diplomatic effort was to create unity and support among the Central American democracies for a hardline policy designed to force Nicaragua to accept an agreement on the Reagan administration's terms or to ensure the Sandinista collapse. Its diplomatic missions to the region in 1986 and 1987 did not involve Nicaragua and did not represent an effort by the United States to have fair discussions with the Central American leaders. The Reagan administration expected the leaders of the Central American democracies to agree with the United States and pursue a course amenable to the will of the larger North American neighbor.

The first Latin American peace negotiations designed to deal with Nicaragua and the Central American crisis, the Contadora talks, began in 1983. Mexico, Venezuela, Colombia, and Panama led these negotiations. These four nations comprised the heart of the Contadora group.[2] Mexico was the most influential player of the four. Between 1983 and 1986, Contadora consistently failed to produce an agreement. The primary reason for this failure was due to the Reagan administration's escalation of military activity in Nicaragua, Costa Rica, Honduras, and El Salvador, which increased the divide between the Sandinista leadership and its neighbors. Further, Mexico was consistently supportive of the Nicaraguan position and angered by the Reagan administration's use of hostile action.[3]

A Mexican-led peace agreement was unacceptable to the United States because it would leave the Sandinista regime stable and intact. The Reagan administration spoke positively in public about Contadora, but undermined the talks with increasing hostility that promoted disunity within the region. In addition, Honduras, El Salvador, and Costa Rica felt that Mexico favored Nicaragua and that the talks provided little concern for their own interests as small nations accustomed to and uncomfortable with the influence of the larger Mexican neighbor.[4] The United States used this situation to create a Central American coalition that it hoped would make the military oriented strategy effective.

By 1986, the United States and the Central American democracies continued to give lip service to Contadora, but through the Habib mission the administration encouraged the demise of the regional peace talks in favor of a united Central American coalition that could facilitate the United States' offensive strategy and create the kind of peace agreement that the Reagan administration desired. The agreement it sought was one that altered the Nicaraguan government.

In the spring of 1986, when ambassador Habib traveled to Central America, Costa Rica was the key state for the administration's diplomatic mission. Honduras and El Salvador were already closely aligned with the Reagan administration, and these two nations sought unity with the United States in hopes of maintaining security against a Nicaraguan state increasingly antagonized by the US-led Contra War. Costa Rica, however, was very important to the Central American coalition that the Reagan administration sought. The small peaceful nation had no military, and its participation was critical if the coalition was to appear in anyway legitimate. Costa Rica, the neighbor to the South, however, was less amenable to the administration's aims. The newly elected president, Oscar Arias Sanchez, was a domestically oriented leader and he did not want his government associated with the continued US effort to use war to isolate and undermine the Nicaraguan government.[5] During 1986, and as directed by Washington, the Habib mission pressured Arias to fall in line and do as the United States desired.

There were two primary objectives for Habib's March mission to Central America. First, the mission sought to guarantee that none of the Central American governments made any statements that could discourage Congress from voting for lethal aid to the Contras. Second, the mission tried to prevent border-states with Nicaragua, particularly Costa Rica, from producing bilateral border patrol agreements with the Nicaraguan government that could undermine the guerrilla's operational capabilities. In part, the goal of the Habib mission to Central America was to prevent positive developments for peace between Nicaragua and its neighbors, while simultaneously implying to Congress and the world that the mission was an honest attempt at a diplomatic solution. Costa Rica and Nicaragua were, in March, on the edge of securing a bilateral agreement. The agreement meant that the two govern-ments would work together to patrol the border. The need for this agreement stemmed from the United States' war against Nicaragua and support of trans-national guerrillas that operated in remote areas and conducted cross border raids into Sandinista territory. The raids were the primary way that the Unit-ed States exerted pressure on the government of Nicaragua, but these were also the root of instability in the region. Because of the continual escalation of US directed hostilities, Costa Rica and Honduras feared major Nicaraguan reprisals into its territory. As a result, Costa Rica and Nicaragua neared an agreement to police the border and effectively put an end to the Contra cross border activity in the southern theater of war.[6]

The Reagan administration perceived the pending agreement between Costa Rica and Nicaragua as a threat to its war aims and the Habib mission sought to halt the agreement. According to Secretary of State George Shultz, the United States opposed the pending bilateral agreement because, "Border agreements with Nicaragua would remove one of the incentives for the San-dinistas to negotiate a regional agreement."[7] The incentive that Shultz re-ferred to was the ability of the United States to make war on Nicaragua through cross border Contra raids that violated the sovereignty of both Nica-ragua and Costa Rica. The regional agreement proposed by the United States referenced a US-backed ultimatum that the Sandinistas disarm and accept the Contras into a new democratic government, or else continue to face the consequences of an increasingly aggressive US war. The goal was not peace with the current governments in the region, but rather a peace that enforced a policy of regime change in Nicaragua brought about by military pressure.

The border agreement that Costa Rica and Nicaragua negotiated in 1986 did not line up with the Reagan administration's overall demand on the government of Nicaragua, but it did represent a promising accord for peace in Central America. Such bilateral settlements promised cooperation as a way to reduce the war making abilities of transnational guerrillas that violat-ed Nicaragua and Costa Rica's sovereign territory. Those fighters represent-ed a danger to peace in Central America. The United States proxies threat-ened the Sandinista government, encouraged its further militarization, and inspired significant cross border reprisals like the Honduran raid that oc-curred shortly following Habib's March mission. Border agreements pro-vided the opportunity to create peace between Central American states, but such arrangements also insulated Nicaragua from the designs of the United States. Such initiatives ran counter to the Reagan administration's objective of regime change.

Even though the two were destined for a positive and productive relation-ship, when Habib met President Oscar Arias Sanchez during their first meet-ing he chastised the newly elected leader for supporting the bilateral border patrol agreement with Nicaragua. The Reagan administration was livid about

Costa Rica's attempt to create such an agreement, and Habib told Arias that, "President Ronald Reagan is not a masochist and will not pay people to dump on him."[8] Habib's sharp words implied that the United States used economic aid as leverage against Costa Rica. To this, the Costa Rican leader, perhaps somewhat intimidated, reassured Habib that "his call for a timetable for establishing democracy in Nicaragua [was] evidence of his opposition to the Sandinista regime."[9] Shortly following the exchange, Arias shelved the border arrangement between the two nations in favor of the demands of the Reagan administration for an agreement that was regional and simultaneous. The United States would only accept an agreement that incorporated direct talks with the Contras and upon which all Central American states agreed. Costa Rica was compelled to align with Honduras and El Salvador and dismiss any bi-lateral understanding that undermined the Reagan administration's goal of using Central American unity to isolate and attack Nicaragua.

While the United States strong-armed Costa Rica into compliance, the other Central American democracies, El Salvador, Honduras, and Guatemala, expressed support for the United States but also concern for the ramifications of US policy. A primary purpose of Habib's missions to these governments in 1986 was to examine any statements or positions that the leaders of the nations might assume publicly or in meetings with members of the United States Congress prior to the upcoming vote in the House of Representatives. The Reagan administration insisted that these Central American leaders, with whom important swing voters in Congress planned to meet, spoke in full support of the administration's policy and, at the least, said nothing that could encourage members of the House of Representatives to vote against a proposal to aid the Contras. The diplomatic effort involved creating the impression of unity among the Central American states with the administration's policy and to use this to facilitate the conduct of an offensive military oriented operation.

Contrary to the intention of the Reagan administration there existed a lack of unity or un-waivered support for its plan from the Central American governments. President Jose Napoleon Duarte of El Salvador was the only Central American leader to offer complete backing for the Reagan administration. On March 12, Duarte expressed his support for the Contras. He agreed to tell US congressional representatives visiting El Salvador that "the Nicaraguan resistance constitute[d] a much needed barrier to Sandinista subversion." Further, he said that at upcoming talks with Nicaragua, scheduled for May in Esquipulas, Guatemala, "he would press his counterparts [the other Central American democracies] to limit discussion to regional matters and to refrain from references to external factors." In other words, Duarte would do everything in his power to support the continued US. offensive carried out by the Nicaraguan Contras, and try and push other states away from individual agreements with Nicaragua.[10] Duarte was a long-time ally of the Reagan administration from which he relied for support in his war against the Nicaraguan backed guerrillas in El Salvador's brutal civil war. His complete and cooperative support was, however, unique. Even President José Simón Azcona del Hoyo of Honduras, the first democratically elected leader since the 1930s, expressed his continued support for the US-Contra program, but insisted that he could not do so publicly due to the controversy in his country over the activity of the Contras.[11]

President Marco Vinicio Cerezo Arévalo of Guatemala also expressed his intention to push Nicaragua to hold democratic elections. Cerezo assured Habib that, "He [would] not publicly oppose military support for the resistance."[12] The Guatemalan leader expressed a sense of homage owed to the United States for his leadership position. His election was praised as democratic by the Reagan administration, and it supported Guatemala in its continued fight against leftist insurgents. Cerezo continued a conflict that ran back to the US-led ouster of the government of Jacobo Árbenz in 1954. Following this overthrow, Guatemala eventually descended into a prolonged period of civil war that began in 1960 and did not end until 1996. Cerezo was grateful to the United States, and he expressed that he would not be in power without the support provided by the United States. However, like Arias, while he promised that his government would not undermine the Reagan administration's policy, he could not give full public backing.[13] Mexico, one of the most powerful states of the region and a nation that opposed the United States' policy with Nicaragua, factored significantly into the decisions of the Guatemalan leader. This relationship made Cerezo unable to join the informal Central American coalition that the Habib mission attempted to create.

Behind closed doors, there was concern among the Central American states that the United States' war effort might cause an escalation of regional state terrorism directed from Nicaragua or lead to a general war throughout Central America. On March 14, Cerezo expressed that he was concerned about "generalized war." To this point, Habib spoke plainly, and Cerezo was not reassured. Habib told the Guatemalan president that, "A Cuba on the American mainland was unacceptable. Nicaragua is a cancer that will destroy an otherwise healthy Central America. The democracies must work together aggressively to expand democracy, or force would be the only option left." The United States was involved in a military offensive and Habib subtly threatened Cerezo that, if it was necessary, the Reagan administration would escalate further. To this, Cerezo insisted that he reiterated this to the Contadora group nations and that even "Colombia and Venezuela [were] beginning to understand that Nicaragua has to be pressured." Cerezo, however, was concerned about an expanded war and afraid that US policy might lead to a return of "Somocismo."[14] The Reagan administration's war on terrorism against Nicaragua caused a continuous escalation of the conflict to the point that Central American governments, like Guatemala, were fearful that the situation could explode into a regional war.

After the House of Representatives' initial rejection of aid to the Contras in late March, Habib went back to meet with the leaders of the Central American states in April. The Reagan administration took the House vote as a setback, but in the wake of its publicizing of the Nicaraguan raid into Honduras following provocative US-Honduran military maneuvers, the administration believed it had a new opportunity to gain support for its regime change approach. The framework of intervention produced by Vice President Bush's task force proposed that a major Nicaraguan offensive into Honduras could substantially shift the opinion of Congress and the American public.[15] The administration brought about this event through provocation and the Honduran raid helped turn the public dialogue in the favor of the administration in late March. Following this escalation in the US-backed war with Nicaragua, Habib found the Central American democracies concerned about the Reagan administration's policy and doubtful that the Sandinistas would sign a treaty at the first meeting of Central American states in Esquipulas, Guatemala, scheduled for late May.[16]

Following the Honduran raid and the positive Senate vote that March, the situation with Nicaragua remained controversial in the United States. Several New England businessmen sued the United States for the sanctions regime against Nicaragua. The sanctions turned one year old in 1986, and was one of the primary methods that the Reagan administration used to isolate states alleged of sponsoring terrorism. Some Americans argued that the sanctions, which prohibited Americans from traveling to or conducting business with Nicaragua, represented a further violation of international law. These individuals were only a small representation of members of the public concerned about the sanctions and the overall approach taken by the Reagan administration.[17]

In 1986, author Salman Rushdie traveled to Nicaragua collecting information for his scathing critique of the United States' sanction program on Nicaragua, which he published as a book titled *The Jaguar Smile*. Even the iconic pop/rock star Jackson Browne, famous for hit songs like "Stay" and "Running on Empty," traveled to Nicaragua and exclaimed opposition to Reagan's policy. Browne reiterated a several year old critique and voiced concerns over the Vietnam-like similarities evident in US policy with Nicaragua and Central America. Since the beginning of the fight over US involvement with the Contras and the conflict in El Salvador, a primary method of voicing opposition to the program was by recalling the tragedy of Vietnam. In 1986, this concern remained a powerful part of the dialogue over the conflict. Not only did Browne consider the conflict similar to Vietnam, so too did opponents in Congress as they fought the Reagan administration's

$100 million Contra aid package. Nicaragua remained an increasingly volatile topic in the United States.

The Honduran invasion caused a relative ground swell of support for the Reagan administration's policy. Its war already involved a unilateral sanctions regime and the legally dubious employment of military pressure through support of proxy guerrillas. Further, the increased use of propaganda that characterized Nicaragua as a state sponsor of terrorism appeared to gain ground in shaping the dialogue over the Contras and the Sandinistas. The growing support for the administration was to a significant degree manufactured. The administration reacted to a peak in a world terrorism crisis that stretched back to 1983, but the allegations toward Nicaragua were largely the result of purposeful manipulation and provocation. The administration applied recommendations from the proposal of the task force and provoked both Nicaragua and Libya. The provocations created momentum for the public diplomacy operations, and Habib's attempt to organize the Central American democracies into an informal coalition capitalized on this momentum.

Despite the dissension of many in Congress and the United States public, the direction of events did not bode well for those hoping to derail US policy in the region.[18] In May, the government of Nicaragua expelled two American diplomats on allegations of espionage. The Sandinista government accused the individuals of using cameras hidden in cigarette lighters. The Reagan administration denied the claims, but responded by expelling two Nicaraguan officials from the embassy in Washington, DC.[19] Reports appeared to provide further confirmation of the administration's position. In the months following Nicaragua's attack on the rebels in Honduras, the momentum in the United States shifted further against the Sandinistas.

In the spring of 1986, a number of influential figures testified vocally in favor of the United States war against Nicaragua, and insisted that it needed to act preemptively. John Norton Moore, an esteemed specialist on National Security Law at the University of Virginia, published an article that supported the approach of the Reagan administration. Moore noted that international terrorism, particularly by Nicaraguans, represented a change in the nature of threat in the world. He insisted that, "The core threat to the contemporary world order has been state-sponsored terrorism, guerrilla warfare and other forms of covert attack." He lamented that, "A policy of non-action against violence and terrorism may lead to a complete collapse of the world order."[20] Further insisting the importance of this shift, Moore argued that, "Perceptions of U.S. and Latin American interests focus heavily on the national security threat of a Soviet base in this hemisphere. But the real, short term issues are . . . the expanding program of state-supported terrorism and subversion that is being used to destabilize other countries such as Colombia."[21] Moore represented a group within the scholarly community that be lieved in the approach implemented by the Reagan administration. Moore's argument evidenced the fact that state sponsorship of international terrorism was not simply a justification. International terrorism, many perceived, was a new kind of security threat that required a new policy and a rethinking of international law and the principle of sovereignty. During Reagan's first term the administration and its supporters sought to side step or ignore the issue of international law. However, after the Reagan offensive was underway the administration and its supporters took the issue head on by suggesting that the principle of international law and protections of state sovereignty were outmoded and that preventative policies of regime change were acceptable methods for dealing with the dangerous and unpredictable threat from international terrorism.

Perhaps the most significant individual to call for a shift in principles of international law that spring was Geoffery Levitt, legal advisor for the Reagan administration. Levitt was an expert on international law. He argued that international terrorism involved a globally coordinated political enterprise directed at the free societies of the world by an international terrorist network. The danger rested in the psychological effect caused by sudden and unprovoked attacks against civilians. Levitt recognized that this was a new danger primarily because the world's growing technologies of communication, transportation, and arms sales made a global terrorist network a dangerous precedent for the future. He cited the events of June 1985, the shooting of six Americans in San Salvador, and the hijacking of TWA 847, as primary examples of the growth of this issue. While Levitt praised certain elements of international cooperation regarding airport security and extradition treaties and of improved intelligence efforts that resulted in the thwarting of many terrorist plots in 1985, he acknowledged that state sponsorship of international terrorism posed a challenge to international law and constraints on the use of preventative policies by the United States demonstrated the international system was antiquated and required rethinking. [22]

Levitt lamented the reality that free world nations had failed to impose multilateral sanctions regimes on leftist states like Nicaragua. He insisted that state sponsorship of terrorism was a new and advantageous way of attacking the free world because it allowed states to incorporate brutal and psychologically damaging attacks, which could eventually involve weapons of mass destruction, but receive no responsibility or punishment for doing so. Levitt reiterated the position of George Shultz and George H. W. Bush and argued that state sponsorship of international terrorism pressed the bounds of international law and that for this reason the United States needed to respond or act preemptively to alleviate what it described as a dangerous criminal threat to the international order. Levitt joined the administration and scholars like Moore and insisted that because state sponsorship of international terrorism posed a unique and elusive threat that the United States possessed the legal right and responsibility to act in a manner that most effectively alleviated the threat.[23] These figures insisted that international terrorism authorized a new form of warfare, a new form of response, that challenged previously accepted norms of international behavior. The United States could no longer guarantee a nation's sovereign rights amid the allegation of international terrorism. Such an assertion by the United States authorized the escalation of activities that violated Nicaragua's sovereign status.

As the critical second vote of the House of Representatives on aid to the Nicaraguan Contras neared, former United Nations Ambassador Jeane Kirkpatrick joined the crescendo of vocal support for the war on terrorism. Kirkpatrick, an authority on foreign policy, insisted that the Sandinistas possessed strong economic and military support from Libya, the PLO, and Iran. Nicaragua, she argued, was the conduit for international terrorism in this hemisphere.[24] Likewise, later that month, *American Legion* published its headline interview with Vice President George H. W. Bush. The title was "We Will Defend Our People." In the article, Bush explained that Nicaragua represented a new menace. Nicaragua was a state sponsor of terrorism, and it was opening up the United States' southern border for terrible attacks against Americans and the allies of the United States.[25] Likewise, on May 13, administration official Craig Coy gave a speech to the National Defense Transportation Association in San Francisco, California, that further built up the argument that the old international system held the United States victim to the threat of terrorism. Coy reiterated the evolving argument of the administration that Nicaragua represented a criminal state sponsor of international terrorism that justified a US policy that challenged the norms of international behavior. Coy was concerned, and he reflected that, "I am not a philosopher, but I have to wonder about the future of a society that refuses to aggressively protect its citizens and interests from wanton killing and destruction by criminal elements or criminal nations."[26] These individuals continued to demand that the criminality of Nicaragua warranted an offensive policy that altered the bounds of international behavior.

The assertions made by Coy, Bush, Moore, Levitt, and Kirkpatrick were, in one sense, rhetorical "old-hat." This was the same argument that the Reagan administration had pushed for over a year. In one respect, propaganda, particularly the criminalizing language of terrorism, was important for the successful implementation of the Reagan offensive. However, vocal proponents in the academic, political, and legal realms showed that many important minds took the terrorism issue very seriously. The terrorism crisis of the 1980s drove a reevaluation of Cold War conflicts by introducing a new kind of national security threat. By 1986, the dialogue of terrorism was beginning to encourage a shift in the meaning of the conflict in Nicaragua and the role of American power in the world.

At this stage, the administration's public diplomacy campaign targeted not just Congress, but also international audiences, particularly in Latin America and in Europe. The Reagan administration defended the program for increased military pressure on the Sandinistas and for the alteration of the Nicaraguan government. The goal was to convince the international community of two main points: first, that the Central American democracies were on the side of the United States and were under siege from Nicaragua, and that the Contras represented an organized political movement. Second, Nicaragua was a legitimate international terrorist threat that required a military-oriented response from the United States. The administration insisted, "That the Sandinistas support[ed] international terrorism and that Sandinista external subversion threaten[ed] the nascent democracies in neighboring countries." Further, the administration insisted that the Sandinistas possessed ties with "terrorists in Latin America . . . and elsewhere (including the Middle East), arms and drug runners [and the] Sandinista practice of providing passports to terrorists."[27] On the cusp of gaining congressional authorization for lethal aid to the Contras, the administration pressed the importance of this action as part of its new and necessary framework of intervention. It emphatically appealed to the language of terrorism in an attempt to create a heightened sense of fear and urgency over the Central American crisis.

Meanwhile, on May 14, 1986, Ambassador Habib met with Contra leaders in Miami, Florida. He met with the three most prominent leaders, Arturo Cruz, Alfonso Robelo, and Adolfo Calero. Habib expressed the importance for the guerrillas to remain united and for them to promote themselves as a legitimate democratic option to Latin Americans, to Europeans and, of course, to the United States Congress. The three guerrilla leaders were pleased that the Reagan administration supported them and expressed a desire to show themselves as a democratic political alternative in what they described as Nicaragua's "civil war."[28] Over the course of the next several months the Contras drafted a concord agreement among the various factions that asserted the guerrillas resolve to pursue democracy in Nicaragua. The Reagan administration also published profiles and biographies of the leaders. In 1986, the Reagan administration's freedom fighters emerged as an apparently legitimate political alternative. This development, along with the support or at least non-resistance from the Central American democracies, further Sandinista entrenchment, and Ronald Reagan's convincing phone calls to swing voters factored centrally into the upcoming second vote in the House of Representatives on the lethal aid package for the guerrillas led by Cruz, Calero, and Robelo.

In May, the Central American democracies met with the representatives of the Nicaraguan government for peace talks at Esquipulas, Guatemala. The meeting did not go well, and the results appeared to implicate the Sandinistas further as intransigent and hostile. The four Central American democracies, led by Arias, presented a proposal that demanded democratization in Nicaragua and a reduction of the Sandinistas military arsenal by 20 percent. This number was far below the figure desired by the Reagan administration and yet Ortega, still concerned and agitated by the United States' proxy war, did not agree to this arrangement.[29] Arias expressed disappointment at the extent of the gap between Nicaragua and the other Central American states.[30] News reports appeared to provide further confirmation of the Reagan administration's position. President Azcona of Honduras reiterated Arias' lament that the Sandinistas refused to downsize militarily.[31] Far from reaching an agreement, Habib left Central America in early June, believing that the United States should continue to "pursue Contra funding as an indispensable element of a two track policy that puts military pressure on Nicaragua at the service of an active diplomacy."[32] With Nicaragua still unwilling to incorporate the Contras into the democratic process, the United States continued to focus on efforts to use military force against Nicaragua as a way of altering the government in a manner that favored the interests of the Reagan administration.

On June 7, Reagan insisted to Congress that a failure of the aid package meant "Nicaragua as a refuge for terrorism." He further reiterated the claim that inaction would result in another Libya in Central America.[33] The following day Vice President Bush publicly disclosed that "drug smuggling [was] a major security threat because it is intimately linked with terrorism."[34] The next day, Reagan administration reported that new shipments of arms from the Soviet Union had arrived in Nicaragua.[35] Capitalizing on the uniqueness of a direct arms shipment from a Soviet vessel, the White House insisted that this was another escalation. The administration, further, suggested that Soviet pilots were conducting reconnaissance in Nicaragua.[36] In reality, this was likely not an escalation, but rather a standard support and resupply operation. The only difference was that the shipments typically went through Cuba and these were direct Soviet shipments.[37] The administration used every opportunity it could to justify war. Shortly after this announcement, Reagan gave his "closing argument" to the members of the United States House of Representatives prior to the critical vote on the Contra aid package. His speech was before Georgetown University's Center for Strategic and International Studies. In this speech, he further reiterated his claims about Nicaragua as a terrorist state and another Libya.[38] With the critical vote in the House of Representatives upcoming, the public diplomacy program was in high gear, and Reagan's political skills proved critical to the success or failure of the controversial measure in the Democrat controlled body.

In addition to the charm and cunning of Reagan in lobbying Congress, the State and Defense Departments together produced another public briefing book detailing the communist-terrorist threat posed by Nicaragua. Titled "The Challenge to Democracy in Central America" the new report reiterated the position that Nicaragua affiliated itself with the clients of international terrorism. According to the report, agents of the PLO and Libya sought to construct a "new Nicaragua." The document was hopeful that the offensive approach of aiding the Contras could prevent further consolidation of the terrorist regime in Managua.[39] Coupled with evidence that the Nicaraguan government was not prepared to talk and that the Sandinistas were further militarized, the Reagan administration's case appeared more powerful than at any other point.

On June 25, 1986, the House of Representatives again voted on the $100 million aid package for the Contras. The spectacle was unique and about as exciting as a CSPAN broadcast could get. The Democratically controlled House of Representatives was broken up into factions, and the debate and amending process ran into the night. When the voting occurred on the $100 million package ($70 million for lethal weapons and $30 million for non-lethal material) cheers and sighs resonated as opponents and proponents responded to the ballots of swing voters. Cheers from throughout the hall rang out when George M. O'Brien, a Republican suffering from cancer, showed up in his wheelchair to vote in favor of aid.[40] This vote in the House of Representatives marked a pinnacle of the administration's efforts with Congress and it was a hard-fought and dramatic moment for Congress.

In all, eleven key members of the House of Representatives switched their votes to favor the administration's plan to provide lethal aid to the Nicaraguan Contras. In this second vote in 1986, the White House succeeded and the House of Representatives approved the measure proposed by the Reagan administration. In her 1993 book, *Crossroads*, Cynthia Arnson suggested that two primary factors caused this positive vote: the pressure and incessant phone calls of Ronald Reagan and the inability of the liberal Democrats to create a viable alternative solution, which, according to Arnson, was the most significant in securing the positive vote. While Arnson is correct in her claim that Reagan's personal efforts and the lack of coherence from liberal Democrats factored significantly in the shift in the House of Representatives in June 1986, her account does not fully explain the reasons for the shift. The support of the Central American democracies and efforts by the Reagan administration to organize the Contras politically were also critical in the motivations of several important swing voters.[41]

Of course, the Senate still had to vote, but this body consistently possessed a narrow majority in favor of supporting the Contras. The vote in the House, effectively, authorized the United States to directly arm the proxy armies on the borders of Nicaragua. For the first time since the war began the government of the United States formerly authorized a non-state actor, not bound by international law, to act in violation of the sovereignty of another internationally recognized state not in a formal state of war with the United

States. Most Americans at the time likely did not comprehend the significance of this moment. The vote was tremendously significant.

Throughout the Cold War the United States used covert operations to
launch coups and topple governments, but when it came to overt armed
conflict the United States relied on containment. The basic principle of containment was to recognize international law and sovereign territory by using
overt force only to prevent the overthrow of a government rather than to
facilitate such a development. The vote was groundbreaking. For the first
time since the beginning of the Cold War, the United States government
openly authorized a policy that made the preemptive violation of another
sovereign nation's borders legal, at least in the eyes of the United States. The
United States government recognized its right to use armed proxies, non-
state actors not bound to any international agreements, to destroy an internationally recognized government. This was a significant moment for the United States and the world, and though none knew it at the time it established a
precedent for the future.

After the House vote the White House directed staff members to create a
report to determine the key motivations for the change. While there was no
single answer, the report noted several important factors in the motives of
swing voters. Some important changes occurred on the domestic front: Reagan's personal phone calls and the constant bombardment of the administration's public diplomacy program. Internationally, however, there were several important developments as well. The effect of the Honduran raid, the
meetings that members like Olympia Snowe (R) had with the Central
American leaders, and the organization of the Contras into a seemingly organized political body served to further vilify the Sandinistas and to motivate
swing voters to favor the military pressure offered by the Contra aid package.
Of course, the Honduran invasion, the testimony of the Central American
democracies, and the political organization of the Contras resulted from tire-
less efforts on the administration's part. Furthermore, Nicaragua's militarization and hostility was a direct consequence of the Reagan administration's
efforts to attack, provoke, and threaten the government. Likewise, Philip
Habib's diplomatic missions guided the testimony of the Central American
democracies. These factored critically in achieving success in the June vote
and in making the Reagan administration's war of regime change legitimate.
The vote was 221 to 209, six Democrats and five Republicans switched sides
and joined in bi-partisan support of the measure. [42]

The success of the administration's program to achieve Contra aid and
increase pressure on the Sandinistas hinged on the Central American coalition's support. However, while the image of Nicaraguan isolation served the
administration's efforts in the House of Representatives, the coalition was
unstable. The Central American alliance was the result of coercion not agreement, but this flaw remained hidden to those in Congress. The aggressive

posture of the Reagan administration forced the Central American democracies to accept, despite reservations, the United States position of using force against Nicaragua. The Habib mission in 1986 amounted to diplomacy used as a tool for obtaining support for military measures, and there was significant objection from the President of Costa Rica and Guatemala. Despite the perception of unity, Guatemala assumed a neutral role, and the administration appeared to threaten and coerce Costa Rica into acceptance of the United States' policy with hard language and the threat of economic reprisals.

Since the Honduran raid and the Habib visits, three of the four Central American democracies came out as public supporters of the Reagan administration. The administration hoped to create unity among all four governments, but Guatemala distanced itself from the process. Guatemala, while not disparaging the United States' policy, adopted a position of "active neutrality" as Cerezo refused to isolate Nicaragua in the manner that Washington hoped. Mexico, which was an ally of the Sandinistas and opposed to US activity in the region, influenced Guatemala. All of the Central American democracies expressed increased concern about Nicaragua's failure at the negotiating table and the growing militaristic posture of both the Sandinistas and the United States. The democracies, particularly Costa Rica and Honduras, found themselves in a difficult position. The United States' support for the Contras, which implicated the two nations in the Contra war, increased tension with Nicaragua. Because of this, Nicaragua had increasingly militarized, tightened its grip internally, and brought cases against both Honduras and Costa Rica at the International Court of Justice. These US allies feared Sandinista aggression and were concerned about the guerrillas, but unable to refuse the increasingly adventuresome United States.

Following the House of Representatives' approval of aid for the Contras in the form of $70 million in lethal aid and $30 million in non-lethal aid, the leaders of the "core three" Central American democracies expressed concern, but also cautious support for the United States' policy. The Central American democracies felt slighted by the earlier Contadora peace talks because major Latin states, particularly Mexico, tended to ignore these small countries. By the summer of 1986, the leaders of El Salvador, Costa Rica, and Honduras felt that the Contadora process favored Nicaragua. For this reason, the Central American democracies aligned, at least privately, with the United States' policy of using war as means to solving the issue with Nicaragua. The "core three" did not fully endorse the administration's approach, but the opportunity to place Central American states at the fore of diplomacy in the region helped draw them together in a weak and tentative relationship.

In early July, Habib was back in Central America to strengthen the alliance as the United State moved closer to the Senate vote and the arrival of support for the Contras. Following up comments made to a group of reporters, the United States diplomat expressed satisfaction at Arias' apparent submission to will of the United States. Pressure in the form of tough language and the threat of economic punishment forced Arias to balk at a bilateral border agreement with Nicaragua and adopt a position more in tune with the will of the United States. Habib noted that President Arias was "more helpful than in the past" for telling reporters that "the U.S. Congress was merely responding to Sandinista aggression and repression when it approved assistance to the resistance."[43]

While Arias seemed to fall in line, the leaders of the three nations were increasingly concerned about the danger that the United States' approach was inspiring an escalation of hostilities and threatened the outbreak of a wider war. President Azcona of Honduras and President Duarte of El Salvador, the two closest supporters of the United States, both expressed concern to Habib that the Sandinistas, in the backdrop of the House vote, assumed an increasingly hardline position and that they feared further escalation from Nicaragua. Increasingly nervous that the United States' escalation might further threaten El Salvador, Duarte sought reaffirmation that the Reagan administration intended to continue its support to his country, which struggled to fight the Sandinista-backed insurgency. The Honduran leadership was, like El Salvador, concerned that the approval of the Contra aid package might lead to Nicaraguan military and terrorist responses. The commander of Azcona's armed forces, General Fallece Humberto Regalado Hernández, expressed his concern that the Honduran government had "intelligence that when the Contra activity begins to pick up, the Sandinistas will react by initiating terrorist actions in Honduras."[44] The "core three" Central American states felt little choice but to support the United States against an increasingly hostile Nicaragua, but they also feared that an expanded war might be a consequence of the continual efforts of the Reagan administration to increase military pressure against Nicaragua. The leaders of these nations were between a rock and a hard place. Opposition to the United States meant threats, economic punishment, and vulnerability to a neighboring government antagonized by the United States' proxy war. However, if leaders of these countries supported the United States' policy then it undoubtedly made escalation of the conflict more likely.

In the summer of 1986, the "core three" Central American states remained cautiously in the United States' camp. All of the leaders faced problems and expressed concerns with Nicaragua, but also feared that the United States' proxy war might result in an expanded conflict. Costa Rica and Honduras were angry for Nicaragua filing a case, along with the United States, with the ICJ for complicity in allowing the Contra guerrillas to use sovereign territory to launch strikes into Nicaragua. When Costa Rican President Oscar Arias sought a closer regulation of Contra activities within its territory, the United States bullied the newly elected leader. At the insistence of the United States, Costa Rica did not accept the bilateral border agreement, but the Arias government did begin to police the guerrilla activity more thoroughly. Likewise, President Duarte of El Salvador continued a war against Sandinista supported guerrillas in his country. By summer of 1986, the three governments were cautious supporters of the Reagan administration's policy. The United States' policy implicated its territories in a cycle of escalating hostilities and with Nicaragua increasingly isolated and intransigent against the war, the "core three" states had little choice but to align with the Reagan administration. Following these developments, the peace process was shelved and the Central American leaderships waited for the new military aid package for the Contras to exert the kind of pressure on Nicaragua that might force it to disarm and reach an agreement that satisfied the Reagan administration's desire of regime change through a pro-Contra democratization.[45] The "core three" states wanted peace, they did not want an escalation of hostiles, but the implication of the governments in the war left little option but to acquiesce to the approach of the United States.

The Contra package was included as a rider attached to the military construction bill for 1987. Congress authorized lethal aid to the Contras with only a few exceptions. First, while American personnel could train Contra guerrillas, they could not do so within twenty miles of the Nicaraguan border, and they could not enter Nicaragua. Second, the aid was scheduled for three installments, $40 million immediately, then $20 million by October 15 (released only if negotiations proved impossible), and $40 million on February 15, 1987.[46] In about six weeks the Senate, amid threats of filibuster, narrowly approved a call for cloture and voted to approve the measure by the predicted margin of 53 to 47.[47] The administration's war on terrorism against Nicaragua was well underway, but this vote represented a long sought shift in Congress and a legal authorization of its regime change policy.

Since the outset of the Reagan administration's surrogate war against Nicaragua in 1981, opponents had challenged the White House that it's policy possessed a dangerous potential to repeat the catastrophe of the Vietnam War. During the majority of Reagan's first term the administration defined the conflict in the guise of Cold War containment, and this rationale found limited support in Congress. However, after the emergence of international terrorism as an expanded and relevant security threat, the administration redefined the conflict and this redefinition marginalized the power of the Vietnam analogy. During the final attempts to undermine the Contra aid package in the Senate, Patrick Leahy, Democrat from Vermont, drew on the Vietnam analogy once more when he remarked that, "There are going to be ugly scenes on nightly television of dead and maimed civilians, destroyed schools, and hospitals, school buses blown up by mines."[48] While no member of that body could predict the future, Leahy understood that this legislation equated to an authorization for war. The Vietnam analogy, used for several years as a way of opposing military support for the Contras, was powerful, but amid a new war on terrorism, this language no longer resonated the way it did during Reagan's first term. Although this was still a divisive issue, the administration had managed to shift the dialogue over the conflict and justify its war.

During the summer of 1986, a *New York Times* reporter gained access to a Contra rebel base. The image painted by the journalist was vivid. He interviewed Contra leaders and observed the pallets of supplies destined to be air dropped to guerrilla units inside Nicaragua. Military leaders made plans for ordering new supplies and prepared to launch offensive operations into Nicaragua. At the base, whose existence the Honduran government publicly denied, there was a military hospital and all the signs of an already brutal war. The report documented those with amputations and injured child soldiers, including a fifteen-year-old girl who had over a year of combat experience. This was a war, and the Reagan administration continually pressed for its escalation. [49]

The Reagan administration's reliance on a military oriented war on terrorism carried significant consequences. Most of these were for the people of Central America. The conflict left thousands displaced, maimed, or killed. Growing tension existed among neighboring states increasingly threatened by a militarized Nicaragua that the United States had backed into a corner by continual harassment and aggression. The unabashed aggression of the United States, however, also carried significant consequences for the administration's own policy. On October 6, 1986, something happened that marked the demise of the administration's efforts at regime change.

On Monday October 6, 1986, a US-built transport aircraft entered Nicaraguan airspace. The transport carried military supplies for the Contras operating within Nicaraguan territory. Shortly after entering Nicaraguan airspace, the Sandinista air defenses shot the plane down. Of the four-man crew, three died. The only survivor parachuted safely to the ground and the Sandinista armed forces took him captive. The United States Congress, the American public, and the international community, were shocked to learn that the survivor was a forty-five-year-old American from Marinette, Wisconsin, named Eugene Hasenfus. Two of the three dead were also United States citizens. While Congress neared the release of authorized lethal support to the Contras, the operations violated long standing restrictions on United States involvement in actions against the government of Nicaragua. [50] Over the course of the following weeks and months, the incident marked the beginning of revelations eventually known as the Iran-Contra Affair. In Central America, the Reagan administration's continual insistence to ignore the accepted bounds of international behavior dealt a fatal blow to its policy.

The downing of Eugene Hasenfus' transport plane marked the eventual end of the Reagan administration's offensive war against Nicaragua, but not without much wrangling and the emergence of a courageous and bold Central

American leader. The event represented the consequences of an arrogant policy that placed military measures before diplomacy and did so with little concern for the norms of international behavior or for the oversight of Congress. The administration's offensive policy of regime change in Nicaragua relied on Congressional backing and support of the Central American leaders. The scandal undermined this support and critically wounded the administration's war on terrorism. [51]

Shortly after Hasenfus' downing the Wisconsin resident testified that he was working as part of an elaborate CIA directed program to drop supplies to transnational guerrillas operating illegally inside Nicaraguan territory. [52] Despite the escalated US-led war, few in the United States, Latin America, or Europe were prepared to openly accept a policy that so clearly violated the sovereignty of another nation. In the coming months, the congressional investigation following Hasenfus' capture led to one of the most damaging political scandals in the nation's history. The Iran-Contra Affair seized the spotlight. President Ronald Reagan, George H. W. Bush, and George Shultz came through the controversy with their careers and credibility intact, but the impetus for the offensive against Nicaragua was lost with that plane crash on that Monday in October.

The Iran-Contra Affair rapidly emerged as one of worst such scandals for an administration in the twentieth century. Directed most intimately by Oliver North, John Poindexter, and Robert McFarlane the administration had conducted an illegal funding and support operation for a number of years. The operation involved illegality on multiple levels: first, despite its own assertion to never negotiate with terrorists the investigation revealed that the administration traded weapons with Iran for the exchange of American hostages, such action was barred by Congress. The proceeds for the sales it embezzled and deposited in the bank accounts of Contra leaders, which at the time were cut off from any direct aid from the United States. Investigations led by individuals like Senator John Kerry revealed that the affair went deeper than simply the embezzlement of illegal weapons sales. Senator Kerry's staff revealed many of the Contras and American citizens were involved in drug smuggling operations as well.

Senator John Kerry began receiving tips that the United States' proxies were involved in drug and weapons trafficking in Spring of 1986. Months before Hasensfus was shot down the Senate Committee on Foreign Relations investigated illegal activities involving the Contras and the role of the Reagan administration. The investigation findings, published in December 1988, were shocking. The Committee insisted that, "It is clear that individuals who provided support for the Contras were involved in drug trafficking [and] elements of the Contras themselves knowingly received financial and material assistance from drug traffickers." Top officials like General Paul Gorman and Drug Enforcement Administration (DEA) Assistant Administrator David

Westrate testified to the Committee that drug trafficking was endemic to Central America and that it was effectively impossible to separate the networks utilized by the Contras, and the Sandinistas before the revolution, from the control and influence of the drug cartels. Drug smuggling and the illegal weapons trade was independent of ideological affiliation. Westrate verified that the FSLN were involved in this before the revolution, and that the Contras filled the void when the United States emboldened its insurgency. Cartels controlled the networks, and this connection was inherent and not the anomaly that the State Department suggested when initially questioned over these matters from 1985 to 1986. [53]

Not only did the committee reveal the link between illegal drug and weapons trafficking with the Contras it also revealed that the United States facilitated the behavior. The degree to which top members of the State Department consciously paid drug smugglers is difficult to know. However, the United States gave nearly $1 million of humanitarian aid authorized by Congress to air transport and supply service companies that smuggled cocaine by air to the United States, particularly South Florida.

On March 16, 1987, the DEA seized a DC-4 in Port Charlotte, Florida just south of the Tampa–St. Pete area. The plane was chased by the Florida Customs Service and it dropped its cargo over the Gulf of Mexico. Contact information for Oliver North's aid, Robert Owen, was found on board. North apparently believed that using drug money to fund the Contras was acceptable in certain cases, and there existed evidence that he pursued leniency and protection of individuals involved in trafficking as a sort of payoff for assistance to the United States war effort. The most notable such case was that of the Honduran General Jose Bueso-Rosa. Buseo-Rosa faced criminal charges for funding a plot to assassinate the Honduran president with $40 million worth of cocaine sales in the United States. The committee revealed that Bueso-Rosa was granted leniency in a case that the Justice Department called "the most significant case of narco-terrorism yet discovered." North feared that Bueso-Rosa might reveal the extent of his involvement with the Contras and so he sought to keep him quiet. Traffickers understood this component of this proxy war and knew that if they worked with the Contras it might facilitate their operations or keep them above prosecution. [54]

The United States interest in overthrowing the government of Nicaragua implicated the United States government in a web of smuggling and illegal operations. Even independent United States citizens were tied up in the network. Most notable was John Hull. Hull was an Indiana farmer that bought land on the remote and rugged Nicaragua-Costa Rican border in 1979. Hull's land, ultimately known as John Hull's Ranch, had six rudimentary airstrips. The airstrips were used for weapons shipments, and refueling for flights of drugs to the United States. Furthermore, the committee investigation revealed that US government owned planes were utilized in some of these operations. Iran-Contra revealed that the Reagan administration's proxy war had implicated the government in a dastardly web of criminal activity.[55]

The development of the Iran-Contra scandal opened a window for Oscar Arias to act as an agent for peace in Central America. The United States' policy with Nicaragua used war to force the Sandinistas to agree to a peace on its terms. The Reagan administration remained uncompromising. The United States demanded that the Nicaraguan government allow the Contras to participate and reform the Sandinista government. This goal was the most efficient way that Washington felt it could achieve the effect of regime change in Nicaragua. For this reason, the pressure of war was the primary tool for the administration. Arias, on the other hand, disagreed with this policy. At the beginning of 1987, Arias revealed his own plan for peace in Central America.[56]

President Arias of Costa Rica was neither a supporter of the United States policy or of the less than democratic nature of the Sandinista government in Nicaragua. Arias perceived leaders in the United States like Reagan and Shultz as blinded by their grand perspective of the Cold War and their associated "obsession" with the Contras. Were the Sandinistas the equivalent of the global struggle of communism? For Arias, the answer was, obviously, no. The President likewise did not feel that Nicaragua represented any true threat to the region. These ideas, he correctly understood as constructs by the United States. Arias supported the FSLN when it emerged as an alternative to Somoza and the embodiment of a truly national movement in 1979. However, after taking power Arias lamented that Daniel Ortega did not fashion the country as a democracy, and Sandinista leadership did not continue the embrace of the mass anti-Somoza movement that brought it to power. Instead, Arias referred to Ortega as little more than a "caudillo" or Central American strongman that had never read the works of Marx or Lenin and was hardly the pawn of a global leftist conspiracy. According to President Arias, Ortega explained to him that because he "won a revolution that he did not need to hold elections." His revolution was like that of Castro, and it granted the Sandinistas a right to rule in perpetuity. A democratically minded individual, Arias found this attitude offensive and problematic, but not the threat alleged by Washington. According to Arias, Nicaragua did not pose any real threat to its neighbors. Instead, the primary problem resulted from a US war policy that created and escalated conflict across the region and violated the sovereignty of multiple Central American nations.[57]

While the Iran-Contra scandal festered on Capitol Hill, Arias seized on his opportunity. The democratically elected leader of Costa Rica went to the United States and met with Democrats in Congress, including Senator Chris Dodd who supported his pursuit of a Central American peace led by Costa Rica. After the peace process was underway Arias, ultimately, remembered Ambassador Philip Habib as his only real friend and ally from the Reagan administration. Arias was grateful to Habib because the ambassador was able to provide communication and continuity between himself and the other Central American states and thereby made his agreement possible.[58] However, while Habib developed as an invaluable ally to Arias some disagreement remained between the United States envoy and the President of Costa Rica. On February 25, 1987, Ambassador Habib reported to Washington on his perception of Arias' plan and his motivations. Habib believed that the plan was inadequate because it did not do enough to guarantee the disarmament of Nicaragua and the incorporation of the Contras into the Nicaraguan political process. Habib was privately skeptical of Arias who he alleged possessed a "distorted and one-sided view of the American political scene" given to him by congressional leaders like Chris Dodd (D). Arias walked a tightrope: on the one hand, the domestically driven leader wanted to achieve peace as quickly and efficiently as possible, but on the other hand, he felt compelled to appease the increasingly disgruntled and embattled Reagan administration, which made veiled threats to encourage Arias' cooperation.[59]

Arias played two opposing cards: first, he promoted a peace agreement that he hoped and believed would succeed and second, he attempted to reassure Habib that he expected his plan to fail. The United States ambassador understood this and reported to Washington his distrust of Arias' intentions by claiming, "at least this [failure of his initiative] is what he says he expects." Habib felt that the plan was an attempt by Arias to take the spotlight for political purposes, and he was concerned that the proposal "could seriously complicate our [US] policy." However, Habib also understood that the Iran-Contra investigation had seriously damaged the position of the United States and for this reason he advised the administration not to publically oppose the proposal and hope for the best arrangement possible. Generally, the architects of US policy opposed the Arias plan. Hardliners wanted an outright opposition to the agreement whereas moderates, like Shultz and Habib, understanding that options were limited, believed that the United States should continue its efforts to support the Contras while going along with the peace plan out of a hope that the war and this process might be enough to discredit the Sandinistas and facilitate its ouster through an electoral process that included the Contras. As Arias developed a plan for a Central American peace deal, the Reagan administration sat on the sidelines, less able than at any point to control the outcome.[60]

The Arias peace plan was a Central American plan for the Central American states. Unlike the original Contadora plan that involved only the major Latin American states, Mexico most significantly, Arias' plan was a five-power agreement among Costa Rica, El Salvador, Honduras, Guatemala, and Nicaragua. These five Central American states planned to vote on the agreement at a second meeting in Guatemala, scheduled for the summer of 1987. The Arias plan and the Iran-Contra scandal, together, was a worst case scenario for the Reagan administration. Following the escalation of its offensive in 1985 and 1986, the United States hoped to use a forceful diplomacy to encourage the Central American democracies to facilitate a policy of regime change. During the summer of 1986, it was clear that Guatemala was not on board with any policy that sought to isolate and attack Nicaragua. President Cerezo of Guatemala, influenced by Mexico, could not go along with the Reagan administration's attempt to use the Central American democracies to surround Nicaragua and bring unyielding force upon the Sandinistas. Without Guatemala, the Reagan administration still felt that it had a winning policy as long as Costa Rica stayed on board with El Salvador and Honduras. However, the emergence of the Iran-Contra scandal mortally wounded the administration's policy and Arias used this opportunity to disassociate himself from the United States' policy.[61]

The Reagan administration was secretly critical of the Arias plan because it placed little emphasis on the need to provide "security" by forcing the Sandinistas to disarm or to enter into a direct and open dialogue with the guerrillas. The plan was a rejection of the administration's original policy of using the Central American democracies as a staging area from which to isolate and make war against Nicaragua. Over the next year, Arias tried to reassure the Reagan administration that he was certain of Nicaragua's rejection of his plan or that it would fail to fulfill the plan after signing. Arias insisted that if the Sandinistas fell short of the agreement then the United States would have the necessary justification to return to its aggressive measures of coercion.[62] Arias knew that the United States' position was increasingly unpopular. Following Hasenfus' capture and the emergence of the Iran-Contra Affair, the Reagan administration was increasingly isolated. No major European or Latin American power supported Reagan's policy of aiding the Contras, and the United States Congress was increasingly reluctant to provide aid to the Contras when the program was up for renewal in November 1987. Arias stepped into this situation and seized an opportunity to make peace and to show the world that Costa Rica was a leader in the process.

The only two governments that remained strong supporters of the Reagan administration were El Salvador and Honduras. Both of these governments privately joined the United States in opposing the Arias plan. However, these two governments did not guarantee that either would not sign Arias' proposal. The leadership in Honduras and El Salvador had since the beginning of the US-Contra war linked national security to the ability of the United States to control and stabilize the region. The United States, however, struggled to control the region and the developing Iran-Contra scandal left a sense of vulnerability. President Duarte of El Salvador and President Azcona of Honduras were concerned that Iran-Contra left the Reagan administration less capable to provide military support than before and that the United States was on the eve of potentially pulling out and leaving the Sandinista government unchanged. While Ambassador Habib tried to convince Azcona and Duarte otherwise, he could not change this sense of concern that El Salvador, for instance, might become just the next Cold War ally sold up the river at the end of a controversial conflict.[63]

After a February 15, 1987, meeting with Arias, the Honduran president asked to delay the Esquipulas summit of the five Central American states long enough for the Contras to leave Honduras and station themselves entirely inside Nicaragua. Arias, desiring a quick solution, felt he made a significant compromise when he agreed to this delay. By June, the Contras operated largely within Nicaraguan territory and Azcona did not want the guerrillas to return to Honduras.[64] The Reagan administration was unlikely to come to the aid of Honduras and President Azcona did not want the Contras return to his country and leave his administration holding the burden of dealing with the transnational army. Both Azcona and Duarte understood that the United States was unlikely to provide the kind of the support that the Reagan administration pledged verbally and neither wanted to be left alone and potentially vulnerable to a Sandinista offensive unchecked by United States power.[65]

In spring and summer 1987, Habib and Arias continued to struggle over the peace proposal. The United States demanded that the Arias plan needed significant changes in order to ensure that the Contras remained viable if

Figure 8.1.   Oscar Arias surrounded by reporters. *Source*: **Archivo Nacional de Costa Rica, Photograph, signature 26258.**

Nicaragua should renege on the agreement, and that there was verifiability in the form of UN inspections to ensure Nicaraguan compatibility. In June, meetings between Arias and Habib grew tense on a number of occasions. In his attempts to promote peace while simultaneously appeasing the United States, he again insisted to Habib that he hoped for the plans failure, either with Nicaragua as the only Central American government refusing to sign or with Nicaragua reneging on the agreement proposed in Guatemala. Arias implied to the United States diplomat that in such an eventuality Nicaragua would appear in the wrong and the Reagan administration might have another chance to use military pressure to secure concessions from the Sandinistas. To Habib, Arias insisted that he sought to use his plan as a way of exposing the Sandinistas. However, the United States did not trust Arias whom Habib called "stubborn." Habib recognized that Arias was emboldened by his consultations with European leaders and opposition leaders in the United States Congress to promote the proposal and oppose efforts by the Reagan administration to increase hardline military oriented measures.[66] The Habib mission insisted that Arias should make necessary changes that would satisfy the demands of both El Salvador and Honduras, but Arias consistently retorted that such changes would result in failure by dividing the Central American states and resulting in Guatemala and Nicaragua voting against the measure.[67]

During their meeting in June 1987 the frustrations between Costa Rica and the United States surfaced in an intense exchange between Arias and Habib. Arias seemed irritated by Habib wrangling with him over the terms of the agreement. Arias demonstrated his nuanced perspective of events and insisted that the United States, following Iran-Contra, was isolated and that its intentional usage of the transnational guerrillas challenged the norms of international behavior and was widely opposed throughout Latin America and the world. Further, Arias was upset over the administration's manipulation of Costa Rica in the previous year as it had basically bribed him to give up on a bilateral agreement with Nicaragua. He exclaimed that the Reagan administration had "used Costa Rica." Arias, in a position of strength and with a degree of annoyance, suggested to Habib that if the upcoming Esquipulas summit failed, he would "walk away" and the United States "could invade Nicaragua!" Arias emphatically asked Habib to stay out of the Esquipulas summit. He tried to reassure Habib that he was confident of the proposal's failure and that when it failed the United States could return to its military efforts to pressure the Sandinistas. However, Arias exclaimed that regardless of whether his efforts succeeded or failed that the United States should not go back to its policy of support for the Contras. The use of those transnational guerrillas threatened the region, violated international law, and implicated states like Honduras and Costa Rica while the Reagan administration avoided the full blame that was due. Arias felt that the Reagan administration had bullied and used the smaller Central American states.[68]

After the Iran-Contra affair was fully exposed the Reagan administration's policy with the Contras was at its most controversial moment. Some in the United States not only supported an end to the administration's war, but expressed their feelings in personal letters to President Arias. George Georges of San Francisco wrote, "Our President Ronald Reagan had a military-oriented ideology and seeks a military solution to the situation/conflict in Central America. Please try to ignore his (Reagan's) obstinances—the people of the U.S. want Peace." Others like Rev. David Duncombe, Frank Winterroth, and Laura Ball of Philadelphia also wrote Arias to encourage the President in his attempt to promote peace and resist the US-Contra war. The conflict was deeply controversial and Americans had throughout expressed fear and skepticism at the Reagan administration's military oriented approach.[69] In these tense hours some Americans voiced direct support for Arias.

Of all the countries most unsure about Arias' plan, El Salvador was at the top of the list. Getting El Salvador to agree was one of the biggest challenges facing Arias. However, unwittingly, the United States facilitated its move into the Arias camp. President Duarte expressed privately to Arias that he increasingly felt that the United States did not care about the conflict in El Salvador, but was instead focused only on the Contras. In his eyes, the Reagan administration, hoping to somehow influence the Arias peace proposal, confirmed these concerns when it pushed forward the Wright-Reagan peace plan. The proposal, which House Speaker and Texas Democrat Jim Wright co-sponsored, hinged on the notion that military support for governments and insurgencies be cut and that the Contras be incorporated into the democratic process in Nicaragua as opposed to support being cut only to insurgencies and irregular guerrilla proxies as the Arias plan proposed. The plan, which many theorized amounted to another ploy by the Reagan administration to derail the Arias peace and promote continued military support for the Contras, unwittingly facilitated the successful completion of the Arias plan. In a private interview in 2016, Arias insisted that President Duarte was so upset, in part, by the notion that no government be allowed to receive military support form a foreign power that he realized that the United States was not a friend of his country, but was rather only interested in its regime change policy in Nicaragua. Duarte expressed to Arias that his government was on a knife edge and that it needed the military support of the United States, but to him the Wright-Reagan plan effectively ignored this urgent necessity. The idea that the United States proposed a cut to this aid as sort of ploy against Nicaragua made him feel as though he was a mere pawn to the Reagan administration. As a result, Duarte joined Arias and became the final critical ally in the support of the Esquipulas agreement, which hinged, in part, on all countries repudiating support for insurgencies in the region.[70]

As the Esquipulas meeting loomed, the Reagan administration, embattled on the domestic front and powerless on the diplomatic side, could do little more than watch its original strategy of using offensive military pressure fade in favor of a Central American peace agreement of which the administration was privately skeptical. Prior to the meeting in Guatemala City that August, the administration secretly hoped for the failure of the Arias plan. However, on August 7, 1987, El Salvador, Guatemala, Costa Rica, Nicaragua, and Honduras all signed the Treaty of Esquipulas. The agreement was a repudiation of the entire Contra support program and acknowledged it as illegal and a violation of the sovereignty of the Central American states. In the following year, the Sandinistas and the Contras agreed to schedule free and fair elections held in 1990 in accordance with the Nicaraguan Constitution. The treaty also began a process that eventually brought an end to the conflicts in El Salvador and Guatemala.[71]

While the Sandinistas and the Contras continued to skirmish over the next year, the two ultimately agreed to a ceasefire and joined political negotia-

Figure 8.2. The Esquipulas Group. Seated from left to right: Nicaraguan President Ortega, El Salvadoran President Duarte, Guatemalan President Cerezo, Honduran President Azcona, Costa Rican President Oscar Arias. *Source:* **Archivo Nacional de Costa Rica, Photograph, signature 26253.**

tions. The Reagan administration and supporters were appalled because the agreement did not necessarily facilitate a change of the Nicaraguan government and potentially allowed the consolidation of the Sandinista regime. The Reagan administration, however, was on the wrong side of history. The world celebrated the agreement and it earned Oscar Arias the noble peace prize in 1987. The Costa Rican leader took advantage of the weakness brought on by the excessive adventurism of the Reagan administration and succeeded in creating a diplomatic solution that the United States preferred to derail.

Often scholars speak of the Reagan administration's activities in Central America as though the United States dictated the terms. Some ascribe a seemingly absolute power to neo-conservative policy makers in Washington. The Reagan administration did exert tremendous influence and will in this story. It went to great lengths: it bullied allies, exerted military violence, encouraged an escalation of the conflict, and used propaganda to build a coalition in Congress and Central America that made an offensive against Nicaragua possible. However, this story is not about the success of overwhelming will exerted by the United States. Rather it is emblematic of the inability of the United States, despite overwhelming capabilities, to control and dictate the future of Central America. The Carter administration had failed to control the course of the government during Somoza's collapse. The Reagan administration attempted to intricately construct an offensive regime change policy, but the capture of Hasenfus and the emergence of the Iran-Contra scandal destroyed this body of work. After these revelations, a majority of Congress lost faith in the justice and legality of the administration's policy and moved against renewing aid to the Contras. Likewise, the loss of congressional support destroyed the loose Central American coalition. Despite the tendency on the part of scholars to emphasize the will of the Reagan administration, leaders in Central America carried through the endgame. A lesson for the United States is its inability to control regions through the use and threat of military force.

In 1990, elections in Nicaragua resulted in the Sandinistas losing its majority control. The new president was Violetta Chamorro, the widow of *La Prensa* editor Pedro Chamorro whose murder in 1978 marked the beginning of the conflict. Her candidacy was championed by none other than President Arias.[72] However, the Sandinistas remained a viable party in Nicaraguan politics. The group suffered from the domestic policies during the embattled 1980s, but the political party and its leaders remained strong and intact. A decade later, the Sandinistas and Daniel Ortega again rose to the majority in Nicaraguan politics. Since 2000, the Nicaraguan people have elected Ortega to the presidency twice. Eventually, the Nicaraguan government voted to suspend term limits for the Presidency. The decision allowed the highly popular Ortega to run for another term of office, and came alongside an unprecedented level of Sandinista political success since the end of the war. Under Ortega the Nicaraguan state has continued to build a close relationship with nations that the United States alleges are potential state terrorist threats, Iran and Venezuela, as well as the United States biggest global competitor, China. Despite being off the public radar, the United States has quietly frowned on the government's move left in the twenty-first century. The George W. Bush administration, for example, withheld military aid and cut off grant deliveries on multiple occasions amid accusations of election fraud. These developments demonstrate the moderation of the modern Sandinista party but also the lasting divide between the United States and Nicaragua caused by a controversial and avoidable US-led war.

NOTES

1. "Announcement of Ambassador Philip C. Habib as Special Envoy to Central America," March 6, 1986, Box 5, John Boykin Collection: National Security Archive, Gelman Library, George Washington University.

2. "Obstruction of Contadora Effort is Charged," *New York Times*, May 11, 1984, http://search.proquest.com/docview/122457093?accountid=14902.

3. "Ambassador Habib's Meetings in Honduras," July 1986, Box 5, John Boykin Collection: National Security Archive, Gelman Library, George Washington University.

4. "Ambassador Habib's Meetings in Honduras," July 1986, George Washington University.

5. Interview with President Oscar Arias Sanchez, by Philip Travis, San Jose, Costa Rica, July 28, 2016.

6. State by George Shultz, "Central American Border Commissions," Box 5, John Boykin Collection: National Security Archive, Gelman Library, George Washington University.

7. State by George Shultz, "Central American Border Commissions," George Washington University.

8. "Habib-Oscar Arias Meeting," March 13, 1986, Box 5, John Boykin Collection: National Security Archive, Gelman Library, George Washington University.

9. "Presidential Evening Reading: Ambassador Habib Meets Azcona, Arias and Cerezo," Box 5, John Boykin Collection: National Security Archive, Gelman Library, George Washington University.

10. "Presidential Evening Reading: Ambassador Habib's Visit to Central America," March 1986, Box 5, John Boykin Collection: National Security Archive, Gelman Library, George Washington University.

11. "Presidential Evening Reading: Ambassador Habib Meets Azcona, Arias and Cerezo," George Washington University.

12. "Presidential Evening Reading: Ambassador Habib Meets Azcona, Arias and Cerezo," George Washington University.

13. Philip Habib, "March 13 Meeting with Guatemalan President Cerezo," Box 5, John Boykin Collection: National Security Archive, Gelman Library, George Washington University.

14. Habib, "March 13 Meeting with Guatemalan President Cerezo," George Washington University.

15. Oliver North, "U.S. Political/Military Strategy for Nicaragua," July 15, 1985, in Kornbluh and Byrne, *The Iran-Contra Scandal*, 51.

16. Habib, "Meeting with Guatemalan President Cerezo," George Washington University.

17. Michael Wines, "Invoked Against Nicaragua, Iran, South Africa, Sanctions Law Has Passed Supreme Court Test," *New York Times*, January 9, 1986, http://search.proquest.com/docview/292222939?accountid=14902.

18. Mary Campbell, "Jackson Browne's Tune is Changing to Reflect his Thoughts," *Orlando Sentinel*, May 4, 1986, http://search.proquest/docview/276838579?acountid=14902.

19. "U.S. Orders Expulsion of Two Nicaragua Envoys," *New York Times*, May 23, 1986, http://search.proquest/docview/110931598?accountid=14902.

20. 132 Cong Rec E1503 (daily ed. May 5, 1986).

21. 132 Cong Rec E1503 (daily ed. May 5, 1986).

22. Geoffrey Levitt, "Combatting Terrorism Under International Law," Folder "Terrorism: Material for Doug Menarchik" 4 of 6, OA/ID 19849, Box 1, Donald P. Gregg Files: George H. W. Bush Vice Presidential Records, Task Force on Terrorism File, George Bush Presidential Library.

23. Levitt, "Combatting Terrorism Under International Law," George Bush Presidential Library.

24. Jeane Kirkpatrick, "Nicaragua's Libyan Connection," *Chicago Tribune*, May 11, 1986, http://search.proquest/docview/290933469?accountid=14902.

25. George H. W. Bush, Interview for *American Legion*, Folder Terrorism- II: Terrorism Article, 3 of 3, Box 1 OA/ID 19849, Donald P. Gregg Files: Task force on Terrorism File, George Bush Presidential Library.

26. Craig Coy, Speech to National Defense Transportation Association, San Francisco, Ca., May 13, 1986, Folder Terrorism- II: Terrorism Article, 2 of 3, Box 1 OA/ID 19849, Donald P. Gregg Files: Task force on Terrorism File, George Bush Presidential Library.

27. "Public Diplomacy Plan for Explaining U.S. Central American Policy in Europe and Latin America," Box 5, John Boykin Collection: National Security Archive, Gelman Library, George Washington University.

28. Memorandum of Conversation, "Ambassador Habib with the UNO Leadership," May 14, 1986, Box 5, John Boykin Collection: National Security Archive, Gelman Library, George Washington University.

29. "Contadora: Visit to Costa Rica, El Salvador and Guatemala," June 1986, Box 5, John Boykin Collection: National Security Archive, Gelman Library, George Washington University.

30. "Ambassador Habib's Meeting with President Arias," June 1987, Box 5, John Boykin Collection: National Security Archive, Gelman Library, George Washington University.

31. "Judge Upholds Embargo on Trade with Nicaragua," *Providence Journal*, April 30, 1986, http://search.proquest/dociew/396575811?accountid=14902.

32. "Contadora: Visit to Costa Rica, El Salvador and Guatemala," George Washington University.

33. Gerald M. Boyd, "Reagan Presses Hard for Contra Aid," *New York Times*, June 7, 1986, http://search.proquest/docview/110919396?accountid=14902.

34. Neil A. Lewis, "Bush Discloses Secret Order Citing Drugs as Security Peril," *New York Times*, June 8, 1986, http://search.proquest/docview/110910339?accountid=14902.

35. "Soviet Arms Deliveries to Nicaragua Resume," *Chicago Tribune*, June 9, 1986, http://search.proquest/docview/290944287?accountid=14902.

36. "Soviets Reported Flying over Nicaragua," *The Globe and Mail*, June 12, 1986, http://search.proquest/386119108/accountid=14902.

37. "Shipment of Arms Called Routine," *New York Times*, June 11, 1986, http://ntserver1.wsulibs.wsu.edu:2184/docview/425925838?accountid=14902.

38. Michael Putzel, "Reagan Presses Contra Aid Plea; Sees Second Libya in Nicaragua if Funds are Refused," June 10, 1986, http://search.proquest/docview/294413274?accountid=14902.

39. State and Defense Department briefing book, June 1986, Folder "The Challenge to Democracy in Central America," Box 16, David S. Addington: Files, Ronald Reagan Library.

40. Linda Greenhouses, "Lobbying Succeeds: President Able to Change Some Minds About the 100 Million$ Plan House, 221–209, Votes Military Aid for Contras," *New York Times*, June 26, 1986, http://search.proquest/docview/110929828?accountid=14902.

41. Cynthia Arnson, *Crossroads: Congress, the President, and Central America, 1976–1993*, 2nd ed. (University Park: Pennsylvania State University Press, 1993), 198–217.

42. Greenhouses, "Lobbying Succeeds."

43. "Ambassador Habib's Meetings in Honduras," July 1986, George Washington University.

44. "Ambassador Habib's Meetings in Honduras," July 1986, George Washington University.

45. "Presidential Evening Reading, Ambassador Habib's Visit to Central America," July 14, 1986, Box 5, John Boykin Collection: National Security Archive, Gelman Library, George Washington University.

46. Greenhouses, "Lobbying Succeeds."

47. Steven V. Roberts, "President Wins Test in Senate on Contra Aid," *New York Times*, August 14, 1986, http://search.proquest/docview/110981288?accountid=14902.

48. Roberts, "President Wins Test in Senate on Contra Aid."

49. James LeMoyne, "For Contras, Prospect of Aid Stirs Preparation for Combat: Contras, Expecting Aid, Plan for War," *New York Times*, July 6, 1986, http://search.proquest/docview/110926533?accountid=14902.

50. "Nicaragua puts Hasenfus on Trial," *Orlando Sentinel*, October 21, 1986, accessed December 12, 2013, http://ntserver1.wsulibs.wsu.edu:2184/docview/276885754?accountid=14902.

51. "Nicaragua puts Hasenfus on Trial," *Orlando Sentinel*, October 21, 1986.

52. "Nicaragua puts Hasenfus on Trial," *Orlando Sentinel*, October 21, 1986.

53. "Drugs, Law Enforcement, and Foreign Policy: A Report Prepared by the Subcommittee on Terrorism, Narcotics, and International Operations" (US Government Printing Office: Washington, DC, 1989).

54. "Drugs, Law Enforcement, and Foreign Policy."

55. "Drugs, Law Enforcement, and Foreign Policy."

56. Oscar Arias Sanchez, "Una Hora Para La Paz: Procedimiento Para Establecer La Paz Firme Y Duradera En CentroAmerica," Folder Presidencia 3429, El Archivo Nacional de Costa Rica.

57. President Oscar Arias Sanchez, interview by Philip Travis.

58. President Oscar Arias Sanchez, interview by Philip Travis.

59. "The Diplomatic Track, My Trip to Central America and Mexico," February 25, 1987, Box 5, John Boykin Collection: National Security Archive, Gelman Library, George Washington University.

60. "The Diplomatic Track, My Trip to Central America and Mexico," February 25, 1987, George Washington University.

61. "The Diplomatic Track, My Trip to Central American and Mexico," February 25, 1987, George Washington University.

62. "Ambassador Habib's Meeting with President Arias," June 1987, George Washington University.

63. "Ambassador Habib's Meeting with President Arias," June 1987, George Washington University.

64. "Ambassador Habib's Meeting with President Arias," June 1987, George Washington University.

65. "The Diplomatic Track, My Trip to Central American and Mexico," February 25, 1987, George Washington University.

66. "The Negotiating Track in Central America, Esquipulas and Beyond," May 28, 1987, Box 5, John Boykin Collection: National Security Archive, Gelman Library, George Washington University.

67. "Ambassador Habib's Meeting with President Arias."

68. "Ambassador Habib's Meeting with President Arias."

69. Letters to Arias from George Georges, David Duncombe, Frank Winterroth, and Laura Ball, Folder Presidencia 3810, El Archivo Nacional de Costa Rica.

70. Oscar Arias Sanchez, interview by Philip Travis.

71. "Esquipulas II," Folder Presidencia 3429, El Archivo Nacional de Costa Rica.

72. Oscar Arias Sanchez, interview by Philip Travis.

Epilogue

On a typically warm spring day in Nicaragua a young American doctor named Keith Graham was on foot on the country's primitive roads. Graham was an independent aid worker that provided medical assistance to the people of a small Northwest Nicaraguan village called Somotillo. The young doctor was trying to find his way into Nicaragua's capital city, Managua. As he journeyed in a world completely alien to a man from the Pacific Northwest he was overjoyed when a car pulled over to offer him a ride. The car was a small Soviet made Lada. Such vehicles were common in Nicaragua. However, more interesting than the car was the driver. Driving the car was perhaps the most well-known of American aid workers in Nicaragua, Ben Linder. [1]

Linder was from Portland, Oregon, and had first traveled to Nicaragua in 1983. From 1983 until spring 1987, Linder worked for the Nicaraguan National Energy Institute on a variant of public improvement projects. Linder, a graduate of the University of Washington, applied his knowledge of power production and assisted in the construction of local hydro-electric facilities in Nicaragua. In 1986, he came back to the United States and went on a speaking tour to raise awareness about the war and obtain financial support for a new local hydroelectric facility. In many ways, Linder represented the core of transnational activism, and of a solidarity movement between the new Nicaraguan government and activists in the United States and throughout the world. [2]

Not surprisingly, Keith Graham knew of Linder before their chance meeting. He heard stories of him riding his unicycle for the children and encouraging vaccinations in rural regions of war torn Nicaragua. As Graham and Linder traveled down Nicaragua's bumpy roads in that beat-up old Lada the two chatted about the war, about the people, and about everyday things. After this relatively short happenstance meeting, Graham, only in his third month in the region, made a friend of Linder. Unfortunately, the short friendship was to remain that, short.

On April 28, 1987, Benjamin Linder and several other Nicaraguans were attacked by the Contras. Linder was wounded and then executed by individuals that the Reagan administration praised in its propaganda messages as "freedom fighters." Linder's death was not connected to any military operation. Instead, the guerrillas attacked the group while they conducted water flow measurements in the remote area of San José de Bocay. The team was working on the construction of a hydroelectric facility designed to provide energy to the Nicaraguans living in this remote area. Linder was first wounded in the legs before one of the guerrillas delivered a point blank bullet wound to the temple.[3] The death carried the markings of an execution.

Prior to his death, Linder wrote letters to his father, David Linder, MD. In these letters Benjamin Linder explained that he witnessed numerous attacks by guerrilla units that at times numbered as many as one hundred. The guerrillas, he explained, destroyed village infrastructure. The Contras burned medical facilitates, destroyed crops, and bombed power stations. From his experience, Benjamin Linder believed that the Contras were conducting a "planned effort to destroy all that is good, every symbol of progress, in the lives of the people." After his death, Linder's father passionately testified before Congress and accused both the United States and the Contras of murder.[4]

Linder, of course, was not the only United States activist working in Nicaragua. Keith Graham, too, was part of a loosely connected grassroots movement that supported the sovereign rights and territorial integrity of Nicaragua and resisted the Reagan administration's policy less by political protest and more by positive actions that built trust and respect with the people. In the United States there were protests, letters, films, legal cases, and other demonstrations that represented a small but present opposition to the United States' war. However, many Americans also expressed their opposition by traveling to Nicaragua and helping the people that the Reagan administration seemed so eager to destroy.

In 1983, Keith Graham worked at a break neck pace finishing his medical training. Graham was an intern at the Medical Center of Vermont located in Burlington. He spent some eighty hours a week working in the hospital completing his training. Burlington had a rich activist culture and while Graham had little time to spend being an activist, he was exposed to individuals and ideas that helped inspire an interest in the increasingly controversial US-Contra war.[5]

After completing his training Graham moved to Anchorage, Alaska, and established his own medical practice. While in Alaska his natural tendency toward active involvement in the United States' democracy led him to his first experience with political activism. Graham took up the difficult position

Figure E.1.   Keith Graham, center left behind the man in the white shirt and black beard, marches in Leon, Nicaragua, in honor and protest to the murder of Benjamin Linder. *Source*: Keith Graham.

of publically arguing in favor of gun control in Alaska, the United States' last frontier. Despite facing significant resistance and little results on his gun control position his activity as a civic minded individual introduced relationships that forever changed his life. After hearing his testimonials about the importance of gun control Graham was contacted by a now long forgotten group that called itself "Alaskans Concerned about Latin America." Graham attended the group's regular meetings and through this engagement his interest in the Reagan administration's counterinsurgency war in Nicaragua increased. It did not take long before Graham decided that he wanted to get involved in the Nicaragua solidarity movement. The young doctor prepared to travel to Nicaragua.[6]

Keith Graham soon learned, however, that going to Nicaragua was not an easy task. He contacted his local priest in Anchorage in hopes of acquiring financial support to travel to war ravaged Central America. He soon learned, however, that the Reagan administration's posture on such activism made obtaining support difficult. Eventually, Graham was connected with a priest in Leon, Nicaragua, named Gerald Stuckey. Stuckey assured him that if he traveled to Leon on his own that the priest could place him in a Nicaraguan community that needed the kinds of services that the young MD offered.[7]

So, in December 1986, with no significant financial backing and only a rudimentary grasp of the Spanish language, Keith Graham left his medical practice, packed up his things, and boarded a plane for Guatemala. In Guatemala, a country also devastated by a war conducted by a repressive US supported government, the young doctor attended several months of language school designed to prepare him for land journey to Nicaragua. [8]

After learning a little Spanish, Graham traveled overland from Guatemala to Nicaragua. His journey gave him a firsthand view of the war-torn region. In Central America, the Reagan administration supported the governments of El Salvador and Guatemala in a fight against revolutionary movements. The use of advisors, and military support brought some controversy in the United States Congress, but this indirect use of proxy war left most Americans almost completely unaware of the reality of the wars being fought. While in Central America Graham saw the results of this war firsthand. In Guatemala, he recalled that the government military forces seemed to target the people in a manner not unlike during Vietnam. The people feared the soldiers and the government went to extensive lengths to fight the guerrillas that included variations of the so-called strategic hamlet program used by the United States and its South Vietnamese ally during the early phases of the Vietnam War. In Guatemala, whole villages were relocated as the government forces sought to isolate and eradicate the insurgents. [9]

Of all the places that Graham visited none, however, shocked him more than El Salvador. The Salvadoran Civil War that began in 1980, and which the United States government went to extensive lengths to end through military support extended to the government, resulted in a massive displacement of the people. In El Salvador, he witnessed widespread homelessness, refugees, and children living in the most decrepit existence imaginable. Graham's experience in Central America lent little sympathy for the policy of the United States government. Instead, it left him shocked and dismayed at how the Reagan administration allowed such a situation to develop while simultaneously insisting to the American people that the policy promoted justice and freedom for Central America. Graham did not witness this, but rather his shock at the consequences of a misguided policy left the physician ashamed and even further critical of the actions of his government. [10]

When he arrived in Nicaragua, Graham experienced a unique situation. The solidarity movement appeared to thrive. Sandinista soldiers did not display the hostility that he experienced from government soldiers in Guatemala and El Salvador. From his perspective, Nicaragua appeared as a nation that supported the ideals of the Nicaraguan revolution. These ideals involved the promotion of justice, equality, and opportunity to all Nicaraguans. It was a revolution that centered on returning Nicaragua from the hands of imperialism and strong-man dictatorship to those of the people, and while criticism was due to the Sandinistas, the population of the country seemed to embrace

Figure E.2. Keith Graham (right hand side of the photo) poses with five Sandinista Soldiers, 1987. *Source*: **Keith Graham.**

the cause despite the Reagan administration's efforts to use the Contras to overthrow the government.[11]

The Contras terrorized people that collaborated with the government of Nicaragua. The guerrillas violated national sovereignty and intentionally attacked soft targets like power stations. In fact, in 1986 the Costa Rican government thwarted a plot by the Contras to launch an organized attack on hydro-electric power stations across much of Costa Rica. This plan was undoubtedly a response to Oscar Arias' efforts to eliminate the Contras from Costa Rican territory. The Costa Rican government referred to the Contras as "terrorists," and the so-called "freedom fighters" use of terrorism was more a rule than an anomaly. However, for the United States the threat of terrorism was less about the act than it was about the motivations of those that perpetrated the act. For the Reagan administration terrorism was more of a political term.[12]

The Reagan administration's policy with Nicaragua flaunted standards of international behavior, particularly respect for national sovereignty, and this unabashed policy brought negative consequences. The covert war that the United States conducted created thousands of refugees and casualties. It also unleashed a political scandal in the United States that caused further damage to the credibility of the executive branch. Perhaps the only silver lining was that the political damage caused by the offensive opened the door for Central Americans to step in and create a lasting peace.

This narrative calls one to question the shortcomings of foreign policy solutions to terrorism that are offensive and militaristic in nature. The United States often relies on military solutions to terrorism, but time and time again such approaches result in an escalation of conflict, and rarely lasting solutions. This story provides a lesson for future administrations that deal with the threat of terrorism. Fighting a war on terrorism with aggressive offensive measures often creates many more problems than solutions. The true solutions rest with the people and the leadership in the region and with the international system of law and justice. The United States should pursue diplomacy and legal measures rather than seek to control such a situation with force. In Central America, the regional leaders created solutions and cleaned up a mess created, to a significant degree, by a militaristic and condescending approach from the United States.

International terrorism was a concept created and defined, by and large, by the Reagan administration. It reconceptualized the manner in which the United States used power in the world. The United States pursued offensive measures designed to fight a new Cold War characterized by the emergence of a global terrorist alliance dedicated to employing the psychologically devastating weapon of terrorism against the free world: at least this was the manner in which the Reagan administration perceived the growth of global revolution and state sponsorship of terrorism. The primary method that the Reagan administration developed to combat state sponsors of terrorism relied on a framework of intervention that culminated in the work of George H. W. Bush's Task Force to Combat Terrorism. This framework used economic, diplomatic, and offensive military pressure as tools of coercion. The United States refused to engage in fair negotiations with an alleged sponsor of terrorism. Instead, the policy of the United States was to provide ultimatums that carried consequences if ignored. The consequences involved crippling economic sanctions, and a wide-range of military measures. Military pressure was a critical part of this new offensive program, and included military and naval maneuvers, covert warfare, support for insurgent movements, threat of war, and direct US military action in the form of air strikes, naval mining and other clandestine operations of sabotage. These were the critical elements of an offensive framework of intervention that the United States developed in the 1980s and continues to use against alleged state sponsors of terrorism in the twenty-first century.

The critical component of diplomacy in this new counterterrorism campaign involved not just ultimatums and non-negotiation, it was also rooted in an invasive and powerful public diplomacy campaign designed to use terrorism as a political weapon that criminalized enemies and created domestic fear and urgency. The war on terrorism of the twenty-first century exhibits one of the most dangerous legacies of the Reagan administration's counter-terrorism program, which is the use of a propaganda surrounding terrorism designed to purposely manipulate reality in an effort to create and exploit societal fear. The terrorist events of the 1980s were not nearly as extreme as those of the post-2001 era. However, the roots of this period are in the 1980s and with the Reagan administration's first employment of the rhetoric of terrorism as a tool of social control that hinged on creating a climate of fear capable of justifying a more offensive form of interventionism.

A number of individuals involved in the development of the Bush doctrine, the use of preemptive attacks and regime change for the purposes of national security and counterterrorism, first cut their teeth as advocates of the Reagan doctrine nearly twenty years earlier. Robert Gates, Paul Wolfowitz and others may come to mind. However, demonstrating a direct continuity in the decision making of specific individuals is, in this case, less important than establishing a wider perspective on the development of the war on terrorism of the twenty-first century. This book does the later by providing an example of how predecessors used techniques similar to the current war on terrorism. It is my hope that this indirect comparison provides greater awareness of the costs and consequences of the aggressive hardline approach that is synonymous with the modern war on terrorism. The approach of the United States in the increasingly unstable twenty-first century, its war on terrorism, is not merely the chance happening of an election or of the influence of one or two people, though, such things are not insignificant. Major foreign policy doctrines, like the containment policy or the war on terrorism, are cumulative developments of the decisions of many policymakers over multiple decades and across political parties. The use of preemptive war and regime change as a formal counterterrorism policy was accelerated after the September 11th attacks, but it was similar in many respects to a longer term change in how the United States responded to and dealt with revolutions and unfriendly governments in the developing world. This work demonstrates that the Reagan doctrine was an important historical point in the development of foreign policy that by the twenty-first century resulted in the normalization of an approach to the world that hinged on violations of the norms of international law and justice.

In the twenty-first century so far and, perhaps, with a touch of irony, the Reagan doctrine seems to resemble most the Obama doctrine. Both of these policies came in the aftermath of controversial and costly conventional wars fought by United States armed forces. For Reagan it was the shadow of the Vietnam War, and for Obama it was that of the Iraq War, the exit to which was a critical component of his 2008 election. Because of constraints from the public, the Congress, and the economy both administrations pursued proxy war and other less visible measures as vehicles for regime change and for the alleged promotion of democracy in the world. For Reagan, the goal was to overthrow the Sandinistas with the use of the Contras. For Obama, a primary target was Syrian President Bashar Al Assad, and Libyan leader Muammar Gaddafi, which it sought to topple by supplying resistance fighters and applying air power. Both administrations sought to use force in increasingly un-conventional ways to deal with its enemies. This approach to the world offered a few direct US actions, but were dominated by proxy armies, drones, hardline economic sanctions, intermittent air strikes and clandestine operations. The objective was the use of offensive tactics with far less controversy and public awareness.

One of the lessons that I hope this book demonstrates relates to the problematic and potentially destructive consequences of not only the policy of regime change and preemption, but also of proxy war. Since the United States emerged as the preeminent world power in the aftermath of the Cold War it adopted extensive measures to maintain its global influence. In short, the United States increasingly found it necessary to make war in a myriad of far off places in the pursuit of maintaining influence in key geopolitical regions. When unable or unwilling to make a large direct military commitment the United States often turns to proxy war as a solution.

A proxy war is almost certain to remain less relevant to most Americans. Even if the media exposes such a policy, as was the case during the Contra War, an administration accepts limited accountability for two reasons: first, American men and women are not dying and so the public cares less, and second, the United States can unendingly deny that it supports or is involved in illegal acts because third parties are acting without its immediate direction and direct evidence is less available. For the Reagan administration these components made proxy war a highly attractive policy choice. In short, it could use force to seek the ouster of an unpopular regime and, at least potentially, avoid the controversy associated with the death of American soldiers and the economic cost of a ground and air campaign. Similarly, the Obama administration accepted that even though it did not seek to commit the United States to a major conventional war in the manner of its predecessor it none the less was committed to playing a decisive role in the forcible alteration of sovereign governments, most notably in Syria. With striking similarity to the Reagan administration, the Obama administration pursued a proxy war in Syria and sought the overthrow of a sovereign government in the name of human rights and democratization.

While proxy war may appear attractive to administrations that seek to influence regions and oust governments on the cheap and with less culpability, these very advantages are, in fact, a great danger of this type of policy approach. First, proxy war inherently implicates the United States with unsavory individuals that often use methods that are illegal or do not align with the principles of international law and justice. The arming of proxies means that once these groups are supplied and put into action the United States is, to some degree, responsible for its actions, but simultaneously powerless to control the actors. Such agents may receive training, arms, and supplies and then conduct brutal killings of civilians, pursue illegal criminal activities like drug smuggling, or defect and join a radical group that opposes the interest of the United States. Arming militants that are not subject to the oversight of the United States or to international law means that the United States implicates itself as accomplices in a myriad of unsavory and illegal activity. In Central America during the 1980s, US-backed guerrillas involved themselves in numerous attacks on civilians and illegal arms and drug smuggling operations that directly threatened citizens at home in the United States. In Syria, the United States supplied militants received weapons, training, and supplies and some of these individuals defected with that knowledge and support to the Islamic State (IS). The United States may not have had a policy designed formally to support IS, but if it armed and trained individuals to fight the Assad regime and these individuals then engaged in terrorist activity then the United States was, in part, responsible for pursuing a policy with little regard for oversight or for the consequences of its behavior.

When Keith Graham returned home from his tour as a medical activist in Central America he shared his experiences with his peers. Graham's experience was transformative, he had witnessed the horrors of war: refugees, maimed women and children, destroyed villages. He intimately understood that the Reagan administration waged a very real and brutal war in Central America. Upon his return to the United States Graham received another shock, nobody cared! Graham went to social functions and spoke to colleagues and friends about the terrible ramifications that the United States' policy had on the people of Nicaragua, El Salvador, and Guatemala. However, the responses he received were unanimous, nobody really cared. Soldiers from the United States weren't dying, and the people of Central America, apparently, were not worth a thought. To Graham this was a soul crushing revelation. People in the United States were supposed to care. The United States was supposed to represent the bastion of democracy and the forefront of justice and human rights yet no one seemed to care that the Reagan administration's proxy war clearly and repeatedly violated these principles. [13]

The second danger of proxy war is the immunization of the public from the reality and gravity of a military oriented foreign policy. This does, in fact, remain one of the reasons why an administration might pursue such an approach, because it will help insulate it from the kind of criticism that a more direct and conventional operation may cause, but for a democratic society this is a very dangerous approach. A proxy war means no dead GIs, no "shock and awe" bombing campaigns, and no soldiers on the news burning houses down. It means back page news stories that few Americans notice because it involves individuals from foreign places, with foreign names. Proxy war results in the United States making war, a real war, but doing so without the public noticing that its country is at war. Even today historians do not refer to the conflict with Nicaragua as a US war. However, a failure to acknowledge this as a US war does a great injustice to the past. Thousands of people lost their lives. The conflict in Nicaragua disrupted the country for a decade, but yet it does not receive mention as a United States war. It was a United States war. The government of the United States trained and armed the militants. It was responsible for the escalation of the conflict and for much of its brutality. By not recognizing it as such, one further justifies the use of proxy war, which is to wage war without accountability to the American public. Proxy war is a dangerous approach because it immerses the United States into war, and implicates it in a wide array of unsavory activities, but does so without the appropriate awareness of the American people, which in a democracy provides the most valuable oversight.

When confronted by the threat of terrorism and state sponsorship the most tempting response is to take up arms and to make war. However, using military means whether through irregular proxy war or through direct and conventional military intervention is perhaps the most problematic. As the story of the United States and Nicaragua demonstrates the use of ultimatum and of preemptive force tended to radicalize the conflicts in Central America. Civil war and domestic terror violence on the left and the right only escalated alongside the US-led intervention. Faced with a war on its sovereignty the Nicaraguan government increasingly turned toward a military build-up, and the conflict deteriorated. It was not until the Reagan administration lost the political capital necessary to wage its war that a peace agreement made by Central Americans was possible. Similarly, in the post-2001 world the United States pursued aggressive military campaigns against its enemies incessantly. Whether in Iraq, Syria, Libya, or Afghanistan the pursuit of conventional or proxy war resulted in an expansion and radicalization of the terrorism problem that personified itself most in the prolonging of conflicts and the radicalization of the opposition, which is most relevant with the emergence of IS.

There are often alternatives to the use of force. In the 1980s, as in the first decade of the twenty-first century, the United States possessed alternatives to the use of military force. These alternatives were, during President Reagan's time, articulated most clearly by Robert Oakley and Parker Borg. Despite an insistence that military measures provided a way to show alleged state sponsors of terrorism the seriousness of the United States, both Oakley and Borg insisted that the use of force would only make matters worse. These two argued that the United States should address terrorism with economic, political, and diplomatic measures that involved improved cooperation with allies, improved intelligence and the recognition that military approaches were not capable of stopping terrorism. Oakley and Borg realized that terrorism was a problem that was too elusive for an offensive military policy to stamp out.

For this reason, they sought to curtail the application of military force and instead encouraged the pursuit of legal, diplomatic, and intelligence-oriented solutions. The Reagan administration ignored Borg and Oakley's criticisms. The Reagan offensive against Nicaragua resulted in more problems than solutions and left the mess to the Central Americans to clean up themselves. This history demonstrates that Washington policy makers ought to heed the criticism of people like Borg and Oakley that military measures to combat international terrorism create more problems than solutions. Sometimes military options are correct, but these should be as a final resort. In the future, the United States may need to use its military, but it should first use every opportunity to address terrorism through diplomacy, intelligence, legal measures, and to consider the history of the conflict before seeking out military means. The case of Nicaragua demonstrates that the application of an offensive and hardline oriented war on terrorism is a potentially dangerous option for all those involved.

Now, well into the twenty-first century it is abundantly clear that the drives of diplomats like Lawrence Pezzullo, Parker Borg, or Robert Oakley to seek non-violent solutions to problems of revolution and terrorism in the world are unheeded. The United States in the post–September 11, 2001, period too eagerly took up the mission of war and in the aftermath it seems that the leadership, no matter which political affiliation, is unable to break free of the tendency to try and solve the problems created by military policies with continual militaristic policies. The result is an emergence of a state of continual global irregular war. The propaganda of terrorism, so emphatically and thoroughly deployed in the twenty-first century, has left Americans fearful and eager to only blame the madmen and crazy terrorists rather than to consider the long historical roots of such issues. Because of a fear inducing propaganda more and more people turn to cries for more war or for the policing and targeting of those of foreign cultural backgrounds or for greater limitations on individual personal freedoms. The United States today is more invasively involved in wars that violate the sovereignty of other nations than at any other time. In the first two decades of the twenty-first century the United States has waged countless air campaigns in numerous countries, overseen the execution or assassination of the legitimate leaders of two sovereign countries and with the exception of the public opposition to the overt conventional war in Iraq it all goes without much of a thought at home in the United States. US irregular counterterror wars have left Americans afraid, but simultaneously almost oblivious to a constant war carried out without any formal declaration from Congress. Increasingly, citizens need to be aware of the potential danger of theses on going irregular counterterror wars to liberty at home and to war and destruction abroad.

NOTES

1. Interview with Keith Graham, MD, by Philip Travis, May 28, 2015, La Grande, Ore.

2. Testimony of David Linder, MD, before the United States House of Representatives, May 13, 1987, *The Digital National Security Archive* (Ann Arbor: Proquest, 2012), NI02993, http://gateway.proquest.com/openurl?url_ver=Z39.88–2004&res_dat=xri:dnsa&rft_dat= xri:dnsa:article:CNI02993.

3. Testimony of David Linder, MD, before the United States House of Representatives, May 13, 1987.

4. Testimony of David Linder, MD, before the United States House of Representatives, May 13, 1987.

5. Interview with Keith Graham, MD.

6. Interview with Keith Graham, MD.

7. Interview with Keith Graham, MD.

8. Interview with Keith Graham, MD.

9. Interview with Keith Graham, MD.

10. Interview with Keith Graham, MD.

11. Interview with Keith Graham, MD.

12. *La Nacion*, Folder Ministerio Seguridad Publica 210, El Archivo Nacional de Costa Rica.

13. Interview with Keith Graham, MD.

Bibliography

ARCHIVAL MATERIALS AND GOVERNMENT DOCUMENTS

Addington, David S. files. Box 16. Ronald Reagan Presidential Library.

Addington, David S. files. Box 11. Series II: Chron file 1987–1988. Ronald Reagan Presidential Library.

Addington, David S. files. Box 12. Series III: Nicaragua file, vol. II–VI. Ronald Reagan Presidential Library.

Addington, David S. files. Box 15. Ronald Reagan Presidential Library.

Addington, David S. files. Box 16. Ronald Reagan Presidential Library.

Anzovin, Steven. *Terrorism*. New York: H. W. Wilson, 1986.

"Argentina, 1975–1980: The Making of U.S. Human Rights." Digital National Security Archive. Ann Arbor: Proquest Information and Learning Co., 2012.

Boykin, John collection. Box 5. National Security Archive: Gelman Library, George Washington University.

Cannistraro, Vincent files. Box 2. Series 2: Counterterrorism (8/8/1985–4/10/1986). Ronald Reagan Presidential Library.

Canas, Richard L. files. George H. W. Bush Presidential Records: National Security Council. OA/ID CF01573, Box 1. George Bush Presidential Library.

Chew, David files. Box 12. Decision Making Information February–March 1986. Ronald Reagan Presidential Library.

Clark, William files. Box 4. Ronald Reagan Presidential Library.

Collamore, Thomas J. files. George H. W. Bush Vice Presidential Records: Office of Operations, Administration, and Staff Secretary. OA/ID 14332–14338, Box 011. George Bush Presidential Library.

Counterterrorism and Narcotics files. Box 91956 no 1. National Security Council Office Records, Ronald Reagan Presidential Library.

Counterterrorism and Narcotics files. Box 91956 no 2. National Security Council Office Records, Ronald Reagan Presidential Library.

Coy, Craig P. files. Box CPC-1; FBI 098. Ronald Reagan Presidential Library.

Coy, Craig P. files. Box CPC-2; FBI 099. Ronald Reagan Presidential Library.

Culvahouse, Arthur B. files. Box 1. Ronald Reagan Presidential Library.

Darman, Richard G. files. Box 2. Ronald Reagan Presidential Library.

Dolan, Anthony "Tony" R. files. 1981–1989, Box 40. Ronald Reagan Presidential Library.

"El Salvador: The Making of US Policy, 1977–1984." *Digital National Security Archive.* Ann Arbor: Proquest Information and Learning Co., 2012.

"El Salvador: War Peace and Human Rights, 1980–1994." *Digital National Security Archive.* Ann Arbor: Proquest Information and Learning Co., 2012.

Fortier, Donald files. Box 18. Ronald Reagan Presidential Library.

Foreign Affairs Oral History Project. Association for Diplomatic Studies and Training, Arlington, Va.

Frank, Robin files. George H. W. Bush Presidential Records: National Security Council. OA/ID CF000943. George Bush Presidential Library.

Friedlander, Robert A. *Terrorism: Documents of International and Local Control.* New York: Oceania, 1990.

The Gallup Poll. Wilmington, De.: Scholarly Resources Inc., 1982.

The Gallup Poll. Wilmington, De.: Scholarly Resources Inc., 1984.

The Gallup Poll. Wilmington, De.: Scholarly Resources Inc., 1985.

The Gallup Poll. Wilmington, De.: Scholarly Resources Inc., 1986.

General Office Files. George H. W. Bush Presidential Records: Task Force on Combatting Terrorism. OA/ID 15394. George Bush Presidential Library.

Gregg, Donald P. files. George H. W. Bush Vice Presidential Records: Office of National Security Affairs. OA/ID 19863, Box 010. George Bush Presidential Library.

Gregg, Donald P. files. George H. W. Bush Vice Presidential Records: Office of National Security Affairs. OA/ID 19849, Box 1. George Bush Presidential Library.

Gregg, Donald P. files. George H. W. Bush Vice Presidential Records: Office of National Security Affairs. OA/ID 19849, Box 2. George Bush Presidential Library.

Gregg, Donald P. files. George H. W. Bush Vice Presidential Records: Office of National Security Affairs. OA/ID 19849, Box 3. George Bush Presidential Library.

Gregg, Donald P. files. George H. W. Bush Vice Presidential Records: Office of National Security Affairs. OA/ID 19850, Box 2. George Bush Presidential Library.

Gregg, Donald P. files. George H. W. Bush Vice Presidential Records: Office of National Security Affairs. OA/ID 19851, Box 2. George Bush Presidential Library.

Gregg, Donald P. files. George H. W. Bush Vice Presidential Records: Office of National Security Affairs. OA/ID 19850/19851, Box 3/1. George Bush Presidential Library.

Kornbluh, Peter and Byrne, Malcolm. *The Iran-Contra Scandal: The Declassified History.* New York: New Press, 1993.

"The Iran Contra Affair: The Making of a Scandal." *Digital National Security Archive.* Ann Arbor: Proquest Information and Learning Co., 2012.

Maseng, Mari files. Box 6. Ronald Reagan Presidential Library.

Mead, Emily files. George H. W. Bush Presidential Records: White House Office of Policy Development. OA/ID 23352. George Bush Presidential Library.

Meyer, Herbert E. *Scouting the Future: The Public Speeches of William J. Casey.* New York: The Heritage Foundation, 1989.

Ministerio Seguridad Publica 210. El Archivo Nacional de Costa Rica.

National Archives. Nixon Presidential Materials, NSC Files, Subject Files, Box 310. Cabinet Committee on Terrorism.

National Archives. RG 59, Policy Planning Council (S/PC), Policy Planning Staff (S/P), Director's Files (Winston Lord) 1969–77, Lot 77D112, Box 361.

"Nicaragua: The Making of US Policy, 1978–1990." *Digital National Security Archive*: Ann Arbor: Proquest Information and Learning Co., 2012.

North, Oliver files. Box 1/2. Ronald Reagan Presidential Library.

North, Oliver files. Box 32. Ronald Reagan Presidential Library.

North, Oliver files. Box 32/34. Ronald Reagan Presidential Library.

North, Oliver files. Box 91173. Ronald Reagan Presidential Library.

North, Oliver files. Box 91715. Ronald Reagan Presidential Library.

Office of Presidential Records: Series II, Domestic Events, OA 16003. Ronald Reagan Presidential Library.

Popadiuk, Roman files. Box 1, OA 18546/18547. Ronald Reagan Presidential Library.

"Presidential Directives on National Security from Harry Truman to William Clinton, Part I." Ann Arbor: Proquest Information and Learning Co., 2012.

"Presidential Directives on National Security from Harry Truman to George W. Bush, Part II." Ann Arbor: Proquest Information and Learning Col, 2012.

Presidential Directive PD/NSC-52. "U.S. Policy to Cuba," October 4, 1979. Jimmy Carter Presidential Library and Museum

Presidencia 3429. El Archivo Nacional de Costa Rica.

Presidencia 3810. El Archivo Nacional de Costa Rica.

Press Office files. George H. W. Bush Vice Presidential Records. OA/ID 14922–14923. George Bush Presidential Records.

Simpson, Christopher. *National Security Directives of the Reagan and Bush Administration: The Declassified History of U.S. Political and Military Policy 1981–1991.* New York: Westview, 1995.

Speechwriter files. George Bush Vice Presidential Records: Policy Office of Speech Writer Research files, OA/ID 14871–14880. George Bush Presidential Library.

Speechwriting files. Box 147, White House: Speech Drafts, 1981–1989. Ronald Reagan Presidential Library.

Speechwriting files. Box 197, White House: Speech Drafts, 1981–1989. Ronald Reagan Presidential Library.

Speechwriting files. Box 198, White House: Speech Drafts, 1981–1989. Ronald Reagan Presidential Library.

Speechwriting files. Box 244, White House: Speech Drafts, 1981–1989. Ronald Reagan Presidential Library.

Speechwriting files. Box 260, White House: Speech Drafts, 1981–1989. Ronald Reagan Presidential Library.

Speechwriting files. Box 261, White House: Speech Drafts, 1981–1989. Ronald Reagan Presidential Library.

Speechwriting files. Box 277, White House: Speech Drafts, 1981–1989. Ronald Reagan Presidential Library.

Speechwriting files. Box 320, White House: Speech Drafts, 1981–1989. Ronald Reagan Presidential Library.

Speechwriting files. Box 372, White House: Speech Drafts, 1981–1989. Ronald Reagan Presidential Library.

Speechwriting files. Box 411, Speech Writing Research Office Series II: General Topic Speech Research, 1981–1989. Ronald Reagan Presidential Library.

Speechwriting files. Box 412, Speech Writing Research Office Series II: General Topic Speech Research, 1981–1989. Ronald Reagan Presidential Library.

Stettner, Carolyn, files. George H. W. Bush Presidential Records: National Security Concil, OA/ID CF01523, Box 04. George Bush Presidential Library.

"Terrorism and US Policy, 1968–2002." *Digital National Security Archive*: Ann Arbor: Proquest Information and Learning Co., 2012.

US Congress. *Congressional Record.* 97th Cong., 1st sess., 1981. Vol. 127, pt. 3.

US Congress. *Congressional Record.* 97th Cong., 1st sess., 1981. Vol. 127, pt. 4.

US Congress. *Congressional Record.* 97th Cong., 1st sess., 1981. Vol. 127, pt. 13.

US Congress. *Congressional Record.* 98th Cong., 1st sess., 1983. Vol. 129, pt. 2.

US Congress. *Congressional Record.* 98th Cong., 1st sess., 1983. Vol, 129, pt. 8.

US Congress. *Congressional Record.* 98th Cong., 1st sess., 1983. Vol. 129, pt. 16.

US Congress. *Congressional Record.* 99th Cong., 1st sess., 1985. Vol. 131, pt. 7.

INTERVIEWS

Keith Graham. Interview by Philip Travis. May 28, 2015. La Grande, Ore.

Lawrence Pezzullo. Interview by Arthur Day. *Foreign Affairs Oral History Project*, Association for Diplomatic Studies and Training. February 24, 1989.

Oscar Arias Sanchez. Interview by Philip Travis. July 28, 2016. San Jose, Costa Rica.

Parker Borg. Interview by Charles Stuart Kennedy. *Foreign Affairs Oral History Project*, Association for Diplomatic Studies and Training. August 12, 2002.

Robert Oakley. Interview by Charles Stuart Kennedy and Thomas Stern. *Foreign Affairs Oral History Project*, Association for Diplomatic Studies and Training. July 7, 1992.

NEWSPAPERS, MAGAZINES AND OTHER PUBLICATIONS

Accuracy in the Media
American Legion
Boston Globe
The Christian Science Monitor
The Globe and Mail
Houston Chronicle
Los Angeles Times
Miami Herald
New York Times
The Orlando Sentinel
The Ottawa Citizen
Philadelphia Daily News
Reynolds, Kevin. *Red Dawn*. DVD. Directed by John Milius. 1984: MGM.
San Francisco Chronicle
Sun Sentinel
Short, Michael. *Speed Zone.* DVD. Directed by Jim Drake. 1989: Orion.
Vianello, Claudia. *El Salvador: Another Vietnam.* 16mm. Directed by Glenn Silber. 1981: Icarus Films.
Wall Street Journal
Washington Post
Zucker, Jerry and Abrahams, Jim. *The Naked Gun: From the Files of Police Squad*, DVD. Directed by David Zucker. 1988: Paramount.

SECONDARY SOURCES

Ambrosius, Lloyd E. "Woodrow Wilson and George W. Bush: Historical Comparisons of Ends and Means in Their Foreign Policies." *Diplomatic History* 30, no. 3 (June 2006).
Anzovin, Steven. *Terrorism*. New York: H. W. Wilson, 1986.
Arnson, Cynthia. *Crossroads: Congress, the President, and Central America, 1976–1993*, 2nd ed. University Park: Pennsylvania State University Press, 1993.
Bacevich, Andrew J. *American Empire: The Realities and Consequences of US Diplomacy*. Cambridge: Harvard University, 2004.
Backman, Clifford A. *Cultures of the West: A History, Vol. 2, 2nd ed.* New York: Oxford, 2016
Brownlee, Elliot and Graham, Hugh Davis. *The Reagan Presidency: Pragmatic Conservatism and its Legacies.* Lawrence, Ka.: Kansas University Press, 2003.
Calhoun, Frederick S. *Power and Principle: Armed intervention in Wilsonian Foreign Policy*. Kent St: Kent St University Press, 1986.
Campos, Joseph H. II. *The State and Terrorism: National Security and the Mobilization of Power.* London: Ashgate, 2013.
Chamberlin, Paul Thomas. *The Global Offensive: The United States, the Palestinian Liberation Organization, and the Making of the Post-Cold War Order*. New York: Oxford University Press, 2012.
Chomsky, Noam. *Hegemony or Survival: America's Quest for Global Dominance*. New York: Henry Holt, 2003.
Chomsky, Noam. *Pirates and Emperors, Old and New: International Terrorism in the Real World*. Cambridge, Mass: South End, 2002.
Chomsky, Noam. *What Uncle Sam Really Wants*. Berkeley: Odonian, 1992.

Clark, Paul Coe Jr. *The United States and Somoza, 1933–1956: A Revisionist Look*. London: Praeger, 1992.

Clarke, Richard A. *Against All Enemies: Inside America's War on Terror*. New York: Free Press, 2004.

Colby, Jason. *The Business of Empire: United Fruit, Race, and U.S. Expansion in Central America*. Cornell: Cornell University Press, 2011.

Collins John, and Glover Ross. *Collateral Language*. New York: New York University Press, 2002.

Cox, Ronald W. *Power and Profits: U.S. Policy in Central America*. Lexington, Ky.: University of Kentucky Press, 1994.

Dumbrell, John. *American Foreign Policy: Carter to Clinton*. New York: St. Martins, 1997.

Miller, Stuart Creighton. *Benevolent Assimilation: The American Conquest of the Philippines, 1899–1903*. London: Yale University Press, 1982.

Elliot, Brownlee and Hugh Davis, Graham. *The Reagan Presidency: Pragmatic Conservatism and it's Legacies*. Lawrence, Ka.: University Press of Kansas, 2003.

Farber, David. *The Sixties: From Memory to History*. Chapel Hill: University of North Carolina Press, 1994.

Fenton, Tom. *Bad News: The Decline of Reporting, the Business of News, and the Danger to us All*. New York: Harper Collins, 2005.

Fisk, Robert. *Pity the Nation: Lebanon at War*. New York: Oxford, 2001.

Foreign Affairs Chronology, 1978–1989. New York: Free Press, 1990.

Friedlander, Robert A. *Terrorism: Documents of International and Local Control*. Oceana, 1989.

Grandin, Greg. *Empires Workshop: Latin America, The United States, And the Rise of the New Imperialism*. New York: Henry Holt, 2006.

Grandin, Greg. *The Last Colonial Massacre: Latin America in the Cold War*. Chicago: University of Chicago Press, 2004.

Hahn, Walter F. *Central America and the Reagan Doctrine*. New York: University Press of America, 1987.

Hass, Richard N. *The Opportunity: America's Moment to Alter History*. New York: Public Affairs, 2005.

Hart, Justin. *Empire of Ideas: The Origins of Public Diplomacy and the Transformation of U.S. Foreign Policy*. New York: Oxford University Press, 2013.

Herman Edward S. and Chomsky Noam. *Manufacturing Consent: The Political Economy of the Mass Media*. New York: Random House, 2002.

Herring, George C. *America's Longest War: The United States and Vietnam, 1950–1975*, 4th ed. New York: McGraw Hill, 2002.

Human Rights In Nicaragua: Reagan, Rhetoric and Reality. New York: America's Watch, 1985.

Hunt, Michael and Levine, Steven. *Arc of Empire: America's Wars in Asia from the Philippines to Vietnam*. Chapel Hill: University of North Carolina Press, 2012.

Johnson, Chalmers. *Blowback: The Costs and Consequences of American Empire*. New York: Henry Holt, 2004.

Judis, John B. *The Folly of Empire: What George W. Bush Could Learn from Theodore Roosevelt and Woodrow Wilson*. New York: Oxford University, 2006.

Judis, John B. "What Woodrow Wilson Can Teach Today's Imperialists." *New Republic* 228 (June 9, 2003).

Kagan, Robert. *A Twilight Struggle: American Power and Nicaragua, 1977–1990*. New York: Free Press, 1996.

Kennedy, David M. "What "W" Owes to 'WW.'" *Atlantic* 295, no. 2 (March 205).

Kirkpatrick, Jeane J. *Dictatorships and Doublestandards: Rationalism and Realism in Politics*. New York: Simon and Schuster, 1982.

Kornbluh, Peter. *Nicaragua, the Price of Intervention: Reagan's Wars Against the Sandinistas*. Washington, DC: Institute for Policy Studies, 1987.

Kruckewitt, Joan. *The Death of Ben Linder: The Story of a North American in Sandinista Nicaragua*. New York: Seven Stories Press, 1999.

Oye, Kenneth A., Rothchild, Donald and Lieber, Robert J. *Eagle Entangle: U.S. Foreign Policy in a Complex World.* Longman: New York, 1979.

LaFeber, Walter. *Inevitable Revolutions: The United States and Central America, 2nd ed.* New York: W.W. Norton, 1993.

Lafeber, Walter. *The New Empire: An Interpretation of American Expansion, 1860–1898.* London: Cornell University Press, 1963.

Laham, Nicholas. *The American Bombing of Libya: A Study of the Force of Miscalculation in Reagan Foreign Policy.* Jefferson, NC: McFarland, 2007.

Latner, Teishan A. "Take Me to Havana: Airline Hijacking, U.S.-Cuba Relations, and Political Protest in Late Sixties America." *Diplomatic History* 39, no. 1 (January 2015).

Law, Randall. *Terrorism: A History.* New York: John Wiley and Sons, 2009.

Lefever, Ernest W. *Morality and Foreign Policy: A Symposium on President Carter's Stance.* Washington, DC: Ethics and Public Policy Center, 1977.

Leffler, Melvin P. "9/11 and American Foreign Policy." *Diplomatic History* 29, no. 3 (June 2005).

Leffler, Melvin P. "9/11 and the Past and Future of American Foreign Policy." *International Affairs* 79, no. 5 (October 2003).

LeoGrande, William. *Our Own Backyard: The United States in Central America, 1977–1992.* London: University of North Carolina Press, 1998.

Macaulay, Neill. *The Sandino Affair.* Micanopy, Fl.: Wacahoota Press, 1998.

Mamdani, Mahmood. *Good Muslim, Bad Muslim: America, The Cold War, and the Roots of Terror.* New York: Doubleday, 2004.

Mamdani, Mahmood. *Saviors and Survivors: Darfur, Politics, and the War on Terror.* New York: Doubleday, 2009.

Mann, James. *Rise of Vulcans: The History of Bush's War Cabinet.* Viking: New York, 2004.

Ninkovich, Frank. *Modernity and Power: A History of the Domino Theory in the Twentieth Century.* Chicago: University of Chicago Press, 1994.

Ninkovich, Frank. *The Wilsonian Century: US Foreign Policy Since 1900.* Chicago: University of Chicago Press, 1999.

Nordholdt, Han Willem Schulte. *Woodrow Wilson: A Life for World Peace.* New York: University of California Press, 1991.

Offner, Arnold A. "Rogue President, Rogue Nation: Bush and U.S. National Security." *Diplomatic History* 29 (June 2005).

Oye, Kenneth A, Lieber, Robert J. and Rothchild, Donald. *Eagle Resurgent? The Reagan Era in American Foreign Policy.* Boston: Little Brown, 1987.

Pach, Chester, Jr., "And That's the Way It Was: The Vietnam War on the Network Nightly News." In David Fabrber, *The Sixties: From Memory to History.* Chapel Hill: University of North Carolina Press, 1994.

Peace, Roger. *Call to Conscience: The Anti-Contra War Campaign.* New York: University of Massachusetts Press, 2012.

Pieterse, Jan Nederveen. *Globalization or Empire.* New York: Routledge, 2004.

Ramirez, Sergio and Conrad, Edgar Robert. *Sandino: The Testimony of a Nicaraguan Patriot, 1921–1934.* Princeton: Princeton University Press, 1990.

Rosenbaum, Herbert D. and Ugrinsky, Alexej. *Jimmy Carter: Foreign Policy and Post Presidential Years.* Westport, Conn.: Greenwood, 1994.

Rushdie, Salman. *The Jaguar Smile: A Nicaraguan Journey.* New York: Random House, 1987.

Solaún, Mauricio. *U.S. Intervention and Regime Change in Nicaragua.* London: University of Nebraska Press, 2005.

Spencer, Donald S. *The Carter Implosion: Jimmy Carter and the Amateur Style of Diplomacy.* New York: Praeger, 1988.

Sterling, Claire. *The Terror Network: The Secret War of International Terrorism.* New York: Readers Digest, 1981.

Toaldo, Mattia. *The Origins of the U.S. War on Terror: Lebanon, Libya, and the American Intervention in the Middle East.* New York: Routledge, 2013.

Walker, Thomas. *Reagan Versus the Sandinistas: The Undeclared War On Nicaragua.* Boulder: Westview, 1987.

Weiler, Michael and Pearce, Barnett W. *Reagan and Public Discourse in America.* Tuscaloosa: University of Alabama Press, 2006.

Westad, Odd Arne. *The Global Cold War.* New York: Cambridge University Press, 2007.

Wheelan, Joseph. *Jefferson's War: America's First War on Terror, 1801–1805.* New York: Avalon, 2003.

Wills, David C. *The First War on Terrorism: Counterterrorism Policy During the Reagan Administration.* Oxford: Rowman & Littlefield, 2003.

Woodward, Bob. *Veil: The Secret Wars of the CIA, 1981–1987.* New York: Simon and Schuster, 1987.

Zakaria, Fareed. "The Reagan Strategy of Containment." *Political Science Quarterly* 105, no. 3 (1990).

Zimmermann, Matilde. *Sandinista: Carlos Fonseca and the Nicaraguan Revolution.* London: Duke University, 2000.

Index

About the Author

Philip W. Travis received his PhD from Washington State University in 2014. Dr. Travis specializes in US international relations during the Cold War, and specifically with Latin America. Currently, Dr. Travis is assistant professor of history at the State College of Florida in Bradenton, Florida.